Indian Muslims and Citizenship

Through the creation of postcolonial citizenship, India adopted a hybridisation of specific secular and western conceptions of citizenship. In this democratic framework, Indian Muslims are observed on how they make use of the spaces and channels to accommodate their Islamic identity within a secular one.

This book analyses how the socio-political context shapes citizens' perceptions of multiple variables, such as their sense of political efficacy, agency, conception of citizenship rights and belief in democracy. Based on extensive surveys and interviews and through presenting and investigating the various meanings of *jihād*, the author explores the usage of non-Eurocentric conceptual approaches to the study of postcolonial and Muslim societies, in particular the meaning it carries in the psyche of the Muslim community. She argues that through means of argumentative and spiritual *jihād*, Indian Muslims fight their battle towards a realisation of citizenship ideals, despite the unfavourable conditions of intra- and inter-community conflicts.

Presenting new examinations of Islamic identity and citizenship in contemporary India, this book will be a useful contribution to the study of South Asian Studies, Religion, Islam, and Race and Ethnicity.

Julten Abdelhalim obtained her PhD from Heidelberg University, Germany, and is an Assistant Professor in Political Science at Cairo University, Egypt. She is also a post-doctoral fellow at Humboldt University in Berlin, Germany.

Routledge advances in South Asian studies
Edited by Subrata K. Mitra
South Asia Institute, University of Heidelberg, Germany

South Asia, with its burgeoning, ethnically diverse population, soaring economies, and nuclear weapons, is an increasingly important region in the global context. The series, which builds on this complex, dynamic and volatile area, features innovative and original research on the region as a whole or on the countries. Its scope extends to scholarly works drawing on history, politics, development studies, sociology and economics of individual countries from the region as well those that take an interdisciplinary and comparative approach to the area as a whole or to a comparison of two or more countries from this region. In terms of theory and method, rather than basing itself on any one orthodoxy, the series draws broadly on the insights germane to area studies, as well as the tool kit of the social sciences in general, emphasizing comparison, the analysis of the structure and processes, and the application of qualitative and quantitative methods. The series welcomes submissions from established authors in the field as well as from young authors who have recently completed their doctoral dissertations.

Indian Muslims and Citizenship

Spaces for *jihād* in everyday life

Julten Abdelhalim

Routledge
Taylor & Francis Group

LONDON AND NEW YORK

First published 2016 by Routledge

2 Park Square, Milton Park, Abingdon, Oxfordshire OX14 4RN
711 Third Avenue, New York, NY 10017

Routledge is an imprint of the Taylor & Francis Group, an informa business

First issued in paperback 2018

British Library Cataloguing in Publication Data
A catalogue record for this book is available from the British Library

Library of Congress Cataloging-in-Publication Data
Abdelhalim, Julten.
Indian Muslims and citizenship : spaces for jihad in everyday life / Julten
Abdelhalim.
    pages cm. – (Routledge advances in South Asian studies ; 29)
    Includes bibliographical references and index.
    1. Muslims–India–Social conditions. 2. Muslims–Political activity–
    India. 3. Group identity–India. 4. Citizenship–India. 5. Jihad–Social
    aspects–India. 6. Islam–Social aspects–India. 7. Community life–India.
    8. Postcolonialism–India. 9. India–Social conditions–1947–
    10. India–Politics and government–1977– I. Title.
    DS432.M84.A2366 2016
    305.6'970954–dc23   2015016115

ISBN: 978-1-138-85971-5 (hbk)
ISBN: 978-1-138-32014-7 (pbk)

Typeset in Times New Roman
by Wearset Ltd, Boldon, Tyne and Wear

To my mother, a great *jihādist*

وَجَٰهِدُوا۟ فِى ٱللَّهِ حَقَّ جِهَادِهِۦ ۚ هُوَ ٱجْتَبَىٰكُمْ وَمَا جَعَلَ عَلَيْكُمْ فِى ٱلدِّينِ مِنْ حَرَجٍ ۚ مِّلَّةَ أَبِيكُمْ إِبْرَٰهِيمَ ۚ هُوَ سَمَّىٰكُمُ ٱلْمُسْلِمِينَ مِن قَبْلُ وَفِى هَٰذَا لِيَكُونَ ٱلرَّسُولُ شَهِيدًا عَلَيْكُمْ وَتَكُونُوا۟ شُهَدَآءَ عَلَى ٱلنَّاسِ ۚ فَأَقِيمُوا۟ ٱلصَّلَوٰةَ وَءَاتُوا۟ ٱلزَّكَوٰةَ وَٱعْتَصِمُوا۟ بِٱللَّهِ هُوَ مَوْلَىٰكُمْ ۖ فَنِعْمَ ٱلْمَوْلَىٰ وَنِعْمَ ٱلنَّصِيرُ ﴿٧٨﴾

And strive hard in God's cause with all the striving that is due to Him: it is He who has elected you [to carry His message], and has laid no hardship on you in [anything that pertains to] religion, [and made you follow] the creed of your forefather Abraham. It is He who has named you – in bygone times as well as in this [divine writ] – "those who have surrendered themselves to God", so that the Apostle might bear witness to the truth before you, and that you might bear witness to it before all mankind. So establish worship, pay the poor-due, and hold fast to Allah. He is your Protecting friend. A blessed Patron and a blessed Helper.

(The Quran, Al-Hajj 22:78)

Contents

Illustrations

Figures

Table

Preface

As I embarked on a quest to understand how Indian Muslims conceive their status as citizens in a secular democratic country, I ended up in Kerala watering tapioca fields with Indian housewives lecturing me about what it means to be a good citizen. This book is about the narratives conveyed to me that aimed at projecting how Indian Muslims, despite their minority-related problems and the failure of the state machinery to grant them their rights, are still proud to demonstrate how they make use of the democratic channels and freedoms of expression and association to achieve intellectual independence and excellence as good Muslims. In their own words, it is democracy that gives spaces for *jihād*.

This book considers the concept of *jihād* differently from the mainstream usage. It looks at how Muslims use the concept to refer to its broader spiritual aspect of striving for what Allah has ordained. Hence it was through this democratic framework and *jihād* that Indian Muslims' goal was lived citizenship, which refers to the practice of citizenship and the attempts to challenge exclusionary processes in everyday life. This is undertaken through a reference to constitutional weapons, collective associations and different forms of agency.

Lived citizenship is about a political space in which opinions and actions make sense to their followers. It goes beyond the Habermasian public sphere because the conditions in which the followers find themselves are not of the western industrial liberal world, but are of a state in which citizens are perceived to be unequal and hierarchical. By observing the processes of invisibilising the self versus visibilising problems, one could witness how Indian youth, especially girls, tried to stage a struggle for presence and overcome marginalisation by bringing to the fore their problems and by making exceptional use of the political and economic liberalisation that led to the expansion of communicative spaces. This study, hence, shows how traditionally labelled illiberal spaces have proven to be factories for citizenship, especially for girls, who acquired a habitus enabling them to realise citizenship ideals.

This book tests the validity of the commonly held myth that Muslims would automatically opt for a *shari'ah* based Islamic system of governance. It is proven that the long political socialisation process has affected the political psyche of the community in a manner leading it to prefer the secular democratic option. *Shari'ah* is conceived merely as a means to achieve justice. This is why voting, as a political right, is not regarded as a sufficient means to maintain a just system. Ensuring justice, as the utmost political aim, is interlinked to the increasing sense of responsibility on the part of Muslims.

One interesting result from my conversations among the youth is the unanimous perception of India as a democratic state and the preference of democracy as a system of governance on a pan-Indian scale. Indian Muslims offer a unique model by accommodating their Islamic identity and presenting a remarkably mature political community in which questions such as political representation (whether Muslims have to be politically represented by a Muslim) and tolerance arise. The Indian case sets a historically fascinating precedent in global history; the majority of Indian religious leaders (*'ulama*) acted as motivators for choosing the secular democratic option versus the promised Islamic regime. The idea of 'composite nationalism' that Madani forged in the first half of the twentieth century as an answer to the partition call was central to this study.

The dynamics of political action and awareness, expressed through the Indian Muslims acquisition of a 'citizen minority' identity, contribute to a subversion of the stereotyped identities ascribed to them. I devised the term citizen minority to describe the status of Indian Muslims, who are full citizens, yet possess in differing contexts different minority cultures. The inability to be critical of the Babri verdict, for example, and hence of the Indian legal system, as shown through many interviews and press review, represents an inclination towards a process of self-marginalisation and a construction of an idea of 'model citizenship' to which an Indian Muslim strives. However, this struggle is combined with another crucial one: the search for life's security.

Finally, I can say that this research provides scope for re-examining the relationship between citizenship and collective group rights. Policies should be changed because Muslims do not necessarily define themselves as a minority. The state's traditional focus on favouring freedom over reform (unlike the case with Hindus) had proven fallacious. The state should promote an understanding and practice of secularism and its legitimacy that gives higher priority to citizenship than to vague notions of collective group identity that are vulnerable to abuse and manipulation by some elite in the name of the community.

As this book is based on my doctoral dissertation, I would like to thank Prof. Subrata Mitra for his faith in my adventure and his guidance throughout the PhD. I am grateful for the funding I obtained from the Cluster of Excellence 'Asia and Europe in a Global Context' at Heidelberg University. I would not be able to do justice to all the informants who shared their insights and who have opened their hearts and, in many cases, their homes to me. However, I would like to thank the students, lecturers and principals of Jamia Milia Islamia and Jawaharlal Nehru University in Delhi, in addition to Calicut University, Feroke College, Rawdhatul Uloom Arabic College, Sulamusallam Arabic College, Mampad College, PSMO College, Irshadiyya College and many others in Kerala. I am also grateful to the *'ulama* and teachers of Nadwatul Uloom and Jamiatul Mominat Alislamia in Uttar Pradesh, Zayid College for Girls in Delhi and Pipli Mazra *Madrasa* in Haryana, who allowed me into the worlds of girls and boys behind the walls of *madrasas* and granted me access to no-woman zones. For the generosity and kindness I have received from my host family in Kerala, I am much obliged. I am also indebted to my husband, who helped me overcome the hard work of doctoral studies in foreign lands. Finally, no words would be able to convey the gratitude I owe my mother for teaching me how to transform dreams into reality.

1 Introduction

A Muslim researcher in a hybrid field

A couple of years ago in Varanasi in North India, a young man on a boat tried to sell me a pack of wooden Indian dolls, asking me if I wanted the Indian or the Muslim one. I looked at him puzzled; the Muslim was also an Indian, but in a black dress. The only answer I got when I enquired why the Muslim was not considered also an Indian was a look of confusion on the man's face. It was a manifestation of how the language of citizenship and inclusion in India remains a puzzle, both in comprehension and in application, despite the long democratic experience.

Being a Muslim female and coming from Egypt, where words such as democracy and citizenship make little sense, India seemed to be the magical zone where people had the right to practise their citizenship. I chose to study Indian politics to understand how Indians managed to develop political mechanisms to ensure their dignity would not be re-usurped, while the Egyptians, to a great extent, failed. India and Egypt embarked on the same postcolonial path simultaneously. While Nehru chose dignity for the people, who were turned from subjects into citizens through the Constitution, Nasser decided to withdraw it from them and retained their subjectivity. In a speech following his alleged assassination attempt, Nasser declared, "It was me who planted dignity and pride in you." Since then, the Egyptians were convinced that the source of their dignity came from the president. Eventually, Egyptians ended up having a very strange history of dignity: a history attached to three presidents in the span of fifty years.

In these fifty years, India managed to be the largest democracy on Earth, and Indians developed a unique sense of citizenship. I only clearly understood what it means to be a citizen when I came to India and listened to nineteen-year-old village girls teaching me what freedom of expression means and how it is indispensable to choose one's leader. The reference to my Egyptian political identity might seem out of context in the introduction to a study of Indian Muslims, but it was this subjective researcher's motivation that shaped the approaches to the study of (a) Muslim community(ies) and the ways they perceive living in a secular democracy.

The path dependency of the political history of Nasser and Nehru's rule is significant to understand the forthcoming political developments in both countries. The anti-colonial nationalism through the transition to mass nationalism in

1919 in Egypt and in the 1920s in India through Gandhism and secular liberalism, the crises of secularism and religious fundamentalism in both countries are the aspects on which these states converge. However, due to, on the one hand, the diversity in the Indian citizenry and the direction of the Congress party to which Nehru was heavily attached and, on the other hand, the autocracy of the military from which Nasser sprung, these leaders radically differed in setting the political systems of their states. This in turn resulted in two radically different political cultures of an Indian citizenry versus an Egyptian subjectivity. Starting from this point, this study investigates the nature of citizenship ideals and sentiments among the Indian Muslims, dynamics of inner changes and the ways they negotiate power relations and create spaces of agency and forms of self-representation.

Through the historical moment of the creation of postcolonial citizenship, India witnessed a theoretically legal adoption of a specific secular and western conception of citizenship, but managed to carefully hybridise it in a quest towards inclusion. The process of adaptation of secular citizenship, which was alien to Muslims, and to their world view (which is in itself based on different interpretations of Islamic *shari'ah*), is reproduced in today's settings by accommodating this revision to the reality of political and social life.

Choosing the Muslim minority, and specifically the educated lower middle class, as a target group and a case study, was based on an attempt to pinpoint the politics of absence. This refers to the absent discourses on how citizens live their lives, and still be political beings without adopting an extremist position, and how these discourses can enrich the debate on citizenship in postcolonial societies, and thus on forms of political action, and help eliminate global stereotypes of Muslim communities. This book identifies Indian Muslims as strong political actors and not mere passive victims or alienated subjects as it is commonly argued and portrayed by the media and political leaders. The case studies also show how feasible it is to argue that, in abiding by the guidelines to 'model citizenship', average Muslims find themselves inclined to adopt an act of 'self-marginalisation' lest their claim for identity and cultural security would be interpreted as disloyalty.

This book is based on my doctoral dissertation that examined Indian Muslims as a case study in two states: one where they constitute a minority and one where they form a majority. By relying on group solidarity, a lived conception of citizenship based on the 'collective' is practised through dynamics of protest on the levels of consciousness, will and action. In this regard, citizenship is also understood as a question of identity and not simply as a legal set of rights and obligations. The main question that guided this study revolved around how Indian Muslims make use of the spaces and channels granted by the democratic framework to accommodate their Islamic identity with the secular one, and to what extent their Islamic identity is conceived (or perceived) as either conducive or conflicting with the political setting in which they live.

To identify the case studies for my research, sampling strategies were employed for geographic *sites*, for *events* related to Muslim politics in India and for *people* to be interviewed. Concerning the geographic sites, two states were chosen to form the basis of the comparative research: Delhi and Kerala. This choice of sites is purposive. The first aim was to look at electoral constituencies with a majority of Muslims and to compare the hegemonic discourses and the forces of social change. This helped in generating insights on how the majority–minority question played a role in theorising on citizenship. I chose the area of Northern Kerala, where Malappuram district has over 60% Muslims, to contrast it with Delhi, where Muslims constitute around 12% of the population. Level of literacy and education among the Muslims was another factor. From Delhi, the urban capital, to Kerala, the rural peripheral setting, other comparative factors were utilised. Other pragmatic reasons of not being able to conduct long-term and political-oriented fieldwork alone without a research guide in states like Uttar Pradesh and Bihar were taken into consideration upon selecting sites for study. This was overcome partly by interviewing young people from these states studying or working in Delhi.

Concerning events, the demolition of Babri Masjid in 1992, the Gujarat carnage of 2002 and the latest Ayodhya verdict in 2010 regarding the division of the site of the demolished Babri Masjid were selected as topics to locate public opinion.

As for people, by limiting the study to the focus on the Indian Muslim middle class, certain groups such as teachers in *madrasas*, colleges and universities, *'ulama*, journalists, students and NGO workers related to community development were selected for lengthy interviews. The decision to choose these individuals was based on their strategic role in the community since they play significant roles in the process of political socialisation as opinion makers and community leaders of Indian Muslims.

Although the nature of the study was qualitative, a survey of around 250 Muslim students in Delhi and Kerala was undertaken to generate general observations on the attitudes and perceptions of Muslim students. The questionnaire was divided into three parts: general information, social and political activities, and conceptions. It was designed to operationalise categories such as political, social and cultural rights, sense of belonging, sense of citizenship versus political subjectivity, political trust, political efficacy, perception of the state, sense of collective memory, forms of protest, civility, participation, role of leaders and *'ulama*, and levels of political analysis.

In addition to reviewing the literature on Indian Muslims, methods of data collection included the following primary sources obtained during interview-based and ethnographic fieldwork conducted in the states of Delhi, Mumbai, Haryana, Uttar Pradesh and Kerala in the period from September 2010 until the end of April 2011 and a short visit in April 2012 to Kerala and Delhi, in addition to interviews in the United Arab Emirates in April 2011 and July 2012. The expert interviews were conducted with historians, intellectuals and university and college professors. Structured and semi-structured interviews were conducted with *madrasa* and 'modern'[1] school teachers, university students, principals, *imams* and *'ulama*, lawyers, journalists, politicians, local government and civil officers, and NGO workers or activists. As for the situational context of the interviews, they were conducted in mosques, *madrasas*, homes, municipalities, and universities or colleges with a certain Muslim affiliation. *Press analysis* was divided among English, Urdu and Malayalam newspapers. I chose the discussion on the Ayodhya verdict in September–October 2010 as a theme to analyse different standpoints from different organisations. Newspapers in the vernacular languages like Urdu and Malayalam covered, to a great extent, the public opinion of Muslims regarding the verdict. In many cases, I found my informants, who are public figures and experts on the topic, unwilling to convey their honest opinion about the verdict. For this I deemed the newspaper's editorial pieces and some reports as a valuable source of information. To overcome the deficiency in finding archived petitions, I resorted to Urdu magazines issued by Islamic organisations based in North India, in which there are several sections on people's problems and opinions in editorial pieces and letters to the editor.

Another primary source was the *fatwas* (religious edicts) issued pertaining to political concerns. In understanding the interaction between the political and the religious, *fatwas* or religious edicts appear in the cotemporary world as a leading international actor or agent (Abdul-Fattah, 2008). Some *fatwas* acquire a global character, like those of the Qatar-based Egyptian Islamic scholar Al-Qaradawy, which are translated into Malayalam and are immensely influential among the Muslim youth in Kerala. Other *fatwas* relating to social issues like work and divorce assumed wide debates in the media in India and played a role in politics of the mainstream versus minorities and perceptions of the Muslim minority. In other cases, purely political issues became religious issues and were introduced by Muslim scholars in public debates, especially in times of electoral campaigns. These latter forms of *fatwas* were crucial for my research to understand how religion became politicised and how politics became religionised. However, as this information is not documented and thus not easily accessible through archival work, I depended on oral narrations from people who had heard an *imam* speaking about a certain political party or issue in the Friday sermon. I also relied on newspapers to see the viewpoints of religious scholars after the Ayodhya verdict as a case.

Brief remarks on positionality and limitations

Through this fieldwork, I have witnessed fascinating interactions and compelling incidents where my agency and conception of my 'self' fluctuated between denial, isolation and recognition. Being a political scientist by training and learning, I lacked the experience of anthropologists necessary for facilitating my initial entry in the field. I was aware of how the task of creation of commonalities between the researcher and the respondents was the first step to gain the required trust, in order to obtain information and access to their lives. However, because of being an Arab Muslim and taking into consideration the historic ties between the Arab world and Kerala, this task was not so complicated. The sharing of practice and understanding of Islamic rituals was the bridge that I crossed to enter the field. As my usage of inter-disciplinary methods for my fieldwork necessitated me to become an anthropologist at times, I was faced with the huge gap between anthropological methods and political ones such as opinion surveys. By living with a Muslim family and trying to adopt the same lifestyle (specific dress code, food, travel limitations and curfew time), I saw how some of the categories I started working with were not only vague but incomprehensibly out of context for the large majority of my respondents.

My triple-faceted profile of a female Muslim foreigner played various roles and interchangeably permitted and denied me access to the field. To start with the latter, there was initially the visa dilemma since I had planned to go to India for a period of eight to nine months and the research visa would have been an almost impossible task. I managed to secure an affiliation with universities in India and obtained a study visa to India, after being interrogated by the consul in Cairo. My Muslim identity contributed to this, besides the fact that the flow of Egyptians to India is almost non-existent. As for being a Muslim, instead of being a stigma like almost everywhere else on the globe, it had granted me access to areas exclusively dominated by Muslims. Being an Arab Muslim was even a prestigious title and status honoured by the Muslims in India, and thus the majority were quite hospitable and helpful in providing me with either contacts or information and opinions on different subjects. The greatest challenge was being a female, on her own, conducting interviews among the orthodox Muslims, especially in rural settings as in Kerala.

In analysing cultural processes and trying to define the laws governing the social and political practice of the subjects of my study, the intersection of my Muslim identity with their assumptions or modes of thinking provided two advantages. The first is context-based and deals with human interactions, while the second advantage relates to the theoretical nature of the topic of my research. First, being a Muslim with similar physical features granted me the benefit of overcoming the processes of what Hayden (2009) calls the epistemology of estrangement. The intriguing observation is that, contrary to the experiences of ethnographers, I was not faced with the typical generalisations regarding my difference. My Islamic identity was sort of a researcher's shield or tool. I practised the same Islamic rituals since I belonged to the same Muslim sect; I also had the same common sense when it came to notions of decency or even humour. For women in the village, I was just like a typical Malayalee[2] Muslim girl with my headscarf and long dress, cooking with them in the kitchen or watering the tapioca field, but once the laptop and the notebook appeared, the reminders of difference chimed again. I observed how logically inverted the generalisations in our daily interactions were. Assumptions about my social habits were made and were fitting to exactly the same social moulds other Muslim girls adopted. My agency was even denied when, for instance, everyone made several assumptions regarding my everyday cultural practices, ranging from tolerating the same level of chilli; not using any cutlery while eating; coming back before sunset; wearing a headscarf; and even being able to understand Malayalam. Only when it came to the non-resident Indians (NRIs) in the Gulf countries, who had some contact with Egyptians and understood the cultural differences, were others alerted that the previously mentioned practices were part of my adjustment mechanisms in Kerala, whereas in fact I eat different food, speak a different language and do not abide by the same social practices. However, the interactions of these NRIs were exclusively with Egyptian male co-workers. As these women had no previous encounters with foreigners, my presence in their villages was conceived as being bizarre and confusing and thus ushered in an undisputable acceptance of treating me like a fellow Malayalee Muslim girl. In other cases, I witnessed a severe case of self-isolation once issues like my marital status or eating habits came up. What happened was that the village women simply overlooked me and for an instant forgot that I could follow what they were saying about me. Whenever a stranger or an outsider from another village visited, they started introducing the 'different' identity I held: being twenty-six years old and unmarried; my strange customs like constantly wearing a wrist watch; not being used to spicy Indian food; and most importantly my free mobility and ability to travel around India on my own.

Returning to the repercussions of being a Muslim, the second advantage was of understanding the nature of hybrid identities when it came to being a Muslim in a secular democratic environment. With the new global settings, the dilemma of accommodating Islam and citizenship centres in many contemporary political debates on democracy, liberalism and secularism. Instead of making dichotomously contending assumptions about religious identity and political behaviour, the case of Indian Muslims offers fascinating insight into showing how hybridity can form a basic tenet of understanding citizenship in an illiberal setting. Here, dualities would be questioned to arrive at an alternative conception of political agency and action. By dualities, I mean those actions accounted for by alluding to hermeneutics that are established in categories such as traditional versus modern, rural versus urban, religious versus secular, *madrasa*-educated versus college-educated and *'alim* versus common man. Related to this is the questionable viability of a dualistic theorisation of political action of Muslims along the continuum of alienation and violent protest. This is not only misleading, but it subscribes to the stereotyping discourses that, in the case of Indian Muslims, are fuelled by right-wing Hindu forces aiming at portraying Muslims as disloyal citizens, failing to integrate and carrying extraterritorial loyalties. Eventually, the differences resulting from living in a dictatorship or a democracy subsume when Muslims are subjected to demands of becoming good citizens and not only morally good persons.

Focusing on the North Indian Muslim, or the Keralite Muslim, as such proved to be a great challenge. The worlds of men and women varied tremendously, and I found myself working with two or four (in this case of comparing North Indian and Keralite) different units or subject groups. This made me rethink the division of my study to accommodate these different four groups, which respond to remarkably different questions of citizenship and subjugation.

One of the limitations that I acknowledge in my research is the representativeness of Muslims who are poor and do not belong to the middle class. However, this research was not intended to be representative as much as to be hypothesis-generative and indicative of certain dynamics in the community. Since it would have been practically impossible for me to deal solely with the urban poor, especially the males, because of my female identity – and this was proven through experience in my fieldwork – the initial declared focus and target of the study was the middle class, despite being a small fragment of the population. This triggered one concern, for if the focus were placed only on those carrying middle-class values, the results would be evidently and starkly biased (for example, the perception of legitimacy or efficacy might vary considerably). However, the middle class is the class generating the highest momentum for social change, and citizenship ideals remain after all middle-class values. Hence, I included in my interviews segments of the urban and rural poor, like rickshaw pullers and illiterate domestic workers.

In addition to this, there were significant limitations to the conduct of my fieldwork. The language barrier was the first. My knowledge of Urdu did not require me to have an interpreter in North India, but when I went to Malabar (Northern Kerala), I found that Malayalam is the only main spoken language, in addition to very broken colloquial Saudi Arabic among the men who have returned from the Gulf, and some English among the professors, teachers and a few students. I was compelled to search for a Malayalee female who was free and able to converse in English. This, on its own, was a difficult task. Later when I found an interpreter, she could not always travel with me everywhere, so I had to depend on myself, especially towards the end of my fieldwork. However, interestingly enough, I managed to pick up some Malayalam, particularly because all of the women in the villages could speak and write a traditional language called Arabi-Malayalam. I will point out the role of this language in creating transcultural identities among the Malabaris further on in my study. What I would like to emphasise here is that, through my knowledge of Arabic and their early schooling in this language besides Arabi-Malayalam, there were basic words that often broke the ice in our first encounter and gave them an incentive or rather the courage to speak with me.

Another obstruction was to overcome the psychological barriers of shyness of women and encourage them to assert their individuality. Sometimes if I wished to meet a group of women in a family and a male member decided to join, then the women would always ask him for guidance. If there was no male sitting around, the women would tend to laugh, get shy, and escape in the name of attending to their babies or housework. Eventually, in many cases our attempts to make them open their hearts to us and explain their views failed, but overall I managed to get extremely valuable insights on the political structures governing their lives and how they perceive their lives in India, politically and socially.

Conceptual framework: *jihād* and youth

The conceptual framework guiding this study is based on the idea of temporal and empirical space as a context, *jihād* as a means and citizenship as a goal. This book hence starts with the temporal space (or in other terms the historical context), then it demonstrates the contemporary socio-political settings in which Muslims live; and finally highlights the case studies where the agents appear in Delhi and Kerala.

In outlining these agents, a brief remark on the gender aspect is due. Emphasis has been traditionally cast on male youth as political and mobilisable actors, whether destructively as in terrorist networks or positively as in NGO activism and protests staged in democratic frameworks. Hence, in many cases the gender factor has been absent. Apart from few studies, such as Tabassum Khan's (2009) ethnographic study of the Muslim youth in Jamia and Winkelmann's (2005) study on girls in *madrasas*, little has been written on girls as agents of change.

This study takes into account this neglected aspect but also surmounts any over-assignment to the role gender plays. Balancing the gender aspect stems from the reality played by both male and female youth in the case studies of Delhi and Kerala. Whereas both share some social and political concerns, others suffer from gender-related problems, such as the males being targeted as potential terrorists or the females fighting with restraining *fatwas* concerning their job prospects. This study, however, focuses more on the political concerns but does not neglect social issues with political implications.

This study overcomes reductionist analysis of youth as passive or alienated masses who are more prone to fight or disrupt the mainstream and create parallel societies. Bayat (2009) establishes youth as a category of active citizenry reclaiming youth habitus and able, through what he terms 'the art of presence', to create social space within which those individuals who refuse to exit can advance the cause of human rights, equality and justice. This is precisely the line of argument I proceed from in my study, where the choice of students relates to their power as political actors and hence active citizens.

Having conducted expert interviews and press analysis, I identified the most strikingly strong agents of social change among Muslims as the youth in general in Delhi and the Muslim women in Kerala, then I gave them distinct reference as *jihādists*. The word *jihād*, meaning struggle, was used by many of my respondents as a description of their everyday reality in India. By calling the agents *jihādists*, I tried not to ascribe western terminology to the actors and reactors of my case study. Employing the term *jihādist* sought to achieve another general aim of the research; that is, to further explore the usage of non-Eurocentric conceptual approaches to the study of postcolonial and especially Muslim societies.

The choice of the term *jihād* as a means of achieving the goal of citizenship necessitates some conceptual clarification. The word *jihād* is an Arabic term that means struggle; it does not essentially connote the military aspect associated with it in relation to anti-Islamic propaganda. The root of the term is *jahada*, meaning to exert effort. The meaning of *jihād* is essential to the meaning of Islam, since Islam denotes submission to God, requiring in turn some form of struggle with the self. The Quran cites *jihād* as a form of resistance to pressures leading a person to disobey God. It also signifies striving to do righteous deeds. In a famous anecdote of the Prophet Muhammad, he was asked: "What kind of *jihād* is better?" He replied, "Speaking a word of truth in front of an oppressive ruler."

Jihād, as an action, has two forms. The first is the greater *jihād*, which signifies struggle and self-discipline, and the second is the lesser *jihād*, which is combative, and means repelling wars of aggression against Muslims. It is the first form of struggling with the self on which I am basing this study. The implication of the concept of *jihād* is in transforming religious rituals into media for social change, or as Smith puts it: "an authentic imperative to bring about change, one deeply imbedded in the Islamic tradition" (Smith, 1970, p. 227). By referring to youth's struggles as *jihād*, I am employing a form of conceptual relevance, instead of obstinately applying an alien concept to a different environment.

One way to conceptually locate my usage of *jihād* is to refer to Maududi, who was known for his scholarly treatises on Islamic nationalism and became interestingly contextualised among progressive Muslims. Having little to share with the Pakistani group, Maududi's ideas on *jihād* and an Islamic life were and still are increasingly circulating among the youth influenced by Jamaati Islami-i-Hind ideas.[3] To him, *jihād* was a revolutionary means to attain the revolutionary core of Islam's message:

Like all revolutionary ideologies, Islam shuns the use of current vocabulary and adopts a terminology of its own, so that its own revolutionary ideals may be distinguished from common ideals. The word *jihād* belongs to this particular terminology of Islam. Islam purposely rejected the word *harb* and other Arabic words bearing the same meaning of 'war' and used the word *jihād*, although more forceful and wider in connotation. The nearest correct meaning of the word *jihād* in English can be expressed as: "To exert one's utmost endeavour in promoting a cause."

(Maududi, 1980, p. 5)

Although *jihād* could not be semantically interpreted as an armed struggle, or holy war, it is the commonly known significance of the term. Historical reasons exist for this disparity between the textual meaning and the popular interpretation of the term, which are embodied in the interpretation of a *shi'a* sect (the *Kharijite*) of the term as legitimate violence against the enemies of Islam (Jalal, 2008). This was reinforced in contemporary times due to the media's usage of the word *jihād* and associating it with any violent or armed action in which Muslims are engaged. Muslim groups themselves tend to use this term to describe violent anti-system activities. An example of this is shown through the *Hindu* newspaper, as it reported the email sent by the so-called India's Jihadist Movement, which was accused of planting bombs outside courtrooms in Uttar Pradesh in 2007 as a means of vengeance of the 2002 Gujarat pogrom. The email ends with the following statement: "Only Islam", it concluded, "has the power to establish a civilized society, and this could only be possible in Islamic rule, which could be achieved by only one path: *jihād.*"

Jihād, as I will show throughout this book, carries very different meanings in the psyche of the Muslim community. For a Jamaati Islami-affiliated North Indian scholar, *jihād*'s contemporary significance is linked to the universality of the Muslim *Ummah* (nation) and how their issues are not considered merely specific or regional. In her words:

> Muslim homes are not just limited to what is inside the four walls of their houses or what is inside the borders of their states. Every Muslim country is one's own homeland and home. Since false news and reports are spreading rumours about *jihād* and Muslims, it is our moral duty to defend these innocent fighters and to clear them in front of the world. *Jihād's* tool is the Quran: Allah asks the believers not to obey the nonbelievers and to do strong *jihād* with them with the Quran. It is apparent from here that there is no call for a fighting place or war, but debate. Women's *jihād* is to stay at home, take care of her husband's comfort, and make sure that her children get an Islamic education and way of life.
>
> (Thanaullah, 2005, p. 114)

The book starts by presenting the historical context in the post-partition era. The main question here concerns the *ijtihād* (independent reasoning) of the Indian *'ulama* (scholars) in the time of partition and their contribution to modern Islamic political theory.[4] This section explicates how the notion of community was theorised and presented within both the broader and the global Islamic discourse and the local context of India as a case study. This impelled me to look at the myth of the *Ummah* as a component of what can be termed as transcultural citizenship and as a new level of analysis in global politics. The Indian case presented us with first: a postcolonial order of an application of a liberal conception of citizenship, coupled with an invention of minority status and adjustments guided by a uniquely secular Constitution; second, these adjustments led to the innovation of concepts such as composite nationalism.

To examine how the given socio-political context of an individual shapes his/her perception of certain variables such as political efficacy, agency, conception of citizenship rights and belief in democracy, I moved from the historical to the contemporary. My points of entry start with the demolishment of the Babri Masjid in 1996, the Gujarat carnage of 2002 and the Ayodhya court decision of 2010. These were selected as events in order to measure public opinion towards identity-related questions. The examination of citizenship as an identity guides the analysis of the hegemonic discourses governing the lives of Muslims in India. The demonstration of these discourses came after a meticulous literature review of what has been written in the past thirty years on Indian Muslims and their varying conditions in different states of India. After indicating the different political, socio-economic and ideological discourses, the aim of this research was to reveal the response of the public with a specific emphasis on the middle class, which is the most evident carrier of citizenship ideals.

The predicaments Indian Muslims face in several parts of India, where their sense of security is critically low, convey a significant part of the story. However, the other less-narrated stories are of youth redefining the meaning of safe spaces. Although the youth are not a homogenous entity (even Hindu youth play major roles in the development of the Muslim community), whether in Delhi or Kerala, they were regarded as the victims of the discourses and the initiators of change.

In Kerala, due to high levels of education among women, high degrees of psychological disorders appeared (amongst women in particular) in the Muslim majority district, Malappuram, where I did my fieldwork. This district interestingly witnessed the highest rates of social change among all other districts in India in terms of education, social mobility and elevated standards of living and income levels. Since women were the subjects of this change to a great extent, I gave them the status of being *jihādists*; although they do not work from gender-based perspectives, but within the mainstream legal and social perspective while utilising Islam as a reference and support to gain more agency.

To conclude, I report the results of the survey I conducted among the students in Delhi and Kerala to consider different correlations between gender, levels of religiosity and political participation. This led me to consider the different implications concerning the betterment of the life-space in which citizenship is practised and felt. This comparison between a metropolis and a periphery was necessary in construing a composite picture of political consciousness in India and is also useful in demonstrating several contradictions of cultural belonging as modes of exercising claims to citizenship.

As this study seeks to bring together different and often contending voices, marking pluralistic political orientations, it does not present a uniform and unidimensional vision. It is a modest attempt to amalgamate different discourses and to present voices of youth. At times the study might also appear to be far from adhering to moulds set by academic standards of categorisation, objectivity or measurement, as folk-based perceptions would be woven in the political narratives, but this is intentionally sketched, for hybrid entanglements are part of everyday life, especially of the Indian Muslim. This study seeks to project an honest picture of how young middle-class Muslims in India think. Hence, readers from different perspectives might find some accounts offensive, reductionist or even biased. I apologise for this and for any unintentional reproduction of undue generalisation, but as reality is so diverse that it is often contradictory, so are many of the arguments in this book. The limitations of being a foreign female doing fieldwork among a community that is always afraid of being targeted by the police are reflected in the shortcomings of the study. No work on India can cover every aspect or be outstanding in itself – perhaps this is a by-product of the difficult living conditions for a foreign researcher, be it the water and power cuts, the bumpy roads, the night curfew for girls or even the intelligence service following me during my research.

Notes

1 I am using the term 'modern' on behalf of both *madrasa* teachers (*ustādh*) and governmental or private school teachers who used this same term and sometimes 'secular' to refer to what is otherwise known as mainstream schools.

2 Malayalee means a person from Kerala. From now on, I use this term interchangeably with Keralite.

3 For a comprehensive study on the Jamaati Islami, see Ahmad (2009).

4 *Ijtihād* is defined by Ibn Al athir as "the effort and endeavour undertaken for attaining some objective". The root comes from *juhd* or *jahd* meaning employing one's complete strength. Whereas *jahd* means hardship and difficulty, *juhd* gives the sense of power and strength. (Ibrahim, 2004, p. 123). For Shariati, *ijtihād* refers to:

> a free and independent endeavour aiming at obtaining a thorough and progressive understanding of Islam in all its dimensions.... It is a tool by which a conscious mujtahid (the person who practices *ijtihād*) presents a new and changing interpretation of Islam according to his progressive and exalted outlook.... Therefore, *ijtihād* is a grand factor in creating motion, life and constant renewal of Islamic culture and spirit as well as practical and legal orders through changing of times.
>
> (Ibrahim M. M., 2004, p. 124)

References

Abdul-Fattah, S. (2008). Ru'ya fil 'ilāqah bain al-dīny wal madani wal siyāsy, moqadammāt minhajiyyah (Methodological Notes on the Relation Between the Religious, the Civil and the Political). In N. Mustafa et al., *Al-'ilāqah bain al-dīny wal siyāsy, misr wal 'ālam ru'a mutanawi'a wa khibrāt muta'adeddah (The Relation Between the Religious and The Political: Various Views and Experience from Egypt and the World)* (pp. 17–43). Cairo: Shourouk International.

Ahmad, I. (2009). *Islamism and Democracy in India: The Transformation of Jamaat-e-Islami*. Princeton: Princeton University Press.

Bayat, A. (2009). *Life as Politics: How Ordinary People Change the Middle East*. Cairo: The American University in Cairo Press.

Hayden, B. (2009). Displacing the Subject: A Dialogical Understanding of the Researching Self. *Anthropological Theory*, 9(1), 81–101.

Ibrahim, M. M. (2004). Ijtihād: A Need of the Hour: A Case Study of Ali Shariati. *Islam and the Modern Age*, 35(1), 123–141.

Jalal, A. (2008). *Partisans of Allah: Jihad in South Asia*. Cambridge, MA: Harvard University Press.

Khan, T. (2009). *Emerging Muslim Identity in India's Globalized and Mediated Society: An Ethnographic Investigation of the Halting Modernities of the Muslim Youth of Jamia Enclave*. PhD thesis. New Delhi: Ohio University.

Maududi, A. (1980). *Jihād in Islam*. Kuwait: International Islamic Federation of Students' Organisations.

Smith, D. E. (1970). *Religion and Political Development*. Boston, MA: Little, Brown and Co.

Thanaullah (2005). *Fikr Islāmi mein jihād ki haythiyat wa maqām* (The significance and position of the concept of *jihād* in Islamic thought). In P. Rehmani (ed.), *Jihād: ma'nā wa mafhūm, ahkām, surati hal (Jihād: the meaning, the concept, the rules, and the state of affairs)* (pp. 111–118). New Delhi: Daawat Publications.

Winkelman, M. J. (2005). *From Behind the Curtain: A Study of a Girls' Madrasa in India*. Amsterdam: Amsterdam University Press.

2 The quest for a community versus composite nationalism

When the two reached a safe destination, the man carrying the box placed it on the floor. "So, what is my share?" he asked.

"One-fourth."

"This is too little."

"I do not think so. I think it is too much. I was the one who found the box."

"Right. But who has carried this heavy load all the way?"

"Do you agree to fifty–fifty?"

"Very well. Open."

The box was opened. Out came a man with a sword in his hand. He cut the two claimants into four.

(Manto, 2000: Taqseem)

India presents a unique case among postcolonial societies. This uniqueness is due to the way the Indian nationalist movement evolved and led to independence triggered by civil disobedience. The secular, civil and constitutionally guided path that India adopted in the postcolonial stage was emphasised and distinguished from the military or unstable political systems that plagued other countries. There is a broad literature analysing how India dealt with this transition and an ample number of theorisations on the Indian model of state and development. The aim of this chapter is to review the literature on the decisional perception of Muslims who opted to stay in India and not migrate to the newly founded Pakistan at the point of independence, and the kind of citizenship they endorsed. The chapter stresses the Islamic justifications for staying and opting for a secular democracy. Indian Muslims offer a distinctive case study among Muslim societies in that they have not just chosen to stay but their decision was also religiously justified. Finally, I will point out how Indian Muslims deliberated strategies of accommodation to their new status as a minority, yet a 'citizen' minority, and how far the term minority applies to them.

Contending impacts of diverse notions of community: Ummah as a myth?

Both British colonialism and Indian independence marked two episodes in the Muslim psyche in India: 'minoritisation' and 'nationalisation'. Muslim supremacy in India, as a ruling class, had ended with the collapse of the Mughal Empire and the defeat of the 1857–58 mutiny. In the Indian context, the intersection of secularism, nationalism and democracy was the field in which an idea of the community was cultivated. Several hypotheses govern the discourse on Muslim identities and politics. Among these is the idea of the Muslim community as an *Ummah* (an Arabic term connoting a specific form of a nation), which poses as a myth to some, and a non-fallacious reality to others. In the following section, I investigate this question by examining the political ideas of Muslim religious scholars (henceforth referred to as *'ulama*).

There are ample studies of the general notion of community. In his study of peasant insurgency, Chatterjee (2000) focused on 'community' as a unifying idea and a fundamental social character, as pre-existing solidarities were themselves the incentives for collective action. The question remains whether collective action in the Muslim community could be approached with the same logic. Being non-monolithic and formed of different classes and castes, it is hard to assert that individual identities are derived from community membership. The endeavour to understand the meaning of community encourages us to build mental maps capturing the relationships between consciousness, everyday social action and perceptions of risks and interests. Communities are thus woven around trust, social networks and shared norms (Mitra, 2003). This, in turn, builds solidarities in the form of alliances.

Contrary to western liberal political theory, in Muslim societies the communal group is considered to be the basic unit of political representation. There are two aspects of community formation and perception. The first is of *group solidarity* and the second concerns the sense of *superiority* of the community. The notion of solidarity or *'assabiyya* is one of the cornerstones of sociological analyses of Muslim societies and thought. There is a particular aspect of the Islamic tradition bearing on the tendency of Muslims to organise on the basis of their faith in politics (Robinson, 2000, p. 182). This is, to a considerable extent, linked to Ibn Khaldun's theory of *'assabiyya*, which he considered a social force, an organisational authority and thus an indicator of social stability.[1] His employment of religion in the analysis of power left its hallmark on contemporary Islamic political thought. However, it could not serve to understand societies in which Muslims did not rule. As such, Islamic political thought remained focused on societies where Muslims ruled and not where they were co-rulers or subjects.

Having formed communities, Muslims started a quest for an Islamic Caliphate after the death of the Prophet Muhammad and managed to form different Caliphates for centuries until the demise of the Ottoman Empire in 1924, thus ending the empirical manifestation of the system of Islamic rule. However, this quest for an Islamic state, according to the legacy of Islamic political history, was circumscribed to the struggle for power, and not for ideals. The civil wars that occurred in the post-prophetic era between the Prophet's followers and relatives were indeed for power. The absolutism that marked the governance and power acquisition was the replacement of a prior democratic setting, where sovereignty had rested with the people, and principles of popular representation

were enacted during the life of the Prophet. Few genuinely innovative books theorising the politics of the state had been written.[2] In this section, I will refer to
Al-Mawardī's book *Alahkam Alsultaniyya* (*The Ordinances of Government*), the
first book on this subject, written in the eleventh century. Although only a small
section of the book was devoted to this cause, most books on the subject were
devised as a loyalty and allegiance tool to a Caliphate. Al-Mawardī's section on
the appointment of the sovereign (the *imam*) had influenced the course of Islamic
political theory until today, since it managed to transform the traditions and
political opinions of the past into a logical system (Khan, 1983). Al-Mawardī
contended that, by executing what was due to the community, the sovereign also
accomplished what was due to God in relation to their rights and duties. Two
changes of policy disqualified him from leadership: lack of justice and physical
disability (Al-Mawardī, 1996, p. 17).

Qamaruddin Khan (1983) points out that Al-Mawardī's work has been based
on dogmatic theology, which has prevented successive Muslim writers from
questioning his authority or introducing new concepts in political thought. In an
innovative measure, Indian *'ulama* such as Maulana Husain Ahmad Madani and
Maulana Abul Kalam Azad contributed significantly to Islamic political theory,
and it is a misfortune that their attempts in generating a theory such as composite
nationalism have not been awarded the respect and recognition they deserve
from Muslim scholars worldwide.

Orientalist and Hindu propagandist writings on Muslims are guided by the
proposition that Islam is a complete reference for Muslims in terms of identity
and moral codes. These writings assume that, as a result of profound attachment
of Muslims to the *'ulama* and orthodox Islam, the Muslim community typically
resists a secular and democratic order of society and politics.

However, the contribution of Indian *'ulama* mainly focuses on the myth of
the separate nation by questioning the proposition that there is an inherent conflict between practiced Islam and forces of secularism and democracy, or tradition and modernity. Stifled voices of Muslim secularists and those opposing the
two-nation theory highlighted, on the one hand, the unresolved issue of how
Muhammad Ali Jinnah, who later became the first Governor-General of Pakistan, together with his colleagues managed to create the two-nation theory and
mobilise Muslims (with their drive of not only ideological but also material concerns);[3] and on the other hand, they underlined Iqbal's[4] insurgence of the call for
dignity of the middle class out of the colonial subjugation, thus deconstructing
the thesis of the inevitability of the partition of India.

Hasan (1997) explains that the eventual success of the mobilisation of
Muslims was not based on ideological grounds, but was due to the context of the
performance and resignation of Congress ministries in 1939, the fluid political
climate during the time of war, the launching of the 'Quit India' Movement and
the British government's willingness to adopt a different political strategy with
the League. All of this provided an opportunity for Jinnah to emerge as a key
political player and to propagate the two-nation theory. However, it must be
stressed that the two-nation theory remained elite-directed. It was taken up by

Jinnah and fuelled by the economic anxieties of certain classes who were the professional groups in Uttar Pradesh (UP) and Bihar, the powerful landed classes in Punjab, Sind and UP, and the industrialists of western and eastern India (Hasan, 1997, p. 56; Hussain, 2006).

Besides group solidarity, the second aspect of the subtle sense of superiority of community appears since the Quran mentions the Muslim *Ummah* as the most benevolent *Ummah*. This has further implications to relations of power and its exercise. The community of believers is privileged as long as they follow four categories of obligations comprising of the theological, practical, personal and social aspects of Islam: faith (*imān*), actions (*a'māl*), exhortation to truth (*twasau bi al haq*) and exhortation to perseverance (*tawaṣau bil ṣabr*) (Quran 103:3). *Ummah* consciousness derives from the Quranic-imposed duty on those "who have attained to faith, enjoining upon one another patience in adversity (*ṣabr*) and [enjoining] upon one another compassion (*marḥammah*)" (Quran 90:17).

The Egyptian Islamic scholar Al-Qaradawy (2010) examines the concept of *Ummah* and presents constructive meanings of the term, in relation to its religious, political, geographical and social aspects. Religion could be the basis upon which the *Ummah* is defined; so we could have a Muslim *Ummah* or a Christian or a Hindu *Ummah*. It is also a political concept, since not only Muslims constitute an *Ummah*; the historical example shows us that Muslims and Jews were two religious *Ummahs* but one political *Ummah*. Geography, as a basis of political identity and citizenship in the modern age, was surprisingly one of the elements of *Ummah*; the endowment of political benefits was only attributed after immigration (*hijra*), meaning after joining Medina and participating in its defence. The solidarity among tribes and inhabitants of Medina incurred another social element to the construction of the *Ummah*. Therefore, the Medina Treaty accepted multiple identities and belongings.

In addition to the Medina covenant, there is also a notion of patriotic brotherhood upon sharing a homeland that finds evidence in the Quran upon the reference to the nations of prophets and the word 'brothers' to denote them.[5] Eventually, the primacy of the human being is the hegemonic principle, which also proves the role of agency of humans in social change, regardless of their religion.[6] The concept of the *Ummah* theologically, therefore, was thought of by Asad (2003) as "a defined space enabling Muslims to practice the disciplines of *dīn* in the world", and not an imagined community or an aspired political entity (p. 197).

As a conceptual unit of analysis, *Ummah* can denote several aspects of community formation, varying from the implications of a people, a society, a nation, a tribe, a culture or a multi-social, multicultural community. For proponents of 'Islamic anthropology', *Ummah* is the basic category of investigation since it is an "*a priori* of the Islamic perspective that mankind is created as a culture-bearing, social being who must necessarily exist in community" (Davies, 1988, p. 128). Sardar (1998) points out the locality of integration as defined by the Friday Mosque and the externality on an international level by the collectivity of Muslims as defined by the notion of the *Ummah*.

Empirically, religion could be analytically treated as the practical translation of faith. When we add the concept of *Ummah* to this analysis, religion or *dīn* (the Arabic term for religion, which also means a path) appears as an active ingredient since every *Ummah* possesses a *dīn*. Davies (1988) expatiates on the concept of *dīn* as it gives the community a realm of meaning of the self and of other communities, where relationships are actualised as system and process. The function of *dīn* acts as a tool of translation of these networks of relationships into patterns of living. Consequently, the concepts of *Ummah* and *dīn* become mutually defining (pp. 129–130).

In the Indian context, the search or construction of a communal identity took place within a broader framework of finding one's place within the 'nation'. Chakrabarty (2008) argues that the first serious attempt to establish the Indian Muslims as a separate community was Rahmat Ali's demand for a separate national status in 1933. Before him, Jinnah showed a determined opinion in the 1916 Lucknow Pact regarding a necessity of separate electorates to ensure communal harmony. The culmination of these demands was evident in the British Communal Award of 1932, which granted separate electorates to minorities (Chakrabarty, 2008, pp. 41–43).

India was faced with a large-scale construction of an idea of a Hindu nation that required the opposite construction of an idea of a Muslim nation to exercise upon it hegemony and majoritarianism. This is one side of the story. The other side is told by some of the Muslim leaders who had crafted an idea of a separate community. What interests me here is not this crafting, but the counter-discourse of Muslim leaders and the ways they envisioned their life in a framework of composite nationalism.

According to Medieval Islamic political thought, the world was traditionally divided into two zones: one of peace (*darul salam*), and one of war (*darul ḥarb*). The benefit goes to the Indian *'ulama* who pioneered the reworking of these divisions. Later, Al-Qaradawy (2010) affirms this point of view. Indian Muslim scholars emphasised the recognition of the concept of homeland (*waṭ an*) in Islam. The love of the place of birth and domicile is a natural tendency and thus, theologically, India is not *dar-al-Islam* (the abode of Islam), but neither is it *dar-ul-kufr* (the abode of atheism) or even *darul ḥarb* (the abode of war). It is *dar-al-'ahd* (of treaty), *dar-al-aman* (peace) and *waṭan* (home) (Shahabuddin & Wright, 1987, p. 157; Wasey, author interview, September 2010).

Wasey (2008) argued that the spirit of coexistence marked the interaction of Islam with the Indian civilisation. Thus a new term in Islamic thought was invented: *ṣulḥ-e-kul*, or peace with all, which was evident throughout Akbar's reign. The division of the world into *darul ḥarb* (war) and *dar al-Islam* had been replaced by *darul aman* (peace) or *darul ṣulḥ or daralmu'ahada* (treaty): the region of peaceful coexistence with those who did not accept the faith of Muhammad. The result of this coexistence is visible today among the Bohras and Memons of Gujarat and Maharashtra, the Mappillas of Kerala and the Muslim population of Bengal. North India witnessed a contrasting picture.

Although the majority of Muslim scholars agree with this classification, among them is a minority claiming the failure of the determination of the nature of *dar*. Shaz (2001), for example, in his critique of *dar almu'ahada*, argues that the *'ulama* missed the point (in their resemblance of the Indian Constitution with the Medina treaty) that the treaty in Medina had brought the Prophet to the position of ultimate authority, while in the Indian situation, the treaty or the Indian Constitution had given the majority a clear edge over Muslims. In addition to this, the treaty was made by the Prophet (who is the ultimate representative of Muslims), but those who claimed to be representative of the Muslim community in the constituent assembly could by no Islamic ruling be called Muslim representatives (p. 90).

This leads us to the wider discussion on the role the *Ummah* plays in shaping political identity. Indian Muslim elites' ideas owe a lot to the past and derive from their historical heritage. Many historians have pointed out that Indian Muslims tended to look less to the international Islamic community and more towards "the organization and solidarity of the local Indian Muslim community for their strength and development" (Esposito, 1987, p. 22).

These politics-based aspirations as to where the Muslim community establishes solidarity networks were reflected in the dilemma of political legitimacy. For the Indian Muslim, justifications for the legitimacy of political orientations shifted tremendously according to historical events. Initially, to a great extent, Muslim allegiance to the British was sanctioned by scholars like Sir Syed Ahmad Khan. By 1857, the *'ulama's* main objective was to adjust to the *raj* (British rule) rather than repudiate it. According to some accounts, the *'ulama*'s role in the 1857 mutiny was almost non-existent, and they were not brought afore to political participation until much later through Azad's introduction in the public scene (Haq, 1970). Interestingly, the Jamaati Islami in India had fought against the 'alien' concept of a territorial state since it challenged the establishment of Islamic rule on a universal level, as imagined by them (Quraishi, 1971).

The later intricate roles that religious identity played in forming political alliances were as manifold as the idea of diversity of communities as inherent in the actual concept of *Ummah*. It could be even argued that one of the concerns that led to the theory of composite nationalism and the negation of the two-nation theory was the fear of the *'ulama* to negate the traditional world view of the *Ummah*.

The rise of Muslims' discontent with the British

Returning to the case of Indian Muslims, the shift from the allegiance to the British was explained in Titus' (1959) study of Islam in South Asia, which demonstrated the effects of occupation on Muslim discontent with the British. The first effect concerned language and the replacement of Persian by English. Second, the abolition of the governmental posts of *Qādhi* (judge) and *Qādhi al Qudhāt* (judge of judges or supreme judge) and the consequent effect upon the administration of Muslim law had a direct impact on the secularisation of the life of Muslims by a non-Muslim power. This resulted in discontent and prompted the question of whether India was any longer a suitable place of residence for Muslims (thus the recurring debate on *darul ḥarb* or *darul Islam*). Consequently, determination to boycott western institutions, led by Muslims, followed. There were continual negative references to western education. Hence, Muslim students fell behind due to pursuing a policy of isolation and self-sufficiency until the mid-nineteenth century with Sir Syed Ahmed Khan's educational movement, which will be discussed later (Titus, 1959, pp. 199–200).

Different historical stages marked the contention between Muslims and the British colonial power. The participation of Muslims in the 1857 mutiny was the first watershed in this series. From Subaltern non-elitist Muslim perspectives, the partition of Bengal in 1905 and its annulment in 1911 was another moment less investigated. Whereas Muslim elites were discontented with the cancellation of the partition, there was rising restlessness on a mass level with the colonial powers. Orthodox leaders of the community played a strong role, especially with the commencement of the Turko-Italian war: either by the inclusion of the name of the Turkish Caliph in the Friday *khutba* (speech) and prayers, or through writings in the Urdu press by Islamic scholars such as Muhammad Ali and Azad. It is argued that the Turkish Caliph had been recognised as the legitimate ruler of all Muslims in contrast to the resisted British imperial power (Karandikar, 1969). The employment of Muslim identity, hence, as a means of resistance to the British by arousing the North Indian Muslim masses could be seen as a resistance mechanism to the colonial powers rather than a reductionist idea of a fascination of the idea of the *Ummah* since their goal eventually was independence from the British and not succession to the Ottoman Empire. Their usage of Islamic symbols and metaphors was a tool for projecting a counter hegemonic performance.

With the defeat of the Ottoman Empire, the Indian National Congress, led by Gandhi, initiated both the Khilafat movement and the non-cooperation movement that included Muslims in its folds. The eventual result was the production of two kinds of spirits amongst Muslims:

> The first is racial, nationalist and linguistic divisions and differences. The second is the approach and thinking that *jihād* should not be for religious and spiritual purposes, but for race and country, so as to divorce the religious spirit from it.
>
> (Madani, 2005, p. 97)

Some of the literature on the Khilafat movement in India indicates that it was less about the Ottoman Empire than about India since it was essentially linked to the Gandhian non-cooperation movement. The use of religious symbols to address a secular demand was a tool often utilised by the colonised to fight imperialism (see, for example, Bamford 1925/1985; Bose & Jalal, 2004; Dale, 1990; Haq, 1970; Hussain, 2006; Jalal, 2008; Madani, 2005; Sanyal, 2005). This was reflected not only in Madani's work, but also in a famous speech by Azad before the Khilafat committee at Agra in 1921:

> We must decide on the goal of the Khilafat movement. Is the goal somewhere outside India? [...] In fact our goal is not outside India. It is not in Iraq or Syria or Asia Minor or Smyrna. Our objective is to test the power of our own belief (*imān*), determination (*azm*) and action (*amal*). Or, let us put it in this way: the goal is in our own country. It is a question of the victory or defer of our own country. Unless you succeed in your own country success will not greet you elsewhere. [...] India is the first goal of the Khilafat movement.
>
> (cited in Haq, 1970, p. 102)

According to Metcalf (2005), this movement drew popular Muslim participation into political movements for the first time through outlining a new role for the *'ulama*, while endorsing Gandhi's ideals and reinforcing an understanding of a bounded society (p. 29). Madani, in outlining the Muslim stance, cited Maulana Mohammad Ali Jauhar's last speech at the Round Table Conference in London on 12 September 1932:

> One word as to the Muslim position, with which I shall deal at length on some other occasion. Many people in England ask us why this question of Hindu and Muslim comes into politics, and what it has to do with these things. I reply, it is a wrong conception of religion that you have, if you exclude politics from it. It is not dogma. It is not ritual! Religion, to my mind, means the interpretation of life. I have a culture, a polity, an outlook on life – a complete synthesis which is Islam. Where God commands I am a Muslim first, a Muslim second, and a Muslim last, and nothing but a Muslim. [...] But where India is concerned, where India's freedom is concerned, I am an Indian first, an Indian second, an Indian last, and nothing but an Indian.
> [...]
> I belong to two circles of equal size, but which are not concentric. One is India, and the other is Muslim world. When I came to England in 1920 at the head of the Khilafat Delegation, my friend said: "You must have some sort of a crest for your stationary." I decided to have it with two circles on it. In one circle was the word 'India'; in the other circle was Islam, with the word 'Khilafat'. We as Indian Muslims came in both circles. We belong to these two circles, each of more than 300 millions, and we can leave neither.... We are not nationalists but super nationalists, and I as a Muslim say that "God made man and the Devil made the nation." Nationalism divides; our religion binds. No religious wars, no crusades, have seen such holocaust and have been so cruel as your last war, and that was a war of your nationalism, and not my Jehad.
>
> (Cited in Madani, 2005, pp. 137–139)

The stance of these *'ulama*, who reflected the state of mind of many Muslims of India, made it predictable that they would join the nationalist struggle of the Indian National Congress. However, at some point, the Muslim League emerged and the Congress lost many of its ties with Muslims.[7]

As a centre of nationalist activity during the Khilafat and non-cooperation movement, Aligarh Muslim University played a pivotal role (Bamford, 1925/1985). Despite the eventual establishment of Pakistan, the Aligarh movement nevertheless had led to the emergence of strong intellectual and political figures that shared the steering of the Khilafat movement and the independence struggle in India. It failed, however, in achieving its initial aim of benefiting from the western experiences by not filling the enormous generational gap of the Muslims who were adherent to their faith (Al-Nadwi, 1965/2005).

The propaganda of misrepresentation was another factor leading to communalism. In a letter written in 1938, Wazir Hasan, a notable Muslim League jurist who propagated for Hindu–Muslim unity, called on Nehru to respond actively to the communal propaganda in order to save the struggle for independence after the defeat of the Muslim League in the 1937 elections. He wrote:

The propaganda of misrepresentation, lies and religious and communal hatred … is being carried on from day to day with ever increasing false statement of facts under the guise of the rights of the minorities and religious hatred. I may refer in particular to the following items:

(1) That the Congress is a Hindu organisation.
(2) That it wants to establish not swaraj but Hindu Raj in India.
(3) That the Congress and its governments in seven provinces are trying to oppress and crush the minorities particularly the Mussalmans.
(4) That the Muslim League is the true representative of the views and ideas of the eighty millions of India.
(5) That there are very few Mussalmans in the Congress and these few are traitors to Islam.

(Quoted in Karandikar, 1969, pp. 250–251)

Prior to independence, the boycott movement against the British yielded influential figures that shaped the course of the Muslim community in India. Among these were Muhammad Ali, Shaukat Ali, Maulana Abul Kalam Azad and Abdulbari Alfarangmahali, who all religiously stood next to Gandhi in boycotting British goods. This movement was then followed by another pan-Indian national movement (Al-Nadwi, 2005). Several movements and names appear most prominently in the struggle for independence and for or against partition. Apart from the Muslim League, Iqbal and Jinnah, who endorsed the call for Pakistan, names of people and movements who rejected separatism are numerous and include Husain Ahmad Madani, Hakim Ahmed Khan, Saifuddin Kitchlew, Mukhtar Ahmad Ansari, Maulana Abul Kalam Azad, the Indian National Congress Muslims, the Ahrārs movement, Jamiyat al-Ulama, the Imarat-e-Shariat in Bihar, the All India Momin Conference (AIMC) and the All India Shiah Political Conference (AISPC).

Whereas the demand for Pakistan was not supported by arguments containing Quranic verses or religious experiences, it was credited with democratic and secular arguments such as freedom and the fundamental right of self-determination (a western-based right and not an Islamic one), and the demand for the unity of India was supported with Quran and Hadith and came from most of the *'ulama*.

Since this study deals exclusively with the anti-Pakistan discourses, space does not allow me to expand on historical studies concerning the role of Muhammad Ali Jinnah (who was portrayed as the major spokesperson for the demand of Pakistan) and the Muslim League in the partition. However, it is important to refer to one observation, namely the limited and vague religious terminology used in most speeches calling for Pakistan, which is remarkably clear in Jinnah's speeches, for example. In his presidential address in 1940, Jinnah urged the workers of the League to "come forward as servants of Islam [and] organise the people economically, socially, educationally and politically" (quoted in Amir, 2000, p. 126). He spoke of an Islamic heritage, the *millat*, the Quran and the Islamic life, without explaining which points he was emphasising; despite this, he later on advocated socialism and nationalism in Pakistan. In his address to the Delhi session of the Muslim League in 1943:

> The people of Pakistan will choose their representatives to the Constitution-making body on the basis of adult franchise.... Democracy is in our blood, our marrow. I could not work for a single day if I thought I was working for the capitalists and landlords who fatten on the sweat of our people. In Pakistan exploitation will not be allowed. If the capitalists and landlords are wise they will have to adjust themselves to the new and modern conditions. If they don't, God help them! We shall not.
>
> (Quoted in Sajjad Zaheer, *A Case for Congress-League Unity*, first published in 1944, Bombay, in Hasan, 2000, pp. 113–132)

The invalidity of Islamic-based conceptualisations of citizenship and the state was also reflected in Muslim League manifestos. The 1936 Muslim League election manifesto was comprised of national democratic terminology. Its main principles included democratic self-government and the utilisation of the legislatures by Muslim League representatives for the benefits of the people in all spheres of national life (Karandikar, 1969, p. 246).

Hussain's (2006) study of the nationalist political processes in Bihar shows the strong opposition to the Muslim League from the Imarat-e-Shari'ah, the AIMC and the AISPC, especially due to the non-Islamicness of Muslim League's leaders. The Mufti of Imarat-e-Shari'ah even issued a *fatwa* declaring it un-Islamic to join the Muslim League because "its claims of protecting and representing the *siyasi* (political) and *mazhabi* (religious) rights of Muslims were not grounded in the Quran but the arithmetic of majority votes" (p. 35).

The struggle against partition was led by both western-educated liberals and traditional religious scholars. Although I do not wish to ignore the role of liberals in the independence struggle, the aim of this chapter is to examine how Islam, not just as a religion, but also as a way of life and a path, has been utilised to further political objectives that resonate with those of the secular liberals.

Those *'ulama* who espoused the case of Indian nationalism and a united India conceived of India as *dar al 'ahd* (based on the Prophet Muhammad's pact with the Jews of Medina) as the model and theological justification for sharing power with non-Muslims, or *dar al aman*, which they described as a territory in which the Muslims live peacefully and have the freedom to perform their religious obligations (Shahabuddin & Wright, 1987, p. 157). It is beyond the scope of this chapter to cite all the movements and activists during the partition time. Consequently, I choose to focus on Maulana Abul Kalam Azad, an independent Muslim scholar who joined the Indian Congress, and Maulana Husain Ahmad Madani, who was affiliated to the organisation of Deoband, as not just proponents but designers of the theory of 'composite nationalism'.

Maulana Abul Kalam Azad: the introduction of Muslim politics

Maulana Abul Kalam Muhiyudeen Ahmed, who was known by his pen name, Azad, lived from 1888 until 1958. Before independence, Azad was a leader in the Khilafat movement and was associated with Gandhi in the nationalist struggle. After India's independence, he became the first minister of education. It is argued that it was Azad who dragged the rather detached Muslim *'ulama* into politics and made them enter the domain almost exclusively occupied by western-educated elites. To Azad, politics were intertwined with religion, as obvious from his main objectives of destroying obscurantism in the religious life of Muslims and establishing a joint platform for Muslims and Hindus to fight the British (Haq, 1970). In 1927, after the emergence of the Khilafat movement, Abul Kalam Azad wrote in al-Hilal magazine acknowledging the largely contested issue that remained a paradox for political theorists till the coming century; namely, the relationship between Islam and nationalism, or in other words the hybrid identity of Muslims: "The large-heartedness of Islam neither negates nationalism, nor is it necessary for nationalism to limit Islamic perception. Both these points are unduly exaggerated. Reality lies not on either extreme, but in between the two. What is this middle course?"[8]

Azad defined nationalism as a concept describing a particular state, that of collective consciousness and social order. By this, nationalism leads to the distinction of certain groups who will incur distinct collective responsibilities. Collective consciousness was initially based on race, but then a stronger force of place of habitat emerged. As Ahmad (1967) argues, social consciousness for Azad had three stages of development: patriotism, nationalism and universalism or humanism. The theory of composite nationalism begins with generalised humanism. Azad criticised the chauvinism of the Arabs as embedded in *'assabiyya*, which, to him, meant enclosures of family, tribe, race and place. The concept of *'assabiyya* was regarded as an Arab hangover from the days of Pan-Arab tribalism and thus was not as valid for application in the Indian context (Ahmad, 1967, pp. 186–187). Azad then argued that the system of conduct and the rituals Islam came with aimed at a designation of the unity of humanity and the implementation of human brotherhood. This was in juxtaposition to the historical evolution of nationalism in Europe that confined rights and liberty to the boundaries of Europe until nationalism became Europe's own greatest threat (Azad, 1927).

A similar point was argued by Azad's colleague in the anti-colonial struggle and the Khilafat movement, Maulana Muhammad Ali, who held a negative view about the western concept of nationalism. According to him, in a speech at the Cocanada Congress in 1923, Indian nationalism should have been described as a 'Federation of Religions' and India, instead of being described as the 'United States of India', could have been referred to as the 'United Faiths of India' (Karandikar, 1969).

For Azad, the Indian nation was an unalterable fusion of differences. It would be impossible to attempt a project of cultural revivalism or to dream of attaining a 'pure' version of either a Hindu or a Muslim culture. The Indian nation became the meeting point of 'caravans of race, cultures and religions'. Consequently, the Indian nation shared a common history and common achievements, which led to an indivisible common nationality (Azad, 1940, p. 162).

The success of the nation, according to him, depended on unity, discipline and confidence in Gandhi. By nation, he meant the Indian nation and never the Hindu or the Muslim. This could be exemplified through this excerpt from his address to the Indian National Congress in 1923:

> When the order of the day is 'Protect Hindus' and 'Protect Muslims', who cares about protecting the nation? The press and platform are busy fanning bigotry and obscurantism, while a duped and ignorant public is busy shedding blood on the streets.
>
> (Azad, 1923, p. 145)

Azad was most probably the first scholar to theorise on common or composite nationalism. By showing how Hindus are nonbelievers with whom alliance should be pursued since there are common interests, in contrast to the British who are harmful, he managed to apply the idea of the Covenant of Medina to a real context. Succeeding him in 1927, Anwar Shah Kashmiri stressed the same prophetic precedent of alliances with trustworthy non-Muslims, integrity of Muslims in keeping their pledges, long historical ties and love of country of the Muslims of India. In 1938, Madani was the last to theorise on the subject of composite nationalism (Metcalf, 2009).

By composite culture, Azad meant a fused and shared culture and not a mosaic (Metcalf, 2009, p. 118). Azad envisaged a similar 'single nation' *(ummah wahidah)* of Muslims and Hindus in India. He wrote, "If I say that the Muslims of India cannot perform their duty unless they are united with the Hindus, it is in accordance with the tradition of the Prophet" (Madan, 2009, pp. 161–162).

Although the term *jihād* was used to describe the struggle to defend the worldwide Muslim community and its Caliph, in an article in al-Hilal in 1912, titled *The Struggle for Independence*, or as the translators put it, *The Crusade for Independence*, Azad refers to the Indian independence struggle as a *jihād*. In the same article, Azad wrote addressing the Muslims:

> Remember, that for the Hindus the struggle for the country's Independence is a part of their patriotism. But for you it is a religious duty and a part of the crusade for Allah. He has designated you Mujahids or Crusaders; the scope of Jehad or Crusade includes every effort made for truth and justice. Jehad means to break the shackles of human oppression and bondage. Those who are, today, engaged in the struggle for country's independence are launching a crusade which you should have initiated. Awake, because now Allah wants you to rise. It is His will that Muslims, wherever they are, should re-dedicate themselves to the duty of this Jehad.
>
> (Azad, 1912, pp. 46–47)

The difference between the stances of Iqbal and Azad or between the theorisation of a Muslim state and composite nationalism was manifested in the division in the stance among the Muslims who were inspired by Iqbal's verses and the *'ulama*, especially of Deoband, who adopted Azad's ideas. The power of verse and nationalist emotions stood against the religious and exegetical analysis by the *'ulama*. It is paradoxical that the same *'ulama* who could not deter the partition and the migration of these Muslims would acquire significant powers in the coming decades as the controller of the Muslim masses in North India.

In an article written in 1912, Azad gave a detailed, yet to an extent vague, answer to a question posed by a friend. The question concerned an inquiry into the preferred political path to be adopted, in the viewpoint of Maulana Azad: whether it was the traditional and historically followed conservative path of Muslims; that of the moderate Hindus in a right-based civil struggle; or the radical anarchical path adopted by extremist Hindus. His answer revealed a fourth path, a Quranic-inspired one. Azad cited the Quran to explain the incentives for political action along a divine path. The verses he cited, however, do not give a detailed and analytical framework. His emphasis on the straight or divine path remains empirically ambivalent concerning political action. However, the straight path option gave insight on his contribution to an idea of unity of humanity and monotheism (*tawḥīd*).[9]

For Azad, this path led to the rejection of submission and humility to anyone, except for God. Political characteristics that Muslims should withhold are inspired from the task of vicegerency (*khilafat*) bestowed upon them by God and are courage, self-esteem and dignity. The principles of justice and moderation are pivotal to all their transactions. Hence, peace and solidarity are advocated. A Muslim is expected to refrain from causing disorder, and to support the common good. The legitimacy of a government, to which a Muslim should show allegiance and respect, is derived from popular consultation (Azad, 1912, p. 35).

Azad departed from this stance in 1920 when he joined the Khilafat movement and the Indian National Congress. He depended on the Quran (40:8–9) to find a basis for this political alliance. Subsequently, he used the covenant of Medina argument, and this was the same argument Husain Ahmad Madani and the other *'ulama* of Deoband used (Ahmad, 1967, pp. 186–194).

Maulana Husain Ahmad Madani: 'composite nationalism' as *jihād*

Maulana Husain Ahmad Madani, who lived from 1879 until 1957, is considered one of the most notable figures in the history of twentieth-century South Asia. As a traditional Muslim scholar, his role was enhanced by the fact that he was the principal of the famous Islamic seminary Darul Uloom Deoband. In addition to his scholarship, he was a prominent figure among the *'ulama* in the nationalist struggle and a strong proponent of Gandhi.

Madani contended that, although the fight for partition was led by secular elites, it was the religious leaders who fought against partition. Before partition, in debating Iqbal's ideas of the Pakistan movement, Madani constructed an appealing argument and stressed the difference between *qawm*, meaning a nation, hence a territorial concept, and *millat*, meaning an *Ummah* and thus a religious concept. Before Madani, there was an inconsistency in the usage of the word *qawm* in the writings of Muslim scholars. The most notable example is Sir Syed Ahmad Khan, who used the word interchangeably to refer to the Egyptians or the Turks as a territorial nation, or to the Muslim community, as a nation of a specific faith. However, in 1884 in a speech, Sir Syed said: "By the word *qawm* I mean Hindus and Muslims both. This is the sense in which I interpret the word nation or *qawm*" (quoted in Amir, 2000, p. 11).

In explaining the difference between *qawm* and *millat*, Madani, in *Composite Nationalism and Islam*, stressed that these two words could not be used interchangeably and that the ancient Arabs, Persians and Turks never used *millat* to denote *qawm*. Furthermore, he made the following comments. First, *qawm* means either a group of men (excluding women), or primarily a group consisting of men where women are automatically included, or a group comprising both men and women. *Millat*, on the other hand, refers to a religious path adopted by a group of people, in other words a *shari'ah* or *dīn*. Examples are found in the Quran, such as *millat Ibrahim* or the path of Abraham. *Millat* could also refer to a doctrine (*tariqah*) or blood money (*diyyat*). Second, there was a pluralist aspect to the word *qawm*, since it has no singular form, but plural forms. *Millat*, on the other hand, is singular and can have plural forms. Third, there was a feminist aspect to the word *qawm*. In Arabic, *qawm* is mentioned in the Quran sometimes as feminine and at other times as masculine. Women are subsumed in the meaning sometimes, and sometimes reference is exclusive to men. Therefore, from a gender perspective, there is confusion in the usage of the word.

A detailed explication of the word *qawm* was found in an Urdu pamphlet distributed by the Jamiat Ulama-e-Hind before partition, entitled *Khatarnaak na'are (Dangerous Slogans)*. According to the pamphlet:

> European experts have not limited their definition of a nation to a religious aspect. They have also stated geographical, kinship and economic status as other elements of components of a nation. In our common usage, when reference to the word *qawm* emerges, the answer is always about one's brotherhood and kinship, so, for example, it is Sayyed or Sheikh or Brahmin or Qadri or others.
>
> In the Quran, there are approximately three hundred positions where the word *qawm* appears, and its application is usually linked to kinship and sometimes geography. However, the Quran in its usage of the word nation does not declare it synonymous with religion. There is no doubt that Islam has put an end to tribal bigotry and divided humanity into two sections. Such tribal-based nationalism was not approved of, and there are multiple *ahadith* (prophet's sayings) condemning it. Actually, according to one of the companions of the Prophet, the word Muslim was applied to a nation. But the *shari'ah* does not base religion as a foundation for a nation. It is the word *millat* which is used to refer to people belonging to the same religion, and not nation. [Then he cites from the Quran: *Millat* Ibrahim (Abraham), and Yusuf (Joseph) who abandoned the *millat* of non-believers.]
>
> It would be appropriate to give an opportunity to copy some of what Sir Syed Ahmad Khan said. The application of the word *qawm* to the residents of a country should be done. Remember that Hindus and Muslims are just religious terms. But Hindus, Muslims and Christians are residents of one country and thus are considered one nation. When all these groups constitute one nation then their country should be one. This is not the time to imagine a country with one religion.
> [...]

In a session of Muslim League in 1938, Mr Abdul Aziz said in a speech:

> This movement for Muslim composite nationalism could only be accepted if it helps in the freedom of India and solving daily livelihood issues. But extinguishing religious identity does not solve issues of livelihood; we should not also worship livelihood issues. It would be never accepted to establish an idea of composite nationalism in which religious existence, specific historical narratives and political rights are annihilated. [Then the writer cites Madani's work on composite nationalism (the action plan of India and the meaning of composite nationalism).]

[...]

The decision of Jamiat Ulama Hind:

> All *Hindustan* is our Pakistan

(Miyan, 1946, my translation)

As for the word *Ummah*, according to the Quran, there are different *Ummam* (plural of *Ummah*) (nations), but despite this acknowledged plurality, there are numerous Quranic verses in which non-Muslims and the Prophet have been addressed as one nation on the basis of kinship.

Madani disagreed with Iqbal's definition of *Ummah*, which, according to him, was not based on any linguistically or historically correct source. Iqbal claimed that *Ummah* denotes people who have forsaken their nations and religions and have embraced the religion of Abraham. Afterwards, the word *qawm* would not be used to describe them. Madani argued that Arabic classical dictionaries were void of these characteristics Iqbal attributed to the word by himself. Linguistically, *Ummah* is singular, but denotes a plural meaning. According to *Al-Munjid* Arabic Dictionary, it connotes a group of men, ways, era and stature, and according to *Mukhtarul Sahah* Dictionary, it means a group of men.

Having the pluralistic significance, the message of Islam contained an essentially binding factor since it was called upon the entire world to follow the same path and the same *shari'ah*:

> Among those who have accepted the call and have entered its fold, Islam has established a magnificent (spiritual bond) that has overshadowed all other bonds prevalent in the world – whether based on regionalism, kinship, economics, nationalism, language and colour, caste and creed, etc. This relationship transcends the bonds of materialism and engulfs them in a spiritual body of Islamic brotherhood.

(Madani, 2005, p. 90)

However, Madani contended that there is no Quranic verse which carried the meaning that only those men who advocated universal brotherhood were to be considered as a single nation and not the people of one country, one race and one colour.

Unlike Sir Syed, who tried to state that loyalty to the British was the religious duty of Muslims, Madani assured his audience in his speech in Delhi in 1921 that the best form of *jihād* was to speak out fearlessly before a tyrannical ruler. He reasoned that, since the British were the greatest enemies of Muslims, then only by being free from their domination could Indian Muslims safeguard their religion and, therefore, in addition to the common goal of independence, Muslims had a religious duty to fight for this freedom. Not only did Madani employ this dual secular–religious discourse on duty, but he also used nationalist and Gandhian terms such as *swatantra* (freedom) and *swaraj* (self-rule) (Madani, 2005, p. 142). In a dateless letter, he reasoned that, since the British had turned India from a *darul Islam* into a *darul ḥarb*, it was the duty of every Muslim to try to liberate India from British influence (Amir, 2000). In Madani's pre-partition action plan for India, he had called on Indians in general to: "make a united effort to throw off the yoke of foreign slavery and open avenues for the progress of the citizens of India. The objective is to establish composite nationalism on the basis of national unity" (Madani, 2005, p. 106).

Madani's nationalist *jihād* or struggles were also focusing on the central place of Muslims in the history of the emerging nation and the contributions of Muslims to India (his book *Our India* and its virtues points out that Muslims made India their home for over 1000 years and most Muslims were descendants from earlier inhabitants). An interesting argument was that not only is India the land where venerated Sufi saints are buried, but also Muslims are the only religious group who get buried; thus they have a strong association with land. This was also a part of his response to Hindu nationalism. Furthermore, according to some texts, Muslims claim to be the original inhabitants of India because of the traditional belief that Adam landed on Earth in India (from heaven).[10] In his writings, he portrayed Muslims as not just anti-British, but as the most anti-British. This was linked to a *fatwa* dated back to 1803 on the status of India after the British occupation of Delhi, the anti-colonial *jihād* of Sayyid Ahmad Shahid, as Madani described it, the Muslim peasant movements in nineteenth-century Bengal and the participation of the *'ulama* in the 1857 mutiny.

Thus through the propagation of the story of Adam and the burial versus cremation argument, it could be argued that Madani adopted strategies of resistance to the colonial discourse that created a process of 'othering' and had been continually used by Hindu extremists to de-nationalise Muslims.

United or composite nationalism was Madani's answer to both Hindu and Islamic nationalism; by composite nationalism, he referred to the analogical application of the Prophet's dealing with non-Muslims in Medina. Madani argued that if the Prophet managed to coexist with non-Muslims who practise polytheism and idolatry (known to be the greatest sins in Islam), then Muslims in India should not have any difficulty in living with non-Muslims in India. To the contrary, they would be following the Prophet's path since they share the same homeland and form one nation. Instead of fighting among themselves or claiming difference, Indians, irrespective of religious and cultural diversity, should wage war against the foreign and alien forces that have usurped their natural rights and deprived them of their common interests.

This was also the same strategy of the Prophet and his companions when they formed a united front with the Jews of Medina that brought them together as a nation. Madani referred to an earlier position of Maulana Anwar Shah Kashmiri, who in his presidential address at the conference of Jamiat Ulama-i-Hind in 1927 echoed the same message (Madani, 2005, p. 107).

Thus, composite nationalism entailed two aspects. The first was realising the unity of inhabitants of India and thus fighting against foreign powers. The second aspect was faith-related. All Indians should be free to practise and propagate their ideology in a peaceful setting. Non-interference in the personal affairs of others should be guaranteed, and majority communities should not try to

assimilate minorities. The same principles were translated in Congress's objectives and proposals.

Madani never abandoned his idea of composite nationalism. After partition
and independence and as he remained in India, the most significant strategy in
his opinion was to keep pursuing *jihād*. This was most evident in education; in
urging Muslims to participate in elections and government plans for economic
development; in learning Hindi since it is the national language; in correcting
school books and the misrepresentation of Muslims; through trade and travel to
Pakistan to normalise the relations; through Islamic endowments; and finally
through uniform laws among the states. After partition, Maulana Madani travelled widely to secure peace and renewed his commitment to seminary education
and Islamic guidance. He stated that: "Jihād against the British and against the
League now over, India's Muslims needed to turn their struggle within. This
would be greater jihād of moral struggle through personal and community discipline, education, and moral reform." Muslims today remember only the word
jihād but they do not remember that, in opposition to rebels against Islam and
enemies of the community, patience, forbearance and high ethics were spoken of
as jihād-i-akbar ("the greater *jihād*"). In this greater *jihād*, there is no need for
sword or dagger, but only strength, resolve and action (quoted in Metcalf, 2009,
pp. 148–151).

In a letter answering a person from Muradabad who wrote to him complaining about life in India after partition, Madani reminded the reader of his earlier
warning of the political incentives behind the call for partition. He demonstrated
how Indian Muslims ended up being a sacrifice to attain the political ambitions
of Muslim League politicians. Madani used nationalist vocabulary and asserted
that there is no point in considering Arab or Afghani help since they showed no
sympathy to the ill fate of hundreds of thousands of Indian Muslims. The zealous
quest for the establishment of majority rule, whether Muslims in Pakistan or
Hindus in India, brought about destructive living conditions for both communities who had to migrate (quoted in Friedmann, 2000, pp. 172–173).

Madani never ceased to blame the British for the failure of composite nationalism. He referred to a work by an English historian named J. R. Seeley, who, in
writing about the means of the expansion of the British Empire, warned of the
thriving of a feeling of common nationality as a threat to the existence of the
Empire. Later on he cites the example of the turning of Sir Syed's thought from
composite nationalism, to later fighting it, as a result of the propaganda by the
British, and so did Iqbal. He warned of the effect of English-based educational
institutions, out of which 80–90% of Muslims were graduating and turning irreligious. The imitation and adaptation of English dress, style of thinking and character were manifestations of the adverse impact they have on the Muslim
psyche:

> Those who wax eloquent about Islam and religion, do not differ in their
> dress and appearance from the British. And why should they? Lord
> Macaulay had said: We must at present do our best to form a class who may

be interpreters between us and the millions whom we govern … a class of persons Indians in blood and colour, but English in taste, in opinions, in moral and in intellect.

(Madani, 2005, p. 130)

Metcalf (2009), in her biographical study of Maulana Madani, eloquently demonstrated the significance of Madani's thought. Even those who differed from him, like Maududi, Thanawi and their followers, and propagated the two-nation theory, were forced to abandon their political ideals. Those who stayed in India realised eventually the value of a secular political setting, and even utilised it to the maximum to achieve their communal goals. What significantly marks the thought of both Madani and Azad is the support for equality of citizenship and building political alliances with non-Muslims. With this, they challenged centuries of Islamic jurisprudence, based on the political supremacy of Muslims (Metcalf, 2009).

Metcalf (2009) argued that there are three key differences between Azad and Madani. First, Azad theorised the legitimacy of universal government as an earthly analogy to the theological *tawḥīd*, while Madani emphasised colonial *realpolitik* at the expense of Muslims. Azad imagined India's Muslims to be under an *amîr*, who would guide and speak for Muslims within the larger society (ibid., p. 117). Azad's later references to India as a secular democratic state appear perplexing, in my point of view, in contrast to Metcalf's opinion.[11] Second, Azad was engaged in finding theological justification for the truth claims of other religions with his key concept of unity of religions (*weḥdat aladyān*) that looked upon religion as an inward aesthetic experience. Third, by 1930 there was a shift, as he abandoned his theological writings and began appearing as a spokesman of Indian nationalists within the Congress by adopting a secularly argumentative approach to the idea of composite nationalism, as most evident in his presidential address to the Indian National Congress in 1940.

Eventually there were four divisions of elite *'ulama* whose stance from the secular state differed accordingly. The first section, like Maulana Azad, Madani and Kashmiri, was termed the nationalist *'ulama*. The second section was the Muslim Leaguers like Shibli and others among the Aligarh Muslim University Scholars. The third group was not exclusively comprised of *'ulama* but included scholars whose writings were influential, most notably Maududi. The fourth section was pendulum-like ones whose attitudes either changed like Thanawi or remained apolitical. The divergence of *'ulama* on their stance from partition breaks the stereotypes about Islamic rigidity, since all these *'ulama*, in basing their viewpoints, had utilised Quranic verses and prophetic anecdotes. By using different religious arguments, *'ulama* managed to lead their followers to favour either Congress or the Muslim League. Haq (1970) metaphorically described this reality when he made the simile of *'ulama* being on the same train but with different and opposite destinations.

Although partition had taken place, it was the concept of composite national-ism, as coined by Azad and Madani, that dominated the ways through which

Muslims accommodated their new status in independent India as citizens and defended the status quo. This notion of common citizenship was also translated constitutionally. Karandikar (1969) contends that the Constituent Assembly had managed to pass a Constitution based upon an idea of common citizenship by stressing equal citizenship and outlawing discrimination on the grounds of religion, caste, race, sex and place of birth. To overcome the issue of granting excessive power to religious authorities, the Constitution guaranteed the freedom of conscience of an individual: "the Individual is granted freedom of conscience and is also ensured protection against the inroads on his equality under the name of religion" (ibid., p. 293).

Adjustment to the new status of being a 'citizen minority'

Having challenged the proposition that Muslims form a separate nation through the alleged *Ummah* framework, it is now necessary to evaluate the proposition of Muslim unity and political mobilisation along communal lines. To date, there has been no attempt to consider a subaltern perspective in the history of partition from the point of view of Muslim masses. Apart from specific studies, focus has been substantial on elite *'ulama*'s perspectives like Azad, Maududi and Madani.[12] With minor exceptions (e.g. Daechsel & Bates, 2014; Mayaram, 1997; Simpson, 2006), the literature on the history of Muslims is either dominated by the upper classes' (the *Ashraf* or *Sayyid* or *Thangal*[13]) histories or by the highly contested Jinnah politics, which was solely representative of the thin Muslim middle class at the time of the Indian independence struggle.

In contemporary India, the differences in viewpoints between the elite, whether emphasising the religious or the secular, and the masses, who are not confined to perspectival boundaries, are large. There is a wide spectrum of orthodox Muslims, revivalist Muslims, socialist Muslims, secularist Muslims, in addition to the regional and class divisions, which are further strengthened by media access and reception. Although secularists and modernists have access to the media, and thus have strong relations with politicians and policy makers, there are contending powers in the small *madrasas*, *maktabs* and mosques, where not-so-famous *imams* and *mullahs* enjoy a certain degree of authority. The extent of the power exercised by the *'ulama* and *mullahs* is further dealt with in upcoming sections of the study. The purpose of this section is to assert these divisions and analytical perspectives to avoid making essentialist arguments, especially that of Indian Islam.

In Joya Chatterji's study of the Bengali Muslims, she puts forward the social constructivist claim of 'true Islam' and how that assertion shunned alternative readings of history. To her, authenticity could only be a "fundamentalist claim that seeks to standardize, essentialize and sentimentalize a past which has been characterized by plurality, multivocality and bitter conflict" (Chatterji, 1998, p. 282). This becomes more obvious once we take into consideration the complex reality of 'plebeian politics' that subverted the myth of the unity of the Muslim community (Hansen, 2000).

There is ample evidence that Islam was not the principal incentive behind mobilising Muslims for the Pakistan movement. It was an aspiration for both political and economic rights that was indeed responsible for the movement. This is first evident in the work of Syed Ahmed Khan, who contended that political rights "were more important than religious traditions, and so long as the Muslims lived freely under British rule they would remain good subjects" (cited in Hasan, 1997, p. 32). Then the argument got crystallised through Azad's own words in his autobiography *India Wins Freedom*:

> It was Gandhiji who first gave currency to the title Qaid-i-Azam or great leader as applied to Mr Jinnah. Gandhiji had in his camp a foolish but well intentioned woman called Amtus Salam. She had seen in some Urdu papers a reference to Jinnah as Qaid-i-Azam, When Gandhiji was writing to Jinnah asking for an interview, she told him that the Urdu papers called Jinnah Qaid-i-Azam and he should use the same form of address. Without pausing to consider the implications of his actions, Gandhiji addressed Jinnah as Qaid-i-Azam. This letter was soon after published in the press. When Indian Muslims saw that Gandhiji also addressed Jinnah as Qaid-i-Azam, they felt that he must really be so.
>
> (Azad, 1988, p. 97)

According to Azad, the Muslim League had pursued a policy of intimidation to the Muslims who held key positions in the Central Secretariat. The League had pressed all of them to leave. This policy was carried out first by disseminating reports to what their fate would be once Congress came into power. Azad then pressed the Government of India to issue a circular to reassure the Muslims that, if they stayed in India, they would not only be given their rights, but would also be treated generously. This had a positive result, and a number of Muslim officers regained their confidence and decided to stay. However, once the Muslim League was informed about this, it started to intimidate those officials by threatening to retaliate against their property and relatives in Pakistan (since many of these officers came from areas that were to become Pakistan). Upon these threats, they had forcibly opted for Pakistan. In Azad's words:

> They had opted for India on the strength of my assurances but when the Muslim League held out threats against their families and their property, some of them came to me in tears and said, "We had decided to stay in India but now after the threat held out by the Muslim League, it is impossible to do so. Our families are in West Punjab and we cannot allow them to suffer. We are therefore compelled to opt for Pakistan."
>
> (Azad, 1988, p. 222)

Apart from Azad and Madani's stance towards secularism, confusion spread among many Indian *'ulama*. Some called to boycott elections because there was an apprehension of Hindu hegemony either through the Constitution (that was not properly understood by the masses) or through elections. Others attacked secularism and democracy and condemned them as an irreligious philosophy and a form of polytheism, respectively. Jamiatul Ulama, however, settled on eschewing politics, while retaining a pro-Congress stance. Eventually, the secular and the democratic ideal, rather than an Islamic dimension, guided the tactics and pragmatic framework that led Muslims' lives to establish and get enmeshed in political and electoral networks and coalitions.

The appeal of Pakistan to the North Indian Muslim community during partition was fuelled by positive and negative factors. For Qureshi (1962), positive factors included the desire of Muslims to maintain a sort of 'separate' identity, in addition to a deep-rooted desire for a Muslim state that had existed in the consciousness of the community. Titus (1959) also mentioned governmental posts being promised and given after partition, especially for upper and middle-class professionals. Negatively, Qureshi (1962) elaborated on the obvious absence of cementing factors in the relations between the two communities. This was evident in minimum-level coexistence. For example, the rate of intermarriage was very low, there was no considerable inter-dining and festivals provided opportunities for rioting instead of a social occasion for coming together. According to him, the communities remained different in everything (culture, thought, outlook on life, dress and cuisine). Besides this, there was no sense of a common history; instead there were two views of such historical happenings. The heroes of the Muslim conquest and the rebels against Muslim domination inspired contradictory feelings. In addition to this, the common bondage to a foreign government did not overcome these conflicting feelings.

Despite these factors, Muslims' attitudes to several issues were radically changed due to their acquisition of a new political identity as citizens in a democratic secular system. Education was one of the main fields of attitudinal change, as they started realising the importance of education, especially that a huge section of the educated middle class had migrated, leaving vast poor and illiterate masses behind. Though it was not new, the religious outlook of Indian Muslims towards other religions was changed. This was manifested through abandoning cow slaughter and joining Hindu festivals that became widely celebrated national holidays.

Mushirul Hasan's works touch best on the issue of accommodation of the Muslim community to their new status of being Indian secular democratic 'citizens'. What made Indian Muslims different from their counterparts in Muslim majority settings in Arab countries was that the Arabs had no clear-cut idea of accommodation between secularism and Islam. Indian Muslims developed many schools of thought and praxis to draw paths to deal with the new condition. This ranged from following the Nehruvian ideology of modern secularism, to the politically Islamist Jamaati Islami perspectives, to the Jamiatul Ulama's Congress-affiliated position, and to the apolitical practices of local and regional organisations, such as the Tablighi Jamaat approach.

Before presenting a summary of the political attitudes adopted by Indian Muslims in the immediate years after partition, a distinction has to be made between two sets of analytical perspectives. The first is of the majority versus minority perspective and the consequent political options available. This is due to the problematisation of the reality of Indian Muslims of being a 'citizen minority', or in other words, a minority not entirely in the political sense since they enjoy the full status of being citizens. The terms of majority and minority, as we will see further on, should be cautiously tackled. The second perspective is of the Islamic divisions among Muslims themselves and the consequent social options with ambivalent assumptive powers on political choices. Whether one is labelled a secularist Muslim, a liberal Muslim, an orthodox Muslim or a revivalist Muslim, there is no scientifically acceptable method of measuring how these variations have an impact on political decisions.

In addition to these two perspectives, there is the factor of externalising the Muslim community and the way they were classified, categorised and perceived by the majority, as shown by historical studies conducted on Hindu nationalism within the volumes of Subaltern Studies. Pandey (1999) shows how politically active Muslims, unlike the Hindus, were not thought of as 'Nationalist Muslims' versus 'Secularist Muslims'. They were divided into nationalist Muslims who were deemed supporters of Indian nationalism, and simply Muslims who were not (ibid., pp. 609–610).

It might appear that, on account of being a numerical minority, Muslims in India had no other path but to accept what the majority sought to establish. Historical evidence shows us otherwise. Millions of Muslims have stayed and chose to be part of India. In India, Muslims were never a numerical majority, the Moghul rule was not in any way linked to the Islamic Caliphate, and thus it could not be argued that Muslim rulers opted to establish a religious state. The evolvement of a Hindustani culture throughout Moghul rule bears witness to the Hindu–Muslim cultural integration (Husain, 1965). With the anti-British struggle, the aspiration to regain self-rule was not directed towards the establishment of a religious state. Although Islam was utilised and armed *jihād* or struggle as a religious duty on Muslims was called for by the *'ulama*, the goals remained secular. With the Congress-led independence movement, the vision of India did not entail any majoritarian role of Hindus, and thus it was the Muslims' decision to 'naturally' follow the path their ancestors followed and achieve self-rule over the land in which they coexisted with followers of other religions.

Logically, Muslims living as numerical majorities have more varied options for political organisation than for those living as minorities, whose best option is a secular democracy that would guarantee their rights, at least of existence. However, utilising Islam and considering giving it a public role or not is still a valid point whether Muslims find themselves in a majority or a minority. The Indian Constitution is unique in the sense that it gives Muslims full freedom of not just practising Islam, but also proselytising it. This led to a sense, although not strongly shared, of being legally equal. Legal equality, guaranteed by a secular and democratic state ideology, was an alternative opposing the realistic one of being subjects to an alien religion-dominated ideology (Pandey, 1999).

There is a difference between the usage and conception of the state of 'minorityness'. Conceptualising the self as a minority or not will be dealt with in the coming sections of this study. Here, I want to focus on the dilemma of usage of the term 'minority' to the discussion on Indian Muslims and their accommodation to the new status of citizenship in a democratic secular state. I acknowledge that neither the study nor the researcher is equipped to resolve this question. However, it is compelling to demonstrate how, on the one side, there is a process of mainstreaming identities fitting into nationalist imagination, and on the other side, there is an over-determination of identities. Identity formation entails a non-ending process of formation of 'Othering'. When one examines the literature written in Urdu, the word 'minority' seldom arises. Instead, 'community' is widely utilised. Weiner (1997) has an interesting point to make when he contends that:

> To regard oneself as part of a minority in India is to suggest that one ought to take group action to remedy one's situation. To declare one's group a minority is, therefore, a political act, in the Indian context, it is a way of calling attention to a situation of self-defined deprivation.
>
> (p. 462)

When the word minority is used away from its initial context of parliamentary politics and numerical calculations, and starts being used to locate certain communities, or rather to dislocate them, then it is automatically burdened with cultural baggage. This in turn overdetermines difference or otherness. Asserting otherness to fit some identities within a singular conception of nationalism is what Mehta (2004) calls 'benchmarking identities', which is considered a risk to minorities.

After independence, there was a secularisation process manifested through democratic processes, progressive social legislation, rapid industrialisation and a massive adult literacy campaign. Whereas this had strengthened Muslims' alignment with the Congress, it did not run smoothly or problem free. Basically, from 1947 till 1962, this era could be characterised with a conviction that political mobilisation along communitarian lines was a threat to security. Muslims opted to take advantage from the multi-party system by lending support to secular-oriented parties. As a result, the share of total votes polled by Muslim candidates rose from 65.41% in 1952 to 75.20% in 1962 (Hasan, 1996).

The second phase was from 1967–80. The last phase of Indira Gandhi's rule witnessed unprecedented levels of religious fervour and sectarian feuds. With the rising tide of communalism and Hindu Muslim riots, the secularisation process that had marked the independence struggle started fracturing (Hasan, 1996, pp. 214–215).

Although most literature cites this relationship between Indian Muslims and Congress affiliation and takes it for granted, there is an aspect of sycophancy to it since, first, it is the better of two evils and, second, it is argued that this affiliation is due to the lack of Muslim representation.

This led to another strategy initiated by Muslims and embodied in the formation of the Muslim Majlis-e-Mushawarat. This body (translated as the Muslim Consultative Committee) was founded in 1964 by bringing together various Muslim leaders ranging from Orthodox members of the Jamiat-ul-Ulama, to the revivalist Jamaati Islami and some modernist Muslims who were either affiliated to Congress or not. Its specific aim was to tactically deal with elections through the endorsement of the candidates who adhered to its position. However, due to strong party loyalty and majoritarian pressures, especially in Uttar Pradesh and Bihar, this strategy failed (Quraishi, 1971; Shahabuddin & Wright, 1987).

Finally, the third strategy of Muslim politics was of non-participation in the political process. Shahabuddin and Wright (1987) argue that a great portion of the Muslim community had rejected this strategy, whether they were in the northern regions that had a long history of Muslim rule or in the southern areas that were not deeply affected by partition. Even with the attempt of some small yet prosperous business communities on the western coast, like the Bohras, Khojas, Memons and Navayats, to adopt this strategy as a means of pressuring the government, their small numbers were deemed anyway ineffective in swaying election results.

The experience of Kerala

At 9 a.m. Kunhi Qadir led an estimated 3,000 Mâppilas from the Tanur area toward Tirurangadi. Some wore the Turkish fez with crescent, others had Gandhi caps, and a few carried flags, one of which had inscribed on it in Arabic:

God is Great The Khilafat
Go to combat light-mindedly and slowly
and you will certainly succeed and God
will be with you.[14]

The omission of the non-Urdu Muslim heritage of South India poses serious difficulty to a non-essentialist analysis of the community's perspectives on nationalism and partition narratives. One empirical finding on the community's perspective is often translated to the meagre number of emigrants to the newly founded Pakistan, and thus the unattractiveness of the idea of partition. Thus as a way out of this analytical shortcoming, the stress on North Indian *'ulama*'s opinions was utilised to comprehend the anti-thesis of Muslim nationalism. The difference in the historical memory and the detachment of Southern Indians from the North and Centre compelled the partition narrative to occupy a humble position in South Indian literature. It could be argued that the English language, as a medium of knowledge, did not hegemonise cultural production in South India and thus a lot of literature is inaccessible to non-Tamil, Malayalam, Telugu or Kannada speakers. A bibliographical search in the state of Kerala has shown that historical literature on the 'Muslim' subject is monopolised by investigations in pre-modern ties with the Arab world, the Malabar Rebellion of the 1920s and the independence struggle. There is a scarcity of literature on partition narratives, apart from those dealing with the quest for Mappilastan or Moplastan.[15]

The modern history of rural Malabar (what is known today as Northern Kerala) witnessed significant events starting with Mappila outbreaks in the nineteenth century, followed by the Khilafat movement, the Malabar rebellion in 1921–22, the call for Moplastan and the emergence of Muslim League politics, which culminated in the establishment of Malappuram district in 1969. The common thread about these incidents is the employment of Islamic identity as a motivating or inciting factor for political action. Panikkar (1989) notes that collective action is, interestingly, an attribute exclusive to the Muslim community and not present among other communities of Malabar.

The starting point is *jihād*, as the Mappilas called their struggle against first the Portuguese then the British and the Hindu upper-caste landlords. What the Mappilas termed as *jihādist* activities against social and economic power of the upper castes, as well as the political authority of the British, was called by the British the 'Outrages'. The translation of discontent into organised collective action within a religious outline that served as a motivating framework is a perplexing issue to analyse due to the absence of concrete goals. To the Mappilas, it was an attempt to counter injustice and inequality, in pursuit for an ideal afterlife or, in other terms, paradise. The influence of popular culture, the nature of the Islamic belief system, the history of its spreading in Kerala and the role of the traditional leaders of that society were all factors that shaped the process of political socialisation of Mappilas and impacted the outcome of their outbreaks (Panikkar, 1989). These events amounted to thirty-two incidents and took place between 1936 and 1921–22, culminating in the Malabar Rebellion. Nearly all of them occurred in the areas of Ernad and Walavanad (Dale, 1980).

These outbreaks were mainly acts of murder of upper-caste Hindu landlords who were aligning with the British and causing further oppression to the peasants and land tenants. This resort to violence should not be detached from the long history of violent collision between the British, the state-landlord collaboration and the Mappila tenants. The violent methods of the struggles were, to a great extent, part of the Mappila cultural political life (Muhammedali, 2004). These struggles were known as the Moplah outbreaks and were characterised by the ritualisation of martyrdom. The participant would wear a white robe, divorce his wife, settle all accounts and after receiving the blessings of a *Thangal* (an upper-class Mappila) would head for his mission and would be considered a martyr (Poonthala, 2004). The *Thangals* and the religious leaders or the *imams* (*Musliyārs*) gave the blessings that had arisen to claim the power vacuum that resulted after the arrest of Congress leaders affiliated to the non-cooperation movement.

In 1919, the Khilafat movement provided an opportunity for Indian Muslims to adopt a pan-Indian identity that was further enhanced by the non-cooperation movement, which established a strong foothold for Congress in Malabar. The feeling that the British posed a formidable threat to Islam fuelled the zeal of the Khilafat movement. The movement also found relevance in the psyche of the Mappila community since, to them, the British assault on the Ottoman Caliph was reminiscent of the Portuguese and British assault on the Muslims of India.

The Khilafat movement climaxed in the Malabar Rebellion of 1921–22, which took place in the southern part of Malabar district. Although the rebellion has been utilised by historians, through Marxist and nationalist lenses, as a quintessential example of peasant rebellion (Panikkar, 1989; Wood, 1987), Dale (1980) in his study on the Mappilas of Malabar, argues counter to this. To him the rebellion, although occurring within the context of the Indian nationalist movement, was actually neither a modern nor a typical peasant revolt. Rather, it was an 'archaic form of protest' with no political vision or goal for the future. It was more about resuscitating Indian Islam than about Indian freedom. Later on, the ideology of the rebellion was actually transformed into the goal. The result was the aspiration to establish an Islamic state. The rebellion was mainly executed by the rural poor, who included labourers, cultivators, traders and a few religious teachers. It resulted in the murder of British officials and non-officials, the destruction of police and government offices, and plundering the property of Hindu upper-caste landlords. The rebellion witnessed a huge involvement of the Mappila population; apart from the official figure of around 3000 rebels who were killed, around 87,000 were involved in the rebellion (Wood, 1987, p. 203).

Simultaneously with the partition discourse evolving in the North Indian context, the Muslim community in Malabar witnessed a call to the creation of Mappilastan (the country of the Mappilas). The idea was to establish a Muslim-majority province in South India within the Indian Union and was first put forward in the Madras Legislative Assembly in 1947 (Miller, 1976).

There are two main factors behind the elaboration of such an idea. The first was the conception of difference in the culture of Muslims from their Hindu counterparts. Although they spoke the same language, Mappilas differed in dress, food and philosophy of life. The evolution of a different identity also came as a quest for independence from Hindu dominance. The second factor was the backwardness of Muslims, and especially of the Malabar region, thus it was thought that if Mappilas were given a province or a federal state of their own, they would have better opportunities for development and growth, void of competition with the fellow countrymen.[16] After the Malabar rebellion, the British had retaliated against the Muslim community by discrimination in the recruitment to revenue, judicial and police posts (Panikkar, 1989). Although the Mappilastan proposal was repealed, it remained on the political agenda of Muslims.

In 1951, the Indian Union Muslim League was formed as a fully-fledged political party. Several factors led to the shift of Mappilas to this party away from the Congress. First, the Congress was assumed to be an upper-caste Hindu-oriented and elitist party (Miller, 1976). Second, the post-1921 rebellion circumstances that resulted in Mappila suppression showed the inability of Congress to support their cause legally or materially or to protect them from the punishment of the British. Third, the formation of the Aikya Sanghom in 1922 (an organisation for Muslim unity aimed primarily at social and educational reforms and thus the upliftment of the community) had fostered the creation of an awareness of a sense of community. The backing of certain candidates by this organisation, especially of the upper-class Mappilas, was a trend that was soon accepted by the masses (Gangadharan, 1995).

The evolution of a backward looking and closed society among the Mappilas was caused due to fear and frustration in the post-rebellion period of the early 1920s. By the 1930s, Muslim separatism appeared as a political solution to their social and economic miseries. It was the British, with their policy of 'divide and rule', who were the first visionaries of a separate Muslim state in India. As a strategic solution, the concept of Mappilastan was materialised in 1969 when Malappuram was formed as a revenue district with a majority of Muslims. The political role of the Indian Union Muslim League managed to forge multiple political alliances and thus obtain a share in the governance process. The League allied with various reactionary groups like church-oriented Christians, caste-oriented Nairs and anti-communist communalists. This led eventually to "think in a different dimension of separative and vertical solidarity" (Kurup & Ismail, 2008, p. 223). However, any notion of communal consciousness in Kerala should be contested because the Muslim League won only one seat in the Lok Sabha in 1957 and two seats in 1962 (Hasan, 1997).

The example of Kerala is significant to show how, on the one hand, demands that seemed communal were integrated successfully in the federal organisational structure of the Indian state and, on the other hand, the Keralite public sphere was transformed. The acquisition of religious leadership of stronger roles in the public space of Malabar was coupled with the establishment and systemisation of religious practices within an institutional structure. *Jihād* against the British was turned into *jihād* for spiritual purification. This was especially manifested with the advent of the Aikya Sanghom. Earlier, the Mappila community shared cultural and religious rituals that gave them the sense of a unified community. The *mala* and *moulid* (praising of Prophet, Sufis and martyrs) recitation in *madrasas* and mosques and the consequent growth of Arabi-Malayalam literature created alternative public spaces in which their identity-related activities were legitimised (Poonthala, 2004).

Summary

It is argued that Muslims are the only group in India who had the choice to leave or stay, and hence to opt for or reject the Indian citizenship status. This chapter has briefly demonstrated the historical context in which Muslims found themselves during the call for partition. The role of Indian *'ulama* as motivators for choosing the secular democratic option versus the promised Islamic regime was a fascinating historical precedent that India set in global history. The choice of this case necessitated a presentation of the ideas of Azad and Madani as two examples of these *'ulama* who supported the case for not migrating to Pakistan. Is it possible to confer here that this decision was considered a compromise made by the Muslims? By a compromise, I mean the consent from the beginning of the Indian independence to start a new phase of governance, where their acceptance of a secular identity as Indian citizens became an obligation, then, gradually, their perception of rights stood still, but unfulfilled (evident in the dilemma of Urdu, education, incursions of Hindu violence, national anthem and history books). This is a question that will be dealt with throughout this book.

With this, India clearly stands remote from other studies pertaining to Muslim minorities. Contemporary literature shows us the trend of ghettoisation and formation of parallel societies (for example, Alcoff, 2006; Alejandro, 1998; Appadurai, 2006; Benhabib, 1996; Jonker & Amiraux, 2006; Kabeer, 2002; Mouffe, 1992). Thus, one of the most common ways in dealing with the reality of being a minority is creating enclaves as a strategy. The Islamic scholar Al-Qaradawy (2001), for example, urges Muslim minorities to create their own micro-societies within the national fabric of the non-Muslim-majority societies where they live. This implies the creation of their 'own' educational, religious, cultural and social institutions. He does not call for ghettoisation or isolation, but openness without assimilation; in his words, this is the openness of an active preacher, not of a surrendering imitator. Despite how complicated this sounds, Indian Muslims have gone a step further in showing multiple ways of living as a 'citizen' minority. This chapter has demonstrated these various ways of accommodating their new political identity.

As this book deals with a comparative study of North India and Kerala, Kerala's entirely different historical background could not have been omitted from the study. Despite the fact that partition did not play any significant role in Kerala's recent political history, a short reference to the general historical context of nationalist politics in Kerala had to be introduced, notwithstanding the vast multitudes of the topic. To conclude, the main emphasis has been to witness how the practice of *jihād* was forged along different regional and historical experiences, interestingly intertwined with a nationalist cause, where a religious tool and objective became mingled with a pragmatically political one.

Notes

1 Ibn Khaldun's theory of solidarity, as explained in his Muqaddimmah, shows how power is the basis of ruling, and every state is established upon violence, and not on a contractual relationship, and when *'assabiyya* reaches its climax, the tribe attains then royal authority, either by despotism or by backing. Thus, Ibn Khaldun denied the possibility of establishing authority on rational bases. He believed that dynasties of wide power and large royal authority had their origin in religion, based either on prophecy or on truthful propaganda, and that religious propaganda gives a dynasty at its beginning another power in addition to that of the group feeling it possesses as a result of the number of its supporters. Thus, in this regard, it is obvious how Ibn Khaldun linked power and religion establishing, in this sense, a domain that provides authority with power; a domain of piety and adherence to religious norms and values.

2 Medieval authors on this subject include Al-Mawardī, Al-Faraa, Al-Juwainy, Ibn Taymiyyah and Ibn al Qayyim al-Jawziyyah.

3 Jinnah was not a practising Muslim and could not speak his mother language well. Being a modernist, he propounded the two-nation theory in a context of power struggles between the Hindu and Muslim elites. It was only after 1937 that his political stance was steered towards this idea, since earlier he was advocating a united India until 1928 (Engineer, 2009).

4 Iqbal was known to be one of the greatest Urdu poets of the twentieth century. His engagement with revivalist Islam and nationalist politics came as a turning point after his return from Europe. He is also known to be among the first who called for a separate state for Muslims in his Muslim League presidential address in 1930.

5 For example, the Quran (26:105–106) states: "The people of Noah denied the messengers when their brother Noah said to them, 'Will you not fear Allah?'"

6 In one of the speeches of Mudavoor, a Muslim scholar in Kerala, India was described as *Darul Insaan*, or the abode of the human being.

7 Robinson (2000) attributed the Indian National Congress's lack of success in dealing with Muslims to four factors. The first is backwardness resulting from the discrimination of the British and the aversion of Muslims to western education. Second, Robinson contends that the British deliberately created divisions in Indian society for their own imperial purpose, therefore, leading to discouraging the Muslims from joining the nationalist movement. Third, the Indian National Congress was infiltrated by Hindu communalism, as manifested in its symbols, ethos, idioms and inspiration. Finally, Muslim communalism and the two-nation theory as propagated by Jinnah played a dominant role (Robinson, 2000, pp. 210–213).

8 Azad, *Islam aur Nationalism*, published in the second phase of *Al-Hilal*, which ran from June–December 1927. Obtained from Hameed (1990: pp. 50–57).

9 The idea of *tawhīd* was further explicated in Azad's Quranic commentary or Tarjuman Al Quran, in which he argued

> the inevitable consequence of this Divinity is also the concept of unity of Faith. Obviously, the path of spiritual guidance prescribed by the Divine force should be for the entire Creation and shown to all. Hence the Koran says that the Revelation is the universal guidance of God and has been present in the world since day one and that it is meant for all human beings.... The same universal truth it calls 'al-deen' (the Faith), that is, the True Faith for all humankind, so it appeared equally in every age and in every country. The Koran says that there is no corner of the world that is inhabited by human race and where a prophet has not appeared. All prophets, whenever and wherever they appeared, showed the same path; all of them taught to be faithful to the universal law of God, that is, the law of Faith and pious conduct.
>
> (Quoted in Wasey, 2008, p. 43)

10 Madani's stance is cited in Metcalf (2009, pp. 134–135). Yoginder Sikand also explains this thesis by alluding to Maulana Miyan's reference to an eighteenth-century North Indian scholar: Ghulam Azad Bilgrami (See: Sikand, 2006, pp. 68–72).

11 As evident through his Convocation Address to the students, delivered on 20 February 1949 at the Aligarh Muslim University:

> You are the citizens of free India – a State which is determined to develop its political and social life on secular and democratic lines. The essence of a secular and democratic State is freedom of opportunity for the individual without regard to race, religion, caste or community ... I have no doubt in my mind that if you can imbibe this spirit of progressive nationalism which is the motto of our secular democratic State, there will no position in any field of life that will be beyond your reach.

12 Abraham (2006), in a conference paper, introduces a discussion on a proposed subject of re-reading Muslim history through subaltern perspectives.

13 The first term commonly refers to East Indian or Bengali Muslims, whereas *Sayyid* is mainly used in North and South India. *Thangal* is a Malayalam term referring to the Muslims who claim Arab ancestry.

14 Quoted in Dale (1980, p. 196) from R. H. Hitchcock (1921) *A History of the Malabar Rebellion*. Madras: Government Press.

15 Mappila or Moplah is the term for the majority of Muslim Malayalees from the Malabar Coast or Northern Kerala now. This section is restricted to a brief outline of their historical role but does not aim at excluding other Muslim groups.
16 These were the ideas presented by Muhammad Ismail and Seethi Sahib, two of the nationalist figures of the freedom struggle in Malabar. Miller (1976) quoted them in his book, *Mappila Muslims of Kerala.*

References

Abraham, J. (2006, October). *A Discussion on the Possibility of a Subaltern Reading of Indian Muslim History*. Unpublished paper presented at the AMSS 35th Annual Conference "Muslim Identities: Shifting Boundaries and Dialogues", Hartford, Connecticut.

Ahmad, A. (1967). *Islamic Modernism in India and Pakistan 1857–1964*. London: Oxford University Press.

Al-Mawardī'. (1996). *The Ordinances of Government (a translation of al-Ahkâm al-Sulâniyya w' al-Wilâyât al-Dîniyya)* (W. Wahba, Trans.). Reading: Garnet.

Al-Nadwi, A. A. A. (2005). *Al-Sirā' Baina Al-fikrah Al-Islāmiyyah wal fikrah al-gharbiyyah fil aqtār al-islāmiyyah. (Conflict: Between Islamic and Western Thought in Muslim Regions)*, Fourth Edition. Lucknow: Almajma Al'ilmy (first published 1965).

Al-Qaradawy, (2001). *Fiqh al'aqaliyyāt almuslimah: Hayāt al-muslimīn wasat mujtama'āt ukhra (The Jurisprudence of Muslim Minorities: Muslims' Life Among Other Societies)*. Cairo: Al-Shorouk.

Al-Qaradawy, Y. (2010). *Al-waṭan wal muwaṭanah fi daw' alusool al'aqdiyya wal maqasid alshar'iyyah (The Homeland and Citizenship in the Light of Jurisprudent Bases and Shari'ah Goals)*. Cairo: Darul Shorouq.

Alcoff, L. M. (2006). *Visible Identities: Race, Gender, and the Self*. Oxford: Oxford University Press.

Alejandro, R. (1998). Impossible Citizenship. In K. Slawner and M. Denham (eds), *Citizenship After Liberalism* (pp. 9–32). New York: Peter Lang.

Amir, S. (2000). *Muslim Nationhood in India: Perceptions of Seven Eminent Thinkers*. Delhi: Kanishka.

Appadurai, A. (2006). *The Fear of Small Numbers*. New Delhi: Cambridge University Press.

Asad, T. (2003). *Formations of the Secular: Christianity, Islam, Modernity*. Stanford, CA: Stanford University Press.

Azad, M. A. (1912). Al-Hilal Objectives and Political Message. In S. S. Hameed (ed.) (1990), *India's Maulana Abul Kalam Azad* (pp. 28–36). New Delhi: Indian Council for Cultural Relations.

Azad, M. A. (1923). Address to the Indian National Congress Special Session in Delhi. In S. S. Hameed (ed.) (1990), *India's Maulana Abul Kalam Azad* (pp. 133–146). New Delhi: Indian Council for Cultural Relations.

Azad, M. A. (1927). Islam and Nationalism. In S. S. Hameed (ed.) (1990), *India's Maulana Abul Kalam Azad* (pp. 50–57). New Delhi: Indian Council for Cultural Relations.

Azad, M. A. (1940). Address to the Indian National Congress in Ramgarh. In S. S. Hameed (ed.) (1990), *India's Maulana Abul Kalam Azad*, (pp. 148–163). New Delhi: Indian Council for Cultural Relations.

Azad, M. A. (1988). *India Wins Freedom*. New Delhi: Orient Longman.

Bamford, P. C. (1985). *Histories of the Non-Co-operation and Khilafat Movements*. Delhi: K.K. Books. (First published 1925).

Benhabib, S. (ed.). (1996). *Democracy and Difference: Contesting the Boundaries of the Political*. Princeton: Princeton University Press.

Bose, S., & Jalal, A. (2004). *Modern South Asia: History, Culture, Political Economy*, Second Edition. London: Routledge.

Chakrabarty, B. (2008). *Indian Politics and Society Since Independence: Events, Processes and Ideology*. London: Routledge.

Chatterjee, P. (2000). The Nation and its Peasants. In V. Chaturvedi (ed.), *Mapping Subaltern Studies and the Postcolonial* (pp. 8–23). London, New York: Verso.

Chatterji, J. (1998). The Bengali Muslim: A Contradiction in Terms? An Overview of the Debate on Bengali Muslim Identity. In M. Hasan (ed.), *Islam, Communities and the Nation: Muslim Identities in South Asia and Beyond* (pp. 265–282). New Delhi: Manohar.

Daechsel, M., & Bates, C. (2014). *Mutinies at the Margins – New Perspectives on the Indian Uprising of 1857: Dalit, Muslim and Subaltern Narratives*. Seven Oaks, New Delhi, Singapore: SAGE.

Dale, S. F. (1980). *Islamic Society on the South Asian Frontier: The Mappilas of Malabar 1498–1922*. Oxford: Clarendon Press.

Dale, S. F. (1990). Trade, Conversion and the Growth of the Islamic Community of Kerala, South India. *Studia Islamica*, 7, 155–175.

Davies, M. W. (1988). *Knowing One Another: Shaping an Islamic Anthropology*. London and New York: Mansell.

Engineer, A. A. (2009). Nehru, Jinnah and Partition. Center for Study of Society and Secularism, 15–31 August. Retrieved on 10 September 2010, from www.csss-isla.com/arch%2017.htm.

Esposito, J. L. (ed.). (1987). *Islam in Asia: Religion, Politics, and Society*. Oxford: Oxford University Press.

Friedmann, Y. (2000). The Attitude of the Jam'iyati-i 'Ulama-i Hind to the Indian National Movement and the Establishment of Pakistan. In M. Hasan (ed.), *Inventing Boundaries: Gender, Politics and the Partition of India* (pp. 157–177). Delhi: Oxford University Press.

Gangadharan, M. (1995). Emergence of the Muslim League in Kerala – A Historical Enquiry. In A. A. Engineer (ed.), *Kerala Muslims: A Historical Perspective* (pp. 207–217). Delhi: Ajanta.

Hameed, S. S. (ed.) (1990). *India's Maulana Abul Kalam Azad*. New Delhi: Indian Council for Cultural Relations.

Hansen, T. B. (2000). Predicaments of Secularism: Muslim Identities and Politics in Mumbai. *Journal of the Royal Anthropological Institute*, 6(2), 255–272.

Haq, M. U. (1970). *Muslim Politics in Modern India 1857–1947*. Meerut: Meenakshi Prakashan.

Hasan, M. (1996). The Changing Position of the Muslims and the Political Failure of Secularism in India. In T. V. Sathyamurthy (ed.), *Region, Religion, Caste, Gender and Culture in Contemporary India* (pp. 200–228). Delhi: Oxford University Press.

Hasan, M. (1997). *Legacy of a Divided Nation: Indian's Muslims since Independence*. Delhi: Oxford University Press.

Hasan, M. (ed.) (2000). *Inventing Boundaries: Gender, Politics and the Partition of India*. Delhi: Oxford University Press.

Husain, S. A. (1965). *The Destiny of Indian Muslims*. Reprint 1993. New Delhi: Har-Anand Publications.

Hussain, M. F. (2006). *Evolving Muslim Cultural Self-Perception and its Impact on the Nationalist Political Processes in Bihar, 1920–1947.* New Delhi: Nehru Memorial Museum and Library.

Jalal, A. (2008). *Partisans of Allah: Jihad in South Asia.* Cambridge, MA: Harvard University Press.

Jonker, G., & Amiraux, V. (2006). *Politics of Visibility: Young Muslims in European Public Spaces.* Bielefeld: transcript Verlag.

Kabeer, N. (2002). *Citizenship and the Boundaries of the Acknowledged Community: Identity, Affiliation and Exclusion.* Institute of Development Studies, Sussex: Institute of Development Studies.

Karandikar, M. (1969). *Islam in India's Transition to Modernity.* Connecticut: Greenwood.

Khan, Q. (1983). *Al-Mawardī's Theory of the State.* Lahore: Bazmi-i-Iqbal.

Kurup, K. K., & Ismail, E. (2008). *Emergence of Islam in Kerala in 20th Century.* New Delhi: Standard Publishers.

Madan, T. N. (2009). *Modern Myths, Locked Minds: Secularism and Fundamentalism in India,* Second Edition. Oxford: Oxford University Press.

Madani, M. (2005). *Composite Nationalism and Islam (Muttahida Qaumiyat aur Islam)* (M. A. Hussain & H. Imam, Trans.). New Delhi: Manohar.

Manto. S. M. (2000). Black Margins. In M. Hasan (ed.), *Inventing Boundaries: Gender, Politics and the Partition of India* (pp. 287–299). Delhi: Oxford University Press.

Mayaram, S. (1997). *Resisting Regimes: Myth, Memory and the Shaping of a Muslim Identity.* Delhi: Oxford University Press.

Mehta, P. B. (2004). Secularism and the Identity Trap. In M. Hasan (ed.), *Will Secular India Survive?* (pp. 72–92). Gurgaon: Imprint One.

Metcalf, B. (2005). Introduction. In M. Madani, *Composite Nationalism and Islam,* translated by M. A. Hussain & H. Imam (pp. 23–54). New Delhi: Manohar.

Metcalf, B. (2009). *Husain Ahmad Madani: The Jihad for Islam and India's Freedom.* Oxford: Oneworld.

Miller, R. E. (1976). *Mappila Muslims of Kerala: A Study in Islamic Trends.* New Delhi: Orient Longman.

Mitra, S. K. (2003). The Morality of Communal Politics: Paul Brass, Hindu-Muslim Conflict, and the Indian State. *India Review,* 2(4), 15–30.

Miyan, M. (1946). *Khatarnāke na're aur jamiat ulama hind ka sirāt e mustaqīm (Dangerous Slogans and the Straight Path of Jamiatul Ulama).* Delhi: Jamiat Ulama Hind Press.

Mouffe, C. (ed.) (1992). *Dimensions of Radical Democracy: Pluralism, Citizenship, Community.* London: Verso.

Muhammedali, T. (2004). Catastrophe and Philanthropy: An Exposition of Ventures of Relief and Reconstruction in Malabar in the Wake of the Rebellion of 1921. In K. N. Ganesh (ed.), *Culture and Modernity: Historical Explanations* (pp. 208–235). Calicut: University of Calicut Publications.

Pandey, G. (1999). Can a Muslim Be an Indian? *Comparative Studies in Society and History,* 41(4), 608–629.

Panikkar, K. N. (1989). *Against Lord and State: Religion and Peasant Uprisings in Malabar, 1836–1921.* Delhi: Oxford University Press.

Poonthala, S. (2004). Community and Political Identity: Emergence of Muslim Political Identity in Malabar. In K. N. Ganesh (ed.), *Culture and Modernity: Historical Explanations* (pp. 245–259). Calicut: University of Calicut Publications.

Quraishi, Z. M. (1971). Emergence and Eclipse of Muslim Majlis-e-Mushawarat, *Economic and Political Weekly*, 6(25), 1229–1234.

Qureshi, I. H. (1962). *The Muslim Community of the Indo-Pakistan Subcontinent (610–1947)*. The Hague: Mouton & Co.

Robinson, F. (2000). *Islam and Muslim History in South Asia*. Oxford: Oxford University Press.

Sanyal, U. (2005). *Ahmad Riza Khan Barelwi: In the Path of the Prophet*. Oxford: Oneworld.

Sardar, Z. (1998). *Postmodernism and the Other: The New Imperialism of Western Culture*. London: Pluto.

Shahabuddin, S., & Wright, T. P. Jr (1987). India: Muslim Minority Politics and Society. In J. Esposito (ed.), *Islam in Asia: Religion, Politics and Society* (pp. 152–176). Oxford: Oxford University Press.

Shaz, R. (2001). *Understanding the Muslim Malaise: A Conceptual Approach in the Indian Context*. New Delhi: Milli Publications.

Sikand, Y. (2006). *Muslims in India: Contemporary Social and Political Discourses*. Gurgaon: Hope India.

Simpson, E. (2006). *Muslim Society and the Western Indian Ocean: The Seafarers of Kachch*. Oxon, New York: Routledge.

Titus, M. T. (1959). *Isla   46m in India and Pakistan: A Religious History of Islam in India and Pakistan*. Calcutta: YMCA Publishing House.

Wasey, A. (2008). *Islamic Response to Contemporary Challenges*. New Delhi: Shipra.

Weiner, M. (1997). Minority Identities. In S. Kaviraj (ed.) *Politics in India* (pp. 241–254). Delhi: Oxford University Press.

Wood, C. (1987). *The Moplah Rebellion and its Genesis*. New Delhi: People's Publishing House.

3 The life-space context and hegemonic discourses

Let us grant that our culture is of a wide variety and many colours. Every place has its own attractive characteristics whether it be the Kashmiri shawls, the Banarsi saris, the Hyderabadi jamewar (which alas! one can no longer get); or the muslin of Dhaka, chickan of Lucknow or silk of Mysore. But consider too that there are some threads in the motif of this culture which are common. Khayal, raga darbari, thumri and dada transcend the frontiers of India, Pakistan and Bangladesh and are heard in every part of the subcontinent. The ghazals which Iqbal Bano sings or the songs of Lata Mangeshkar are all based on the raags which, for thousands of years, have resounded in the gardens and markets of our country. When the cry goes up in the darbar of Khwaja Moinuddin Chisti:

> Khwaja pia, mori rang de chundaria
> aur rang bhi chaukhe aaye
> dhubayya dhoye sari umarya
> Beloved Khwaja dye my stole, and let the colour
> be so bright and fast,
> Even though the washer-woman washes it
> all her life

(Ansari, 1999)

In the previous chapter, I introduced the historical setting in which Indian Muslims were both self-situated and forcefully located. As is well known, the transition of postcolonial India into a secular democratic state was stained with unprecedented violence and mass movement. The subsequent Hindu–Muslim riots that were witnessed mainly in Northern and Eastern India throughout the years tainted the socio-political fabric of the body of Indian citizenry and, to a substantial extent, also led to a specific political culture in which state–society and community-to-community relations were considerably shaped. This chapter will tackle these relations by first demonstrating the nature of the political sub-cultures of postcolonial Indian citizenry and by briefly looking at the ways Muslims are engaged in politics in India. Second, a frame of reference to the current life-space of Muslims in India will be expounded through portraying the conditions as 'hegemonic discourses' governing the lives of Indian Muslims.[1]

These hegemonic discourses are not independent of each other; rather they are interrelated and correlated. After a literature review coupled with interviews with North and South Indian Muslim youth, I have categorised these discourses into political, ideological and socio-economic ones. Finally, this section will overcome the review of the predicaments of Indian Muslims by presenting their counter-discourses to these narratives, through both reflection and action.

By discourse, I borrow Foucault's definition of it being not only about signs or language, but also practices that form the objects of which they speak. A discourse creates a 'space of multiple dissentions' (Foucault, 1969/2009). As we are talking about political discourses, this in turn leads us to relations of power and contentious politics of domination. There is a continual process of mixing between the hidden and the obvious, and in turn between what is prevalent and what is hidden or intentionally hidden from the discourse. Scott (1990)'s idea of hidden versus public transcripts is hence useful. By hidden transcripts he means the discourses that take place away from the direct observation of the power holder and could consist of elements such as speeches, gestures or practices that aim at contradicting public transcripts. Throughout this chapter, I will be locating the sites in which the dominant discourses are prevalent, and in the coming chapters, I will show the spaces of contention where there are counter-discourses and where, in Daechsel's (2006) words, "the politics of self-expression had to 'outflank' the world of the everyday by creating alternative spaces" (p. 128).

The idea of space is also inherently important for this study. By space, I do not necessarily mean physical or material space, but the scope of opportunities granted to the subject, or in other words mental space as defined by Madanipour (1998). Usually mental or even social space gets translated into physical space (Bourdieu, 1993). The significance of space is evident in urban settings where it plays a strong role in the integration of groups. In social constructivist logic, the context of power and domination is the sphere where ambivalent and ruptured politics of culture and identity take place (Werbner, 1997).

Sites, as spaces for the emergence of public and hidden transcripts, differ. Whereas public transcripts appear most evident in the intended encounter with the subordinates, either through public meetings, political party campaigns, police encounters or media, the hidden transcripts usually appear in different contexts. Throughout this book, I will be tracing specific sites of the appearance of these political discourses. Unlike the European examples set by Scott (1990), this case study of a religious community includes alternative sites, such as the university, the Islamic associations, the mosque, the press and media, especially the vernacular.

Political subcultures and impediments to Muslim politics

> It is a shame that Muslim leaders managed to agitate thousands of Muslims over a mosque that is no longer in use, while at the same time, it is hard to fill one line with men in many mosques in UP during namaz time.
>
> (A Muslim barber from UP commenting on the
> Babri Masjid issue, October 2010)

Muslims in India constitute around 13.4% of the Indian population (Census of India, 2001); this makes them the second biggest religious community in India after the Hindus. In fact, the nature of social reality in India is incredibly fragmented, to the extent that even the categorisation of Hindus as a single religious community has been contested on the basis of the radical differences in castes and practices, which called for a sense of quantitative insecurity among some Hindu groups. Indian Muslims in turn are also comprised of different groups, and their homogeneity is greatly contested. It is thus hard to define who an Indian Muslim is, since not just demographic and regional differences exist but also caste issues divide them into separate communities. For example, the south-western state of Kerala had long-term ties with Arab countries, and the Keralites continue to migrate in large numbers, where they find ample job opportunities in the Gulf countries. They speak Malayalam, and their diet and dress code resemble their Hindu counterparts to a great extent. Muslims are a majority in the state of Jammu and Kashmir, but they have a dominant Kashmiri identity, and do not necessarily identify themselves with the rest of Indian Muslims. In the Hindi-speaking region where the two-nation theory was developed and attained support, around 64% of Muslims consider Urdu as their mother language in addition to Hindi (Weiner, 1997). In Bengal, Muslims speak Bengali and share a lot of traditions with Hindus that are even considered non-Islamic by a lot of other Muslim communities in India and elsewhere. In Andhra Pradesh, Muslims lived under Muslim rule until 1947 and are overwhelmingly Urdu-speaking (91%). Politically, especially in Andhra Pradesh and Kerala, Muslims formed their own confessional parties, while North Indian Muslims have frequently participated in mainstream political parties (ibid.) and mainly showed support to Congress.

This myriad of communities precludes any generalisation on a particular political culture among Indian Muslims. As a non-Arabic speaking minority, there is a definite attachment to *'ulama*, but it is impossible to quantitatively pinpoint it and it is often an orientalist mistake to assume any correlation between religiosity and a resistance to democratic and secular orders. In fact, Indian Muslims' life-spaces are dictated by multiple series of oppressions, such as caste, class, gender and religion, which are justified by dominant groups to preserve the status quo (Sikand, 2004b).

The study of the Muslim question in India is inherently complicated since it should be ideally addressed on different analytical levels: the local (village or town), the district, the state, the region and the country levels. In each, there is a variation in the democratic composition, a difference in the nature of socio-political significance, and specificity of the situation or the problem (Engineer, 1985). If we add the class level to these analyses, the difference in the discourses governing the lives of upper, middle and lower classes will be apparent. Between the two discourses lies the common man or woman who struggles through the construction of the majority setting to overcome the minority problem on the one hand, and simultaneously on the other hand conserves the aspect of Islamicness. As the Indian Human Development Survey, conducted by the National Council of Applied Economic Research (NCEAR), revealed, 31% of Indian Muslims live below the poverty line (Babu, 2010). A prompt problem arises once the ordinary Muslim is defined. There is an apparent problematic of opposing them and their problems applicable to middle-class Muslims. However, when issues of Indian Muslims are discussed, it seems that the problems addressed tackle community-wide concerns, often transcending class-based distinctions.

Two strands of discourse appear when we raise the Muslim question in India. The first is related to the minority position and the second to the issue of religiosity or 'Islamicness'. Whereas development-concerned secular activists mark the first discourse, Islamists, on the other hand, outline the second and fight for issues of education, power and *fiqh* (jurisprudence). As I have previously mentioned, although most secular intellectuals employ the term minority in writing about Indian Muslims and their predicaments, while interviewing *'ulama* and looking through Urdu literature, I found that the term minority rarely appears, whereas the most common way of talking about Muslims is through the word community or its Urdu equivalent, *brādry*. As a fundamental category like caste, religion and village, community in its turn is an indispensable conceptual tool as a shaper of social and collective identity. Not only are there spaces of contention where the sense of majority and minority oscillates, but also the self-perception of agents in these processes is crucial to the understanding of the politics of power and citizenship in India. Interestingly, within the Muslim community, there are some voices criticising the persistent representation of the community in both a homogenously holistic manner and a victimised fashion. On the other hand, as I will show in a forthcoming section, despite structural predicaments that the community faces, there are counter forces trying to portray them as unmerited recipients of excessive state benefits who employ the minority card.

The treatment of 'community' within Indian sociology has traditionally assumed a substantive character. It could be argued that communities act as collective personalities with enormous powers of policing individuals' personal behaviour and morality (Alam, 2004, pp. 77–80). Upadhya (2001) reviewed the works of Sudipta Kaviraj (1992), Nicholas Dirks (1997), Dipesh Chakrabarty (1995) and Partha Chatterjee (1998), who share the opinion that caste and community were invented under colonialism by the operation of certain political and discursive processes. This construction of a sense of identity was intricately linked with the political argument of belonging that was raised along the partition narratives and led to the necessity of the idea of the natural citizen and the disciplining of difference (Pandey, 2004).

Mahajan (2005) points out two different ways through which a minority could be disadvantaged with a nation-state: first, through policies of cultural homogenisation and non-recognition of difference, and, second, through systematic misrecognition and selective targeting of a community and its members. What happened in India through the constitutional and legal framework was an attempt at a curtailment of the former way. However, the second means is still evident through the media (for example, the *fatwa* concerning women's work and how it was misportrayed).[2] Negative stereotyping is increasing, not just by the media but also by political groups who are actually, or potentially, affiliated with the government. In addition to this sense of anxiety resulting from such policies, religious minorities in India suffer from potential physical threats through the eruption of communal violence in which the state has proved to be either complicit or a spectator.

To study this mentality and how far it is an integral part of the self-perception of the community, one could consider the concept of the life-space, and how it is translated into the reality of Muslims' lives in India. The concept of 'life-space' was utilised by Lewin (1951), who emphasised that studying the behaviour of an individual derived from the psychological facts that exist in his/her life-space at a given moment (cited in Hasan, 2006). Several incidents are considered landmarks in the life-space of Indian Muslims. The first was the moment of partition in 1947 and the consequent migration and fear concerning life and property. A major move was the resulting Constitution guaranteeing Muslims equal legal status as citizens of India. In the same year, however, the process of the displacement of the Urdu language commenced. The next historical point was the 1965 Indo-Pakistan war and the communal violence in Jabalpur, Ahmedabad and other places. In 1971, Bangladesh attained its independence from Pakistan and hence the myth that religion is a key element in defining nationalism had been shattered. In the subsequent years, India witnessed a series of riots, most notably in Aligarh between 1978 and 1982, in Moradabad in 1987 and in Meerut in 1987, where the complicity of the police was a notable factor.

The conversion of the Harijans in Tamil Nadu in 1981 was another landmark, followed by the famous Shah Bano case of 1986 when a sixty-two-year-old woman sought court to demand maintenance from her divorcee. Being Indian, the Supreme Court granted her the right to maintenance from her ex-husband under the Criminal Procedure Code. As the Supreme Court invoked the need for uniform civil code and made some controversial remarks on *shari'ah*, significant groups of Muslim leaders and organisations treated this issue as an attack on Islam and initiated campaigns challenging the judgment. Parliament, under Rajiv Gandhi's rule, passed the Muslim Women (Protection of Rights on Divorce) Act of 1986, which limited women's maintenance to a four-month period. Another incident in 1988 spurred great attention concerning identity politics: the ban on Salman Rushdie's *The Satanic Verses*, in which the decision of the state to ban the book violated the principle of freedom of expression in order to listen to the demands of Muslim organisations. Ironically, Hindu nationalists used the same logic in their attack on Babri Masjid (An-Na'im, 2008). The Babri Masjid demolition of 1992 was one of the watersheds that transformed the way Muslims perceive their citizenship in India. Later in 2002, the Gujarat carnage added to the fissured psyche of the community. Such incidents make it almost unmanageable to generate generalisations regarding the life-space of Indian Muslims and hence the political culture of the state and the political subcultures they bear. However, several remarks have to be made in this regard.

There is an inherent democratic puzzle in India that resulted from the classical belief that the survival of democracy is negatively related to the persistence of poverty, illiteracy and oppression. However, India is incomparably high in every one of these indices. These societal sections suffering from these problems have undeniably become the important supportive actors in the sustenance of democracy, albeit producing also the phenomenon of 'collective unfreedom', as Alam (2001) calls it. What concerns us here are Indian Muslims and how debates of democracy and secularism are discussed differently than among other Muslim communities worldwide. Unlike their Arab and Pakistani counterparts, they manage to overcome parochial lenses of a blind adaptation of *shari'ah* to everyday life and politics.

India presents a model in the developing world of a moderate statehood. What is unique about India is the inheritance of a hybrid political culture that joined the earlier pre-modern humanistic traditions and western political values that came to India in a dynamic way. Thus, freedom and democracy, national self-determination, equality and social justice were all terms that were translated in the Gandhian concept of *swaraj* and in the postcolonial stage. The result was a tradition of social pluralism, differing from the traditional European idea of political pluralism (Kothari, 2000).

Oommen (1995), in outlining the nature of state–society relationships in India, contends that they are not governed by any of the traditional models of governance as pointed out by Worsley (1984): the hegemonic, the uniform and the pluralist. Oommen argues that these relationship patterns lie some-where between the hegemonic and the pluralist models. Though the state operates according to a democratic setting, there is a witnessed state of oppression to several sections in society. Responses to oppression differ according to the conditions and contexts of operation. The first set of responses revolve around the practice of self-enclosure, which is considered a response to failure. The oppressed here limits his/her ambitions, holds on to traditions and escapes to the past. Another strategy is to take the group as a shelter and to assimilate in it.

A second type of response consists of imitating the oppressor. A noted obser-vation in postcolonial societies responds to the Khaldunian logic[3] – that the oppressed copies the oppressor, is manifested in the postcolonial societies wishing to copy their masters, and this explains the adoration for democracy. However, India poses an exception to other postcolonial states that failed in or severely grappled with their democratisation process because India succeeded in sustaining the democratic Constitution it had from the beginning, and it nurtured among the state subjects a sense of citizenship that allocated the Constitution a sacred place.

Due mention of the colonial heritage in the formulation of political subcul-tures of the oppressed is noteworthy. A significant part of this heritage was the manipulation of knowledge and the successful perpetuation of myths and stereo-types in order to deepen divisions among people and acquire a stronger hold over the subjects. Perhaps this could be related, in a manner, to Asad's (2003) analysis of the role of myths in the formation of the secular versus the profane.

Political discourses: practising and participating in democracy

What is noteworthy is to locate the history of Indian Muslims in the Indian environment and not in the wider scope of the 'world of Islam'. Because unlike their Muslim counterparts in different countries, their shared experience and political environment in India are one of democracy, secularism and "a pragmatic engagement with the social, political and economics processes" (Hasan, 1997, p. 21).

Mayer's (1981) study negated the myth of Muslims as a monolithic community and showed that they act as active participants whose regional cultures are reflected in their perceptions and behaviour. The space in which their sociopolitical reality is set is not measured through a narrowly democratic lens. Hence, the democratic reality in India is not just about voting rights and equality, but there are normative questions that must also be addressed. There is a sustained predicament of structural inequalities caused by a history of discrimination and marginalisation due to the Hindu caste system and partition narratives. Partition dictated a certain path dependency, which should not be omitted from the analysis. The division into India and Pakistan resulted in a sort of transfer of the bulk of the middle-class Muslims and Sikhs, where the Muslims headed to Pakistan and the Sikhs to India (Mitra, personal communication, July 2012). This explains, to a great extent, the current overrepresentation of Sikhs versus the underrepresentation of Muslims in governmental bodies (Figure 3.1).

The political discourse lies in a grid of striking a balance between the sense of a separate religious identity and the collective sense of national solidarity,

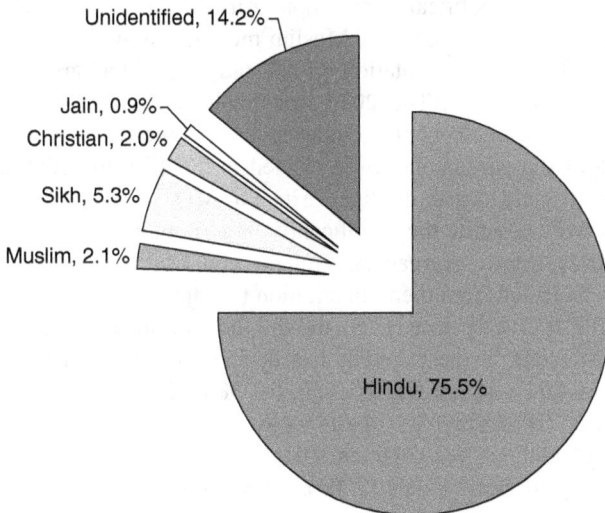

Unidentified, 14.2%

Jain, 0.9%
Christian, 2.0%

Sikh, 5.3%

Muslim, 2.1%

Hindu, 75.5%

Figure 3.1 Social background of the Indian Administrative Service (ISID; statistics obtained from Goyal, 1990).

legitimacy and integration. Seeking to ensure the secular order as a guarantee of their enjoyment of an equal status as citizens, while at the same time overcoming the threat of alienation, remains the biggest challenge minorities are faced with in democracies. There are different methods of tackling religious identity as either a precursor or a determinant of political action, or as independent from it. One valid assumption that is endorsed by Williams (2011) holds that religion is not necessarily a primordial identity, but a transformed and mobilised one according to the changing political situation, and especially manifested in electoral politics and within urban public spaces. The reference to 'urban' here is substantial since Muslims predominantly live in urban areas, despite the fact that India is mainly a rural country. In fact, the level of urbanisation among the Muslim population is higher than the average level; in 2001, 35.7% of the Muslim population was urban compared to 27.8% of the overall population (Census of India, 2001).

Limiting the analysis to one coherent political discourse that the Muslim community in India possesses is impossible. This is due to the existence of multiple Muslim communities and not simply a single one. These communities, spread all over India, are guided by regional political differences that determine their political choices.

I focus further on two issues in this section: the problem of representation and voting patterns. Representation, and especially its political aspect, is a source of continual frustration among Muslims. There is widespread discontent when it comes to the disparity between the political representation of Muslims and their share of the population in India (Shahabuddin & Wright, 1987; Ansari, 2006b). Muslims constitute more than 20% of the electorate in 197 out of 545 parliamentary constituencies, but their presence in legislatures remains dismal (Khan, 2006, p. 156).

Labelling this feeling as political deprivation, Ansari (2006b) conducted a meticulous study showing the statistics of Muslim members in parliament from 1952 to 2004. Figure 3.2 is a representation of this study after I had grouped the percentages compiled by Ansari. The 2014 Lok Sabha elections yielded the lowest number of Muslim members since independence. Whereas only twenty-three Muslims (4% of the parliament) were elected in 2014, in the 2009 elections, the parliament yielded twenty-eight Muslim MPs and, in the 2004 elections, thirty-six MPs. Despite the significantly large population of Muslims in the states of Maharashtra, Karnataka, Gujarat and Madhya Pradesh, no Muslim MP has been elected from them, in addition to Rajasthan and Orissa. As for the Indian Administrative Service (IAS) and the Indian Police Service (IPS), the percentage of Muslims in these bodies has declined over the years, from 4.5% in the IAS and 4.04% in the IPS in 1960, to 3% in the IAS, 1.8% in the Indian Foreign Service (IFS) and 4% in the IPS (Shah, 2007; Sachar Committee Report, 2006). Municipalities are another space where Muslims are poorly represented. According to Bandukwala (2006), no Muslim could be elected to the municipal corporation in the state of Gujarat because Muslim localities are deliberately partitioned into different municipal wards. This raises the issue of communalism and ghettoisation.

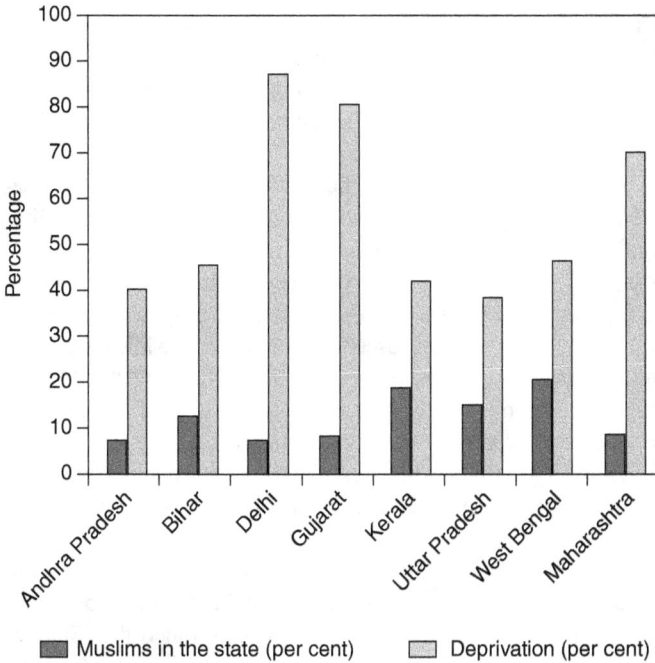

Figure 3.2 Political representation of Muslims in India, 1952–2004 (statistics source: Ansari, 2006b).

The dilemma of political deprivation was closely related to the nature of political participation in India. Although at the time following the independence of India there were calls to boycott the political process, such voices have disappeared from the contemporary political scene. However, several tactics pertaining to voting behaviour have been utilised. Still, it should be noted that emphasis has to be made concerning some of the structural reasons accounting for the low representation of Muslims. These reasons include under-numeration in the census, gerrymandering in the delimitation of constituencies and exclusion of Muslims from the electoral rolls, either due to contested citizenship proof as in the border areas (Shahabuddin & Wright, 1987, pp. 159–160) or due to marriage or change of residence.[4]

Political deprivation cannot be divorced from the problem of Muslim leadership in India. In an opinion poll conducted by a Jamaati Islami magazine in Delhi, only 4% showed trust in Muslim leadership in India. One of the interesting answers was, "currently, Muslim Leaders are definitely a phoenix". The same sentiment was shared among many students:

> One of the problems facing Indian Muslims is that they have no single united platform to participate in the political system. Other political parties

have many constraints to support Muslims wholeheartedly. Many Muslim majority places are very backward in basic necessities. The only exception is the state of Kerala where Muslims have a united political party, which helped a lot to attain their rights without damaging others' rights.

(North Indian student's comment in the online survey, December 2010)

The absence of this platform is also linked to the previously mentioned bifurcation among Indian Muslims according to divisions based on caste. These divisions resulted in the difference of united interests and demands.

Voting as a democratic tool of political participation in India has been often associated with the idea of vote banks. Two main strands govern the issue of voting behaviour among Muslims. The first ascertains vote banks, while the second regards it as a myth. The first strand shares perceptions concerning the Muslim community as being a homogenous, monolithic minority group (hence, treated by parties as a uniform vote bank). Another shared conviction is that voting behaviour is determined by *fatwas*, thus Muslims are generally viewed as a distinct and separate political community aloof from mainstream political processes. During the UP election campaigns of January–February 2012, both English and Urdu media reported the speeches of Delhi's Jama Masjid Imam Bukhari and his incitement to the Muslims to vote for the Samajwadi Party. Interestingly, in the 2004 Lok Sabha elections, Imam Bukhari's appeal was to the BJP as he had joined the 'Support Vajpayee Committee'. However, the BJP candidate did not win in the Chandni Chowk constituency (Hashmi, 2012). In 1996, the same *imam* had issued an appeal in favour of the BSP (Bahujan Samaj Party); this was erroneously termed by the media as a *fatwa*. The fact that BSP got only 20% of Muslim votes indicates how the majority of Muslims do not regard the opinions of religious leaders, especially such a famous one (Asif, 1998).

However, the second group that challenges these assumptions contends that, first, vote banks are a reality in India in general because of caste, linguistic and religious diversities (Rab, 1998). The popular notion of communal consciousness, as an element of political participation that is usually associated with the Muslim community in India, is negated by several intellectuals (Hasan, 1997, p. 217). Alam (2009) shows that the political participation and the voting patterns of Muslims are highly contextual and do not reveal any specific pattern. In states like Kerala and West Bengal, the overall turnout has been historically high and so was the Muslims' and the contest was usually between the left (non-BJP) and the Congress, unlike in the remaining states, where Congress usually harvests more Muslim votes. Eventually, Muslim voting behaviour is determined at state-level politics and cannot be generalised on a pan-Indian scale; different contexts in Indian states offer divergent voting behaviour patterns.

Voting en masse or, as it is referred to, enbloc or group voting was also regarded as a mechanism, employed by community leaders to prove to be politically efficacious, and is considered a universal phenomenon with minorities as a means of bargaining for their common interests and advantages. It is argued that the political behaviour of Indian Muslims has always been in tune with the general political traditions of the country (Rab, 1998, p. 53), therefore, negating arguments or 'exploding myths' of monolithic political behaviour in the matter of choice of a political party and enbloc voting.

Another myth dominating the discussion on Muslim political participation and their usage by political parties as voting banks is related to the idea of Muslim appeasement. Journalists and intellectuals respond to this argument by counting the incidents in which Muslims have been not only marginalised but also threatened, compelled to be ghettoised and deprived of developmental services and security. Thus, it becomes questionable to retain the appeasement hypothesis.[5]

According to Shahabuddin and Wright (1987), the Muslim community majorly adopted a political approach that resulted in a "class of powerbrokers" (p. 174). In addition to the awareness of their bargaining power, the need to form such bodies came as a result of the dissatisfaction with the failure of national political parties in helping to overcome the under-representation of Muslims. The fact that some Muslim individuals received nomination by national parties to contest elections is not in itself a guarantee of legitimate representativeness. Often these nominees are seen as "symbols of tokenism" (Shahabuddin & Wright, 1987, p. 160). Following the party line prevents them from publicly serving the community and forwarding their demands; this is because they aim to pose as being more national than the national and not be deemed communal and thus lose the chance for re-nomination. This fact serves to partly answer a question I am posing throughout this study. The fear of a member of a minority community of being labelled as disloyal to the 'nation' leads him/her to adopt a self-marginalisation position and, in the case of a politician, it is to refrain from being a voice of that community in many cases. Eventually this led to a 'communication gap' between the Muslim community and the state, leading to further alienation and withdrawal from the political mainstream.

In order to have a measurably comparative perspective, it is vital to refer to some quantitative studies conducted concerning Indian Muslims. Nandy (1975) reports that findings of a survey in 1971 showed that two thirds of Muslims were satisfied with territorial non-communal representation. In 1975, he conducted studies on the acceptability of democratic norms and could not find any differences in respect of support for the democratic norms among Muslims and Hindus. Intergroup differences, in fact, mainly occurred in the frequent blaming of the police by Muslims (Hasan, 1987, quoted in Hasan, 2006) and in having more dissenters and outsiders (Nandy, 1975). On symbolic issues (such as the destruction of Babri Masjid and support for separate personal law), there is a notable and sharp difference between Hindus and Muslims (32% to 86% and 41% to 67%, respectively). However, when it came to a sense of personal efficacy and legitimacy of the political system, Muslims' percentages were actually higher than Hindus (60% of Muslims believe their vote matters, as compared to 58% for Hindus, and 72% of Muslims believe that better government is not possible without parties, assemblies and elections, as compared to 68% for Hindus) (Mitra & Singh, 1999).

The report titled the *State of Democracy in South Asia*, conducted by the Centre for the Study of Developing Societies, located in Delhi, shows that there is no radical conceptualisation of democracy that is specific to Muslims. The majority of Indians, according to this survey, share the conception of democracy as justice and are almost equally satisfied with democracy (50% average versus 43%, and 38% average versus 41% among Muslims, respectively) (SDSA, 2008, p. 242).

These figures demonstrate strong congruence between the pan-Indian and the Muslim average since the differences are slight or, in some cases, even surprisingly higher when it comes to the support of democracy. Although it is common-sensical that a minority would be supporting a secular democratic order to guarantee its existence, the figures provide an answer to the strong discourse labelling Indian Muslims as anti-social elements whose political loyalty to the system is questioned, as I will demonstrate in an upcoming section of this chapter. Surveys show how the preference for elected representatives gets the highest level of support among Indian Muslims, not differing in this from the Indian average. A surprising difference between the Indian average and the Muslim average records relates to the index of general institutional trust; the India average recorded a percentage of 64%, while Muslims had higher rates of around 70% (SDSA, 2008, p. 59). What is also significant about these figures is how they challenge the misconception that Muslims give top consideration to religious interests while deciding their vote (Engineer, 1995).

Ideological discourses: otherness and Hindu nationalism

Media and the role of the press

The double-edged role of the media in India is significant to see how it both voices the concerns of the marginalised and at the same time demonises them. The large Muslim population in India prompted a phenomenon called 'Muslim press', which are mainly newspapers owned by Muslims, circulated in vernacular languages (most commonly in Urdu and Malayalam), and which prioritise issues related to the Muslim community. In this section, I tackle Urdu and Malayalam Muslim press separately due to the contextual differences of North India and Kerala. These differences induced a disparity not only in content, writing style, professionalism and distribution, but also in the role of the media, especially the written one, in serving as an apparatus for mobilisation, awareness and socio-political change.

To start with, Muslim press is usually associated with Urdu press (with the exception of non-Muslim Urdu press in Punjab and Delhi and Muslim press in other vernacular languages). Most, if not all, of the studies on Muslim press would mean, and refer to, only Urdu press. In India, in 2012, there were around 5519 registered Urdu media publications (newspapers and magazines), the majority of which were in Uttar Pradesh (around 1646) and Delhi (around 1013) (The Registrar of Newspapers for India, 2012). However, in an article written in

2009, Farouqui draws attention to the limited number of Urdu publications that actually reach public hands. Interestingly, the initial number of 347 publications that he gave lags behind the official number obtained in 2012 from the Registrar of Newspapers for India website. Farouqui goes further to explain that the exaggerated number could be accounted for because of the role of the government in granting concessions and advertisements to Urdu newspapers. Eventually, each publication does not give realistic figures on the number of issues published and thus the high number of registered publications does not reflect the reality of readership or distribution.

Although Urdu is identified in contemporary India as an identity marker for Muslims, not all Muslims are able to speak or read Urdu. The southern Indian Muslims, with the exception of those in Hyderabad and Bangalore, do not speak Urdu. Even the new generations in North India, where Urdu is commonly spoken, have difficulty reading the language since they mainly learn Hindi and English at school. This causes a severe language problem when it comes to Muslim press, and also justifies the absence of a pan-Indian newspaper for Muslims. The thin distribution of Muslims over India is another related demographic predicament of Muslim press. English is also not a useful language in this case, since most of the literates cannot speak it.

The spirit of Muslim press was characterised by frustration over the loss of power of Muslims since British colonialism. In a pendulum nature, Muslim press often ranges from self-congratulation to lamentation (Shahabuddin & Wright, 1987); however, the sense of lamentation usually dominates. This feeling was carried along since post-partition and the material chosen to be reported only proves this sense of pessimism and negativism and pushes Muslim masses to both a sense of alienation and protest (Farouqui, 2009; Khan, 2009). Wahiduddin Khan (2009) points out an important observation: unlike non-Muslim press, where both backwardness and underrepresentation of Muslims are reported, Muslim press intentionally omits all reference to lack of education and thus backwardness of Muslims as causes for their misfits. Being an Islamic scholar and preacher, Khan adopts a Quranic approach to the understanding of problems and solutions of Muslim press. To him, Muslims not only neglected the first Quranic commandment of 'Read', but also forgot that the power of peace was greater than the power of war. Instead of forwarding positive action, Muslim journalism is charged with negativism and protest that built up a paranoid mentality. Khan expands his argument by presenting solutions to these problems through proper training of Muslim youth and cultivation of journalistic consciousness, giving more importance to publishing in mother languages and opening a Muslim school of journalism.

The significance of the media in this section on ideological discourses lies in the role in forming political identities. Examining Urdu, as well as English press, explicates this point. In the Urdu newspaper *Sahafat*, for example, the section related to national news is termed as '*apna waṭan*' (our homeland). Here, the utilisation of the Arabic term of *patria* is symbolic and appears as a response to the questioning of political loyalty of Indian Muslims. The interaction between the religious and the political through a secular sphere is evident through many news pieces, including, for example, one reporting on the third Friday prayer of Ramadan, which was titled "Mosques were filled up: thousands rise for the safety of their country and faith (*mulk aur millat*)" (Sahafat Urdu Daily, 20 August 2011).

On the other side of the spectrum, as the Janata Party came to power in 1977 and LK Advani became the Minister for Information and Broadcasting (Asif, 1998), the media became a tool used by the Hindu right-wing or the *Sangh Parivar* in spreading its ideology and in consolidating the derogatory discourse on Indian Muslims, with little reference to changes in the community's social and economic outlook. Amanullah (2004) points to an observation concerning the hijacking of the letters to the editor section in newspapers by *Sangh Parivar* members.

Two strands in the English media are described to be antagonistic and patronising. Issues that are not relevant to the community get more attention in the media, whereas others of more significance do not (such as Muslim students, police force, administrative service examination, dropout ratios). The media, accordingly, suffer from an elite phenomenon (Mitra, 2009). Another stereotyping project was directed at the issue of freedom of expression and the attitude of Muslims towards it. One clear example was the Salman Rushdie affair, which started with the banning of *The Satanic Verses* and the huge media coverage it gained, and then its recurrence in 2012 with the Jaipur book festival. What was noted by several Muslim writers is that the media do not allocate the same interest to other books being banned especially covering Hindus.[6]

Activists usually point out the negative role played by the English media, especially *The Times of India* in the coverage of the Batla House Encounter and the ensuing stigmatisation of Muslim youth. Scholars and intellectuals emphasise the need to issue a counterbalancing press publication in English. In an interview from Nadwatul Ulama in Lucknow, a Muslim scholar asserted:

> Mainstream media are not concerned with the news of the Muslim minority; on the contrary, reporting is often biased and incorrect. In one of the functions, a newspaper reported that around a thousand attended, while the actual number of attendees was multiple thousands. This is why we decided to issue an English weekly.
>
> (Maulana Nazrul Hafiz, Lucknow, 2010)

In 2000, the first English newspaper run by Muslims and directed at Muslim issues in North India was established. The *Milli Gazette* was made available online in 2008 and is published on a biweekly basis. In an interview, the founder and editor in chief, Dr Zafrul Islam Khan, contended that the media in India had propagated images of Muslims as being backward, illiterate, dirty and a burden, and having done injustice to Hindus during their rule. By the 1990s, this trend had become very powerful and these kinds of media started asserting themselves. As for Indian Muslims, according to him, they do not have the power to counter it. The Hindu-biased media have numerical and financial power. Muslim resources are too limited to counter them. Mainstream media, he argues, created a hostile atmosphere and connected it to President Bush's war on terror. Interestingly, it was the US itself that admitted that there was not a single Indian in Al-Qaeda, and thus Indian Muslims had nothing to do with the terrorism discourse.

Although the picture in Kerala is quite different due to the different historical setting, there are some shared concerns relating to the issue of stereotyping and representation in the English press. In several interviews with Muslim students in Kerala, the feeling of bias of the English media was prevalent, as they argued that it was usually 'anti-Muslim' as evident from its coverage of issues such as the incident of the chopping off of the hand of a Christian teacher, the recruitment of terrorists and their capture in Kashmir, 'love *jihād*' and the inferiority complex of Muslims. A student in Calicut University related:

The problem with media is that there are no investigative media now. But not all media give wrong images of Muslims; it depends to which party it is affiliated. In Shaheena's case,[7] even media people were giving bad images about her being a terrorist. In Kerala, we cannot know what is happening exactly by reading one paper. At the time of Eid, Mathrubhumi, for example, published a bigger photo on an insignificant festival in Kerala and next to it a smaller photo on Eid.

The coverage of the state of Muslim women in the media was also a significant point that emerged in several public meetings and conferences, such as the Muslim Student Federation's (the Indian Union Muslim League Youth wing) conference in Calicut University campus in February 2011, where Fatima Muzafar, an eminent member of the Indian Union Muslim League (IUML) in Tamil Nadu, stressed how the media focus on trivial issues such as triple *ṭalāq* or *pardah*.

Counter to the complaint that there is no mainstream Muslim media house in North India, a different image is projected in Kerala, where it has one of the leading mainstream newspapers with Muslim ownership affiliated to the Jamaati Islami, *Madhymam*, which is said to have the third highest rate of circulation among Malayalam dailies in Kerala (Sikand, 2009). The importance of the Malayalam newspaper originates from their readership rates due to the high literacy rate in Kerala. According to the Indian Readership Survey of 2012, Malayalam newspapers and magazines were in the top ten dailies and magazines in India (*Manorama* came fourth and *Mathrubhumi* came tenth as dailies, while the top language magazine was the *Vanitha*) (Indian Readership Survey, 2012). Unlike other regional newspapers, the Malayalam press has Gulf editions, whose sales contribute to the success and even the financing of the original Kerala edition.

A worthwhile study would be to look at matters of discussion in both the English and the Urdu press and see how the focus has changed over the years.

Qamar Hasan (2006), for example, shows how the press of the 1970s was by a discussion on job reservations for Muslims, modernisation of Muslims, the status of Aligarh Muslim university and management of Muslim trust (*awqaf*, plural of *waqf*). By the 1990s, there were additional captivations, such as the alleged illegal immigration of Bangladeshi Muslims, the use of the Terrorist and Disruptive Activities Act (TADA) and the restriction on construction of *madrasas* and mosques.

Through reviewing major headlines of a daily Delhi-based Urdu Muslim newspaper titled *Sahafat* from December 2009 until March 2012, I generated a list of the main topics frequently discussed and reported. The most featured issues were the fake police encounters and the critique of UPA government, the Rashtriya Swayamsevak Sangh (RSS), national and international reporting on terrorism and excessive surveillance on Muslims, in addition to significant critique of Modi and the RSS, especially the oppression of Muslim youth in Mumbai by RSS and Bajrang Dal (looting their shops and houses, and harassing pregnant women) and the case of RSS books in Bhopal. Condemning the description of the city of Azamgarh as a terrorist hub and working on improving the services and the living conditions in the city was a recurrent theme, which was complemented by reporting the achievements of Muslim students and showing positive success stories, especially of model *madrasas*. In addition to this, there was a noted difference in the intensity and volume of coverage of the Moradabad riots of August 2011 compared to the English press, where there was little coverage. Much was reported on communal harmony, especially in festivals (as an example, there was an image of Muslim male children during Ramadan tying *raakhi* on Hindu girls).

It remains to be said that, through reading reports or articles written on the predicaments of Indian Muslims, especially in the North, twenty years ago and now, we find them almost identical in the spheres of economy, education and security. In fact, some problems have worsened, like the deprivation of Muslims of government welfare schemes, and new ones have appeared (like the Gujarat carnage and fake encounters). Muslims are still calling for:

1   Better representation in security forces and government, in addition to reservations and quota for Muslim students and for Muslim women in particular.
2   More responsible leadership (a magical equation: not too religious, not too irreligious).
3   More emphasis on education, especially in the North (*madrasa* reform, increasing the number of higher education Muslim-run institutions).
4   Human rights.
5   Islamic financial banking.

They are also critical of the conspicuous consumption of Muslims working in the Gulf.

Security aspects

> There is much that the murdering mobs in Gujarat have robbed from me. One of them is a song I often sang with pride and conviction. The words of the song are:

> Sare jaha se achha
> Hindustan hamara...
> (In all the world, our India is the best)
> It is a song I will never be able to sing again.

> (Mander, 2004, p. 30)

Although this book is about everyday life, there are many stories which should not be left untold. Everyday life for Indian Muslims cannot exclude sometimes the 'painful' or the extraordinary. Violence, as related to the feeling of insecurity, is one of these stories and is one of the main processes behind the backward social and economic conditions of Muslims. Community-related factors such as the decline in level of education are not always absolute or independent variables, but are closely related to other processes, such as violence. Recognition of direct, structural and cultural violence inflicted on Muslims through discrimination and structural processes, such as institutionalised communalism in everyday life, is significant to the understanding of the life-space of a majority of Muslims in India.

Any discussion on direct violence exercised on Indian Muslims cannot omit the 2002 Gujarat carnage, in which not only were the police complicit, but so was the state itself and its machinery, from the governor to the chief minister, the home minister, the BJP allies, the district administrators, judicial magistrates and even hospitals (Abdul Rauf, 2011; Jaffrelot, 2007). Although what happened in Gujarat cannot be generalised to the rest of India, such incidents could be revealing to inherent symptoms. The widespread expansion of the BJP in India is an alert that must be taken into consideration. That is in addition to the remark that the atrocities committed in Gujarat had symbolic attributes. The violence did not stop at killing, but extended to burning corpses and killing unborn babies. The emphasis on raping women and killing babies carried subtexts that reflected the mentality of fear on the Hindu race and the apprehension of Muslim high fertility rates (Abdul Rauf, 2011; Jaffrelot, 2007; Sarkar, 2002).

The role of the police in the Gujarat pogrom cannot be independently considered from its general role in Indian society in relation to minorities. Muslims were not the sole group that suffered because of the complicity or passivity of the police role, but also other minorities, such as the Sikhs in 1984 in Delhi. India suffers from a peculiar predicament in the realm of security of minorities; despite any advancement on the democratic or secular ladder in India, there is always a constant fear that violence might erupt and clash with one's identity as a minority. In recent times, however, the police have been notorious for their role in executing fake encounters against Muslim youth, which usually end up with the killing or detainment of innocent victims.

One of the most exhaustive studies on the role of police in communal riots was conducted by V. N. Rai, a senior police officer in UP, whose findings confirmed the partisanship of police during riots, the discrimination in the use of force at police stations against Muslims and the diametrical opposition in the perception of the police by Hindus and Muslims: where Muslims consider the police as their enemies, while Hindus perceive them as protectors and friends (Subramanian, 2006).

The frequency of this type of violence shows the significant clash between fundamental rights inscribed in the Constitution and their violation on an everyday basis by the police. Extra-judicial killings (Ansari, 2006a; South Asian Human Rights Documentation Centre, 2003), denial of bail (Khan, 2006) and prejudice in representation that led to the communalisation of the police are all forms of these violations. It has also been noted that no direct and formal action on the part of the state has been taken to circumvent these policies (Subramanian, 2006; Khan, 2006). Special emphasis is directed at the illegality of terror investigations in the cases associated with fake encounters and state-wide arrests of youth and the use of torture in their interrogations (Ali, 2012; Subrahmaniam, 2011; Setalvad, 2010).[8]

Considerable media evidence reports the increasingly politicised actions of the Indian police and how some factions of the governing party and local bodies have used it against minorities. In addition to this, in many ethnic conflicts in Punjab, Gujarat, West Bengal and UP, the police have been ineffective (Weiner, 1997, p. 488). In specific contexts like Gujarat and Rajasthan, Indian human rights activists confirm that the only relationship Muslims had with the police was of terror. To overcome this, organisations like ANHAD (Act Now for Harmony and Democracy) have started, from 2007, organising the internally displaced victims in Gujarat and conducting public hearings in Gujarat and Delhi.

On a side note, gender concerns have to be emphasised. With Gujarat being the most striking case of violence committed against women in India, several studies and activists have focused on the impact of the Gujarat carnage on Muslim women and children (e.g. Sarkar, 2002; Setalvad's articles in *Communalism Combat*; Bharatiya Muslim Mahila Andolan Indian Muslim Women Association). Though being devoid of communal violence, the state of Kerala has been witnessing rising rates of violence against women and has thus called scholarly attention to it (see, for example, the works of J. Devika and Usha Zacharias). Most studies on the remaining states of India have focused on the low educational status among Muslim women, especially in UP, Bihar and West Bengal.

What happened in Gujarat ushered in the empirical reality of the transformation of some communities in India into alien communities. This was first made possible during colonial times through the British system of census and enumeration, then was consolidated through the instrument of separate electorates and institutionalised through the study of Indian history and its epochal divisions into Muslim versus non-Muslim rule (Abdul Rauf, 2011; Hasan, 1980; Pandey, 1989).

Cultural violence could be embodied in the Hindu-nationalism discourse, tackled in the next section. The compulsory singing of the *Vande Mataram* in schools was considered, by some, as the veneration of a country in the form of a deity or goddess that excluded them from a pan-Indian cultural fold.[9]

The division among different kinds of violence is also linked to the two different types of power diffusion: as a material force and at the level of consciousness or culture (Mitchell, 1990). Domination through creating an environment of fear not only shows physical vulnerability, but also indicates the integration of fear in everyday life in people's minds. The history of the fear psychosis in Delhi, for example, goes back to partition and the massacres witnessed in Old Delhi and *Qutub Minar*.[10] It is often recalled that the area of *Qutub Minar* had 90% Muslim inhabitants and thousands of Muslims were massacred, to the extent that people were saying there was another *Qutub Minar* of the bodies of the Muslims (Interview with Manzoor Alam, September 2010). The result of this psychosis is the inability of future planning since the main concern is survival. Identity, hence, features as a top priority and a precursor for survival.

This lack of a sense of security among Indian Muslims necessitates the reality of spatial segregation among Muslim and Hindu communities. On the one hand, there is the 'mini-Pakistan' phenomenon, where urban Muslims get ghettoised, especially in Mumbai, Delhi and the state of Gujarat. However, this term seems controversial as it is used in Hindu-nationalistic speeches referring to the difference between their ghettos (Muslims') and our shining cities (Hindu nationalists') (Abdul Rauf, 2011). In addition to tainting the ghettos with an anti-social criminal outlook, I once heard a Muslim auto rickshaw driver describe Meerut as a Mini-Pakistan, where Muslims form a collective power. It seems imperative to note the surprised look on the face of a Muslim university lecturer I interviewed, once he knew of this driver's story and that he was a Muslim. The logical story, to him, would have been that he was a Hindu driver complaining of the Muslim population and reflecting the Hindutva's sense. On a Hindu upper-middle-class level, this sense is evident in the marketing strategies of new residential projects along community lines, where one can live without the troubling presence of the 'other', which have been supplanted by a Supreme Court decision to approve restrictions of membership to persons from the same caste or religion (Abdul Rauf, 2011).

In her study about the Emergency in Delhi, Tarlo (2003) narrates the targeting of Muslim urban poor in the sterilisation campaign led by Indira Gandhi in 1976. Tarlo expounds that individual and collective fear and anger could be discerned from victims' reports. The feeling of insecurity dominates the way they perceive not just their past but also their future. It is not just the mere experience of a riot or communal violence that shapes a Muslim's perception of fear, but also a strong anticipation of violence that could erupt in any moment. She cites the following quotation of a young Muslim man: "We are, after all, living in a country which is governed by others. Whatever they want to do to us, they do it whether we want or not" (Tarlo, 2003, p. 134). She explained the context of this quotation as a continuation to a discussion on the exclusion of Muslims in a specific colony from the electoral roll in the recent local elections and on the police participation in the riots.

During my fieldwork, I happened to be in Jamia Nagar in Delhi on the day of the verdict of the Ayodhya dispute on 30 September 2013. There was an overall sense of pensive anticipation in the country and people were expecting curfews. As I started an interview in Batla House, my respondent kept on reminding me that by 1 p.m. I should be out of Batla House. The reason he gave was a statement said in a matter-of-fact way: "We do not know what will happen. If the verdict is pro-Hindus, then nothing wrong will happen, but if it is pro-Muslims, fanatics might come and kill us. Just make sure you are out of here before the verdict is announced." This insecurity, as an everyday fact that citizens are accustomed to, signals one of the biggest mishaps of Indian democracy. As a remedy, most studies recommend the inclusion of Muslims in law enforcement agencies, such as the police and the judiciary, which would result in monitoring and curbing the communal elements on both societal and state levels (Khan, 2006).

The success of state management of communal riots in the South versus the North should be noted. This is accounted for by the strength of the middle and lower caste mobilisation around a Dravidian identity in the South. In the case of the Ayodhya mosque dispute, the leader of the Indian Muslim League party in Kerala invited the opposition leaders (the communists) and threatened to dismantle the coalition with Congress unless the state managed an overhaul of the police and bureaucracy against any elements inciting anti-Muslim riots (Wilkinson, 2002). This is in addition to the speedy trials, like the Marad riots case (explained in a forthcoming chapter).

Nationalism: the ideological discourse

> But to make the future of Muslims in India more secure will require a new political imagination that combines principle with prudence to defeat the forces that are putting the interests of Muslims – and all citizens of India – at risk. The sad fact is that since partition there has not been any form of meaningful Muslim politics for a variety of reasons. Politics, in the genuine sense of the term, requires the availability of a public space and a public discourse where issues of common concern could be debated without let or hindrance. Such spaces have been in an effective sense closed to Muslims.
>
> (Mehta, 2004, p. 82)

The Indian state employs two principles evidently through the Constitution. The first is called in Sanskrit *sarva dharma samabhava* (equal attitudes towards all religions) and the second, *dharma nirapekshata* (religious neutrality) (Mitra, 2003). Although the stress on these two significant markers of the Indian state is evident through many political and social studies, the dominance of upper-caste Brahminical influence on the social and political everyday life in India cannot be negated. This dominance is manifested in the Hindu nationalistic discourse that emerged in the nineteenth century, but was codified only by the early 1920s through the work of V. D. Savarkar (Jaffrelot, 1996). The term Hindu nationalism has been incorporated into the study of Indian politics. Although its conceptual linkages have more to do with fundamentalism and communalism, the term nationalism has been attributed to it, and the whole term of Hindu nationalism is often associated with other derogatory phenomena and institutions of Indian politics, such as the Sangh Parivar, the RSS, the Shiv Sena, the saffron wave and *Hindutva*.[11]

Zavos (2000) explains that the transformation of nationalism into communalism occurs upon the instrumentalism of the elites of an extreme form of nationalism to create a violent political force. The political manifestation of Hindu nationalism was historically evident in two organisations. The first was the Mahasabha, which was founded in 1915 and by the 1920s assumed a high political profile on the national and anti-colonial level. It came as a counterpart to the Muslim League, and thus sought to represent the Hindus as a political party. The second organisation was the Rashtriya Swayamsevak Sangh (RSS), which was formed in 1925 as a regional organisation, and it was around the late 1930s that it began to have an impact on national politics (Zavos, 2000). Significant members of the Mahasabha joined the Bharatiya Jana Sangh, which was later transformed in 1980 into the Bharatiya Janata Party, currently the second biggest national political party in India on a national level. Another Hindu nationalistic organisation is the Shiv Sena. Unlike the RSS, it is regionally based in Maharashtra, and had started its work by targeting South Indian immigrants in Mumbai, regardless of their religion, in addition to communists. Today, it mainly targets Muslims (Gupta, 2005).

The Hindu nationalistic discourse started by extending the history of domination to incorporate the Muslim rule over India and, therefore, to designate Muslims as foreigners (Alam, 1999). This helped the Sangh movement to actively describe Muslims as a dangerous and undesirable community who do not qualify to be equal citizens. Throughout the Ram Mandir movement, this was clearly manifested (Khan, 2006) and was in turn reflected in government-managed schools, history books, modes of greeting and formal cultural programmes.

The Bharatiya Janata Party's ideology and policies echo this discourse on a national level. Das (2004) cites examples of the BJP's discourse against Muslims in what has been published in the BJP newspaper *Swastika*. These include stating that not only do Muslims practise foreign religions and have extraterritorial loyalties, but they also constitute a 'drag' on the nation because they are ignorant and stubborn, resist education and, unlike Hindus, refuse to practise birth control (ibid., p. 385). The BJP ideology places the 'Hindu' ideology at the core of the nation, criticises Muslims for failing to integrate and for being 'disloyal' and thus critiques the practice of secularism as having wounded the Hindu ethos (Singh, 2005). This is what makes the BJP disapprove of the term secularism and argues that it has become a creed in itself that has destroyed the principles of *sanatan dharma* (the eternal creed of Hinduism) and *bhartiya samskriti* (Indian culture) (Chowdary, 2007), thus leading to its replacement with the hegemonic 'integral humanism' (BJP website, 2012).

Statements of BJP politicians reflect these discourses in a rather obvious way, hence questioning the nature of secular democracy. These include the current prime minister and former Gujarat chief minister Narendra Modi's statement: "all Muslims are not terrorists but all terrorists are Muslims"; in addition to former prime minister Atal Behari Vajpayee's proclamation that "Muslims are the source of problems all over the world" (Abdul Rauf, 2011) and hence find bitter resonance among the Muslim community. In many of my interviews with Muslim students, they mentioned these statements while expressing their grief and their frustration at having to deal with such declarations. Engineer (1998) is of the opinion that it is the educated modernist middle class that is directly involved in power struggles and thus gets involved in rightist or fundamentalist movements. This explains why the BJP, VHP, Bajrang Dal and RSS are not pro-vided by orthodox Hindu priesthood. It is through matters of education like history text books, the singing of *Vande Mataram* and *Saraswati Vandana Mantra* in schools and the Vidyabharti syllabus that the role of BJP becomes most obvious. What is enforced is a vision of a 'one-dimensional man' and an educational system based on centres of acknowledgement and recognition.[12]

There is a noted failure of the state to check the *Sangh Parivar* and the parti-ality of judgment and communalism. This is evident in bureaucrats attending cultural events of RSS, career development of police personnel involved in com-munal riots, mainstream media coverage of communal forces, ceremonial pūjas and anti-Muslim speeches by politicians. Jaffrelot's studies on Hindu national-ism show how, in addition to the creation of communal organisations such as the RSS, and complicity in Hindu–Muslim riots, there was a new strategy imple-mented in bomb blasts or, as he calls it, "emulating Islamist terrorism" (Jaffrelot, 2010). The Abhniav Bharat organisation, responsible for the Malegaon blast, resorted to two tactics. The first was of bomb blasts, and the second was the search for outside support, mainly from Israel and Nepal, for the purpose of acquiring training, equipment and political asylum (ibid.).

The discourse on terrorism

> The police would register their deaths as foreign terrorists, take pictures of the bodies and then, late at night, go to the villagers demanding that they be buried, quickly and quietly.
>
> (Peer, 2011)

This quote was taken from a newspaper article unveiling some of the atrocities committed by the police in Kashmir. Although Kashmir is an exceptional context, with different political settings, the discourse on terrorism in general has assumed a hegemonic role. The issue of terrorism has been identified on a national level as the biggest threat to the Indian nation, as the former prime minister Manmohan Singh has declared. However, despite the previously mentioned terrorist activities conducted by Hindu right-wing organisations, this discourse on terrorism seems to be exclusively linked to Muslims. Alternative Muslim media often remark how even after the discovery of Hindu nationalists' complicity in some terrorist attacks, like the Abhinav Bharat, no actions of massive hunts for associated Hindu youth takes place, but once a Muslim is caught, he is immediately dubbed a terrorist, without sufficient proof (An Indian Muslim Blog, 2012).

In an interview, the human rights activist Shabnam Hashmi from ANHAD (Act Now for Harmony and Democracy) related the following:

> As far as terrorism is concerned, there is a relationship between the Hindu right-wing and the state.... The state in the last twenty years has become very communal because during the period that BJP was ruling India, they have successfully placed right-wing people almost everywhere: in the army, the media, in military, police and bureaucracy. And those people have reached now almost either the middle or top ranks in various public spheres in the country, so the fact is that they are in the government and they breed this hatred within the system. It is not only that you have to counter right-wing forces who are organised communal forces but their ideologies have also seeped in all public spaces, including these so-called secular political parties. Even their way of thinking and acting has become highly communal.
>
> (Author interview, October 2010)

Reversing the weapon of accusation of Muslims of terrorism, directing it towards the Hindus and calling it ideological terrorism has been a significant counter-discourse that Muslims have been trying to disseminate through the media and literature. Police-induced terror combines symbolic, physical and ideological violence. The terrorism discourse becomes inverted and assumes legitimacy when the projected perpetuator is the Muslim. However, looking at the counter-discourses of Muslims, it is obvious how they not only reject the whole terrorism discourse and condemn it, but also present their own reality as being victims of another terrorism discourse – that of the police.

There is also an emphasis that terrorism in India claims more Muslim victims than others, whether injured or falsely detained (Khaliq, 2011). In addition to this, there is an emphasis on resorting to factual information de-linking Muslims from international terrorist networks (Ansari, 2006a). Singh (2005) commented: "It is significant that of the 150 million Muslims in India, not one joined the Taliban or Al-Qaeda" (p. 15).

As a result of the discourse on terrorism, there has been a phenomenon of which the Muslim community in India severely suffers – that is, of 'fake police encounters'. Instead of reforming the police and correcting the impartial control of communal violence, the Indian state, in its pursuit of a vision of good govern-ance, chose to adopt Draconian laws such as TADA (Terrorist and Disruptive Activities Prevention Act) and POTA (Prevention of Terrorism Act) that contributed to the alienation and frustration among the Muslim community since these laws were mainly targeted at them to terrorise them (Ansari, 2006a).

Media and investigative reports demonstrated police barbarism against Muslim students at Jamia Millia Islamia University in New Delhi. Records show that fake encounters have been prevalent for many years, but not enough media attention has been cast upon them. In April 2000, there was an incident characterised as "one of the worst ever incidents of police terror against students since the Emergency" (Ansari, 2006a, p. 168). The police selectively and communally targeted Muslim students with distinct features, such as beards or kurta-pyjama. Iqbal Ansari cites sections of the observations of the People Union for Civil Liberties (PUCL) report:

> The ones (students) sporting beards had their beard pulled, while doing this the police was using filthy words, and abusing the students for following a particular faith. [...] The taunting, tortures and humiliations of the students on the ground of faith is a serious matter. It shows increasing communalization of the Delhi Police.
>
> (Ansari, 2006a, p. 169)

Discourses on socio-economic backwardness: discrimination and marginalisation

Muslim Personal Law(s)

The situation in which Muslims find themselves is based on multiple oppressions, including caste, class, gender and religion. Traditional understandings of religion are part of the problem rather than the solution. The set of laws comprising Muslim personal legal codes are argued to have been formulated by dominant groups to justify their own interests, preserve the status quo and justify these multiple oppressions (Sikand, 2004b). In common discussions about applying Islam in everyday life, there is a recurrence of the term *shari'ah* and its application. This is embodied mainly in the whole debate of Muslim Personal Laws in India, being the area where Islamic rules of *shari'ah* are applied or believed to be applied. To make things clear, *shari'ah* simply means a path or source[13] and consequently it means the basic laws set by God that one follows in religion and are derived from the Quran and the *Sunnah* (the prophet's sayings and traditions). There is a misconception that *fiqh* or jurisprudence is synonymous with *shari'ah*, since *fiqh* refers to the knowledge or the know-how to apply these basic laws and thus is linked to the observance of certain rituals and also tends to focus on details not set out clearly in the *shari'ah*. In India, the creation of the Muslim Personal Law was equated to a *shari'ah* body. This is falsely conceived and has been criticised by many scholars due to the injustices it holds for women and thus the violation of *shari'ah*, since justice is its basic underlying principle (Sikand, 2006). The unbalanced gender concerns relate mainly to divorce laws, inheritance, polygamy and maintenance issues (Vatuk, 2005).

Another serious predicament is the division of Muslims along sects and religious rifts: for example, Deobandi, Barelwi, Ahl-hadith, Shia, Tablighis and Jamaati. The consequently created AIMPLB (All India Muslim Personal Law Board) faced difficulties because of these sects, since it is hegemonised by self-appointed Deobandis who claim to be the dominant ones, and thus are not representative of the Muslim community. One of the latest controversial debates concerns the call by *'ulama* to the creation of state-recognised *shari'ah* courts that would be manned by *madrasa*-graduated clerics instead of state-appointed judges. This demand comes as a replacement to the system employed in India in which the Muslim Personal Law is applied by civil courts and judges regardless of their religion.

One of the most alluded-to cases in Indian intellectual debates and the media over the Muslim question is the problem of Muslim Personal Laws, and the reference to the Shah Bano case. For the media, the case is juxtaposed as an inclination by the Indian state to Muslim appeasement, insurance of Muslim votes or even tolerance of Islamic fundamentalism. For a variety of Muslim intellectuals, it is regarded through different lenses; either as touching an essential aspect of cultural rights of citizens or as an embodiment of the "Sovereign's will in the realm of law making which Parliament was honour-bound to enforce after what the Supreme Court did in the Shah Bano Case" (Rizvi, 1998, p. 45).

An inherent problem with the discourse on a Uniform Civil Code is the hijacking of the arguments supporting this cause by Hindu nationalists. The Hindu nationalist discourse presents a model citizen, who is supposedly an upper-caste Hindu male idealised as the universal citizen expounding the secular ideas of the middle class. That same model citizen is turned into a victim by the oppressors who fight against these ideals he carries. The Hindu right has presented the case of the UCC (Uniform Civil Code of India) as an example of this. Within the folds of these discourses, the voices of the feminists, who are not subscribing to the Hindu nationalist project, get dissolved and neglected. Roy (2002) speaks of this phenomenon by stressing the feminism of the new woman who is an active political subject, who struggles for her rights of freedom and equality as a citizen before being a woman.

The Urdu language

There is a strong link between language and legitimacy, and thus the sense of citizenship in a nation-state. Trust in the political system and believing in its legitimacy enhance the sense of citizenship. There are many remarks, for example, on how Bengalis, before the independence of Bangladesh, deemed it unfair to consider Urdu as an official language and to be expected to be proficient in it to attain a governmental post. India did not suffer from this syndrome because of the incisively managed role of federation and state powers and the acknowledgment of regional languages.

However, the question of Urdu in India and the huge debate on it in literature on Indian Muslims arose because of the colonisation of the discourse on language by the question of nationalism. Historically, Urdu has been seen as a political instrument utilised by pro-partition forces and thus appeared threatening to a Hindu Nationalist imaginary (Rahman, 2012; Rumi, 2012). Urdu, as Mehta (2006) argues, is "one of the few languages in the world that is treated, not as a language, but as an icon, a marker of an identity that puts the project of nationalism at risk" (p. 15).

Employing Scott's idea of hidden transcripts, we would arrive at the conclusion that the Urdu press represents a site for resistance and for the embodiment of hidden transcripts against the public and hegemonic discourses. According to Scott (1990), "the social sites of the hidden transcript are those locations in which the unspoken riposte, stifled anger, and bitten tongues created by relations of domination find a vehement, full-throated expression" (p. 120). One aspect to be considered is, despite the fact that a very small proportion of the non-Muslim Indian population could read Urdu, the majority of the Urdu press, and the totality of the Muslim-owned Urdu press, caters to a Muslim audience, and thus is, to a great extent, away from the control and surveillance of the non-Muslim public and especially the dominant sections, such as the Hindu nationalist forces. Whereas a Muslim citizen would seem intimidated to talk or would feel obliged to stick to a certain path, we find examples in the editorial pieces of the ability to cast one's opinion freely without repression or inhibition. The following is a quote from a letter to the editor of the *Sahafat* Urdu daily dated 26 January 2012 and titled "Happy Republic Day", reflecting typical middle-class Muslim concerns:

> Today is a historically dear day to us as it put an end to the age of slavery and subjectivity to the British. The newly independent state was supposedly built on the secular premise of non-discrimination among its citizens. However, there is strong discrimination falling on Muslims who constitute the second biggest *majority*. In Gujarat, when the lives of Muslims were improving and when they were advancing, the chief minister prepared a staff to kill them.... Students in Azamgarh were falsely accused of terrorism to force them to discontinue their education and ruin their careers. Now Azamgarh has turned into a *Terror town*.... Mosques are continually targeted and whenever Muslims clear any allegations against them, new ones start appearing.
>
> (M. I., Delhi, translation and italics mine)

Backwardness

> We have received the news of our release from the prison; lamps of flowers are burning bright
> But there is so much light that the door of the cage is invisible
> The empty hands and dry sleeve is a commentary on our poverty,
> There is not even a drop of perspiration of labour on our forehead.
>
> (Feelings of freedom and partition as expressed by the Urdu poet Siraj Lakhnavi, quoted in Hasan, 2008, p. 153)

During the colonial struggle in Algeria against the French, Malik Bennabi emerged as one of the most prominent philosophers, whose work surpassed the traditional analysis of colonialism, to develop a notion of colonialisability. Bennabi asserted the agency of the colonised Muslims in creating a state of civilisational backwardness and weakness that made their colonisation inevitable. In a similar fashion, when asking different people, ranging from auto rickshaw drivers to employees at an electricity company, to professors at central universities, regarding the reasons of the Indian Muslim predicament, they relate the backwardness created by the Indian Muslim himself.

This oppression neurosis directly relates to a minority complex, which according to Hasan (1987), consists of two aspects. The first is educational backwardness (Hasan, 1987, pp. 168–176), attributed in India to causes such as poverty, the accumulation of backwardness over generations from the time of establishment of British rule and Muslims' indifference to education or the reluctance to send their children to Christian schools. Backwardness, as a discourse, was attributed to the colonial times and the British policy to kill the nerves feeding the Muslim community through killing or exiling *'ulama* and blocking resources to the *madrasas* (Qasmi, 2005).

In addition to this, there is the partition narrative in which a large part of the Muslim educated class migrated to Pakistan.[14] Other reasons include discrimination, infatuation with conservatism, Muslims' hesitation to send their children to governmental schools because of the lack of facilities for the teaching of Urdu and the lack of visibility of Muslims' presence in the service sector. This gave rise to a perception of discrimination in jobs in public and private sectors (Ansari, 1989), the gearing of language and history books to Hindu ethos and the unacceptability of an essentially Hindu culture of schools, illiteracy of mothers, attitude of Muslims towards white-collar jobs and the use of children as earning members of the family. Before moving to the second aspect of the minority complex, the emphasis on the Muslim collision with the Hindu dominant culture should be contested. Figure 3.3 manifests an aspect of the composite nationalism that religious scholars like Azad and Madani tried to emphasise. The Muslim celebration of Republic Day in *madrasas* throughout India is also another indication, as I will later show.

The second aspect of the minority complex is social and political malintegration. Conceptually, political integration is understood in terms of the in(congruence) of people's orientations and the political system (Almond & Verba, 1989). Bonds of affiliation between people and the system are strengthened by people's competence in their role as citizens and subjects (Hasan, 1987, pp. 177–179). This is challenged by incidents of institutional exclusion, like those witnessed in festivals and sports, or through the formation of a nation-*rāshtra* (Das, 2004).

What Indian Muslims in certain spheres in India suffer from is structural socio-economic discrimination and cultural exclusion. Looking at various official reports and listening to narratives from Muslims from all classes, we see that socio-economic discrimination mainly refers to employment, housing and the

Figure 3.3 A Muslim mother with her son
dressed as the Hindu Lord Krishna
for a school function (source: *Hindustan Times*, 1 September 2010).

credit market. Cultural exclusion, as defined by Madanipour, is a situation in which group members are marginalised from the symbols, meanings, rituals and discourses of the dominant culture (Madanipour, 1998). Points made by Ansari in a report presented to the United Nations World Conference against Racism, Racial Discrimination, Xenophobia and Related Intolerance in 2001 in Durban clarify this exclusion. Regarding Islam as an adversary of Hinduism, the hype created about Hindu lower-caste converts to Islam and a chauvinist reading of Indian medieval history that portrays Muslims as oppressors of Hindus are such examples.

In 2006, the first detailed and government-commissioned report on the social, economic and educational conditions of Muslims in contemporary India (known as the Sachar Committee Report) was presented to parliament. The report divided the problems of Muslims into the following categories: identity-related, security-related and equity-related issues. These categories, just like the hegemonic discourses I have been presenting throughout this chapter, are not mutually exclusive or independent. To the contrary, they are deeply interrelated and causal.

The identity and security-related aspects in the report directly relate to the political and ideological discourses, especially as evident in the politicised actions of the Indian police. One of the major triggers of this is the visibility of Muslims in public spaces. Lack of security, due to the fear of eruption of ethnic violence and concerns about police impartiality, led to the reduction of safe spaces for women and the transformation of common public spaces into segreg-ated spaces. Thus, an apparent clash with citizenship ideals appears when the feeling of being at home gets redefined. This fear-triggered and self-imposed ghettoisation led to another complicated chain of deterioration on socio-economic levels. There is a reported short supply and neglect by municipal and government authorities when it comes to infrastructure (water, electricity, sanita-tion, roads, transport facilities) and schools, public health facilities, banking facilities and ration shops. This indeed led to poverty and sustained low levels of education due to poor access to school and pessimistic perceptions of one's chil-dren's futures. The literacy rate among Muslims in 2001 was 59.1%. This is far below the national average (65.1%).

Now Muslims are realising that the key to their security is education, and par-ticularly in riot-affected areas like Gujarat, there is a high demand for quality education, especially for girls. Girls are indicators of the change happening in the community. They are slowly breaking the confinements of being a minority within a minority (Bandukwala, 2006). Considerable stress has been placed on the significance of education both as a marker of the Indian Muslim dilemma and as a solution. Muslim scholars such as Al-Qaradawy have pointed out the irony that, despite the importance of knowledge in Islam (since Islam considers acquisition of knowledge as a medium of attaining success in this world and the world hereafter) and how its concept of education encompasses all disciplines of secular as well as religious society, two-thirds of Muslims in the world are illit-erate and three-quarters of female Muslims are illiterate (Shahid, 2006). Despite this, the initiatives of the Muslim community to enhance its welfare through *madrasas* and *waqf* associations should not be neglected.

In India, dropout rates among Muslims are highest at the levels of primary, middle and higher secondary schools compared to all the socio-religious cat-egories. As a result, there is a higher percentage of Muslims among the self-employed, and lower percentage than the backward classes in regular jobs. There is also a noted high percentage of self-employed female Muslims that amounts to 70%. The National Sample Survey provides data for workers engaged in "Public Order and Safety Activities" both at the state and at the central govern-ment level. The available estimates show that the share of Muslims in these activities at the central government level was only about 6%, while that of the Hindu–Upper Caste was 42% and both Hindu–Scheduled Castes/Scheduled Tribes and Hindu–Other Backward Classes had a share of 23% each (Sachar Committee Report, 2006, p. 186).

According to data from the Centre for the Study of Democratic Societies, if we were to take out 6–7% of those who belong to the gentry or the middle classes among the Muslims, then the condition of the ordinary Muslim is no better than that of the Dalit or the most backward castes (Alam, 2001). Reserva-tions for Muslims who are listed as Other Backward classes are found in Tamil

Nadu (3.5%), Andhra Pradesh (still contested 4%) and Kerala, where the entire community has been classified as 'backward'.[15] The acquisition of the right to reservations has enabled the community to overcome the predicaments posed by job discrimination. The problem prevails since job discrimination is more persistent in the private sector, except in a few Muslim-owned enterprises or in Muslim-dominated labour divisions, such as the skins trade in South India or silk weaving in Banaras (Shahabuddin & Wright, 1987, pp. 163–164).

This sentiment of discrimination sadly not only still lingers but gets enhanced every day in North India, as voiced by a Delhi-based journalist in an interview:

> When I am in the system, I have no problem, but when I try to act for the Muslim interest then I am crushed, discriminated, and completely denied.... I am talking from my experience; I have been a very famous journalist but after I started writing on Muslim issues, I was denied jobs and my articles would not be published. As long as you have no problem with the state, as, long as you are in accordance with the system and its ideas, then there is no problem.

The most commonly cited factors for Muslim backwardness in India relate to the pre-independence struggle against imperialism, the intra-community's opposition to the educational system of the British and hence the reliance on the establishment of *madrasas*. In the post-independence period, external and internal factors intertwined. Externally, campaigns of defamation and demonisation conducted by communal organisations against Muslims, the partisan role of the police and paramilitary forces and complicity of the local administration during communal riots, discrimination against Muslims by governmental agencies and the biased role of the media were all interplaying and inducing the state of backwardness. Internal factors, however, were deemed more powerful and dangerous. These included the apathetic attitude towards education, the low achievement motivation, endemic disunity and dissension, lack of communitarian engagement and grassroots mobilisation, self-complacency and lack of initiative for self-improvement, in addition to the dearth of dedicated leadership. For girls, additional causes such as the scarcity of segregated schools for girls were conducive to the marked low rate of literacy among Muslim females, hence labelling them in the contemporary time as the most disadvantaged group in India. The weakness of Muslim institutions is measured through their weak role in management of educational institutions (in 1997, only fifty-four out of 3604 degree colleges were managed by Muslim institutions) (Kutty, 1997).

Despite all these factors, there have been sincere efforts to reverse these conditions. The first step was the establishment of *maktabs* and *madrasas*. *Maktabs* are small institutions usually linked to a mosque in which children go to learn how to read and recite the Quran. *Madrasas*, on the other hand, are more educationally complicated institutions, and could be regarded as alternative schools in which children go to learn basic religious studies, but also, to a large extent, language, some mathematics and sciences. This step catered to the needs of a large portion of the Muslim population in marginalised areas, providing education up to fifth standard, enabling students to get admission in sixth standard in vernacular schools. The noted parents' concern to let their children join mainstream schools once the *madrasas* had completed their role, or once conditions suited them, is a remarkable indicator of the resilience of the marginalised sections of the community (Shahid, 2006). This is in contrast to claims of their alienation and rejection of the 'system' or the 'mainstream'. Their role in combating illiteracy is also clearly noted since government efforts have not been successful even after five decades of governance. However, *madrasas* are bringing good results – "they are working as NGOs with meagre resources" (Shahid, 2006, p. 124) – they act as a deterrent against human trafficking and their graduates become medical practitioners, Urdu teachers and translators.

Thus, the perception of responsibility for backwardness is divided between blaming both the government and the Muslims themselves. In an interview, a recognised *imam* and community leader in Delhi answered my question on whose responsibility it is:

Both! The government ignored the situation and this is why Muslims became backward. The kind of care that Muslims expect from the government is not met. Today there is discrimination in every office. It is not that we are blaming the government. No. Everyone should try his best. Nowadays Muslims do not think of their lives carefully. If there is money, it is spent on building a house and not on education, money is spent on luxury, cars, and if there is a wedding, then two to four lakhs are spent on food.

(Imam Makrami, Shahi Imam of the Fatehpuri Mosque, Delhi, December 2010)

In another interview with a Muslim middle-class clerk living in a small town in Haryana, he cast full blame on the Muslims for not paying due attention to education. He cited how it was always the case that if someone got highly educated then they in turn would be able to achieve some social status; otherwise how would the Muslims think they would be able to find decent employment without a corresponding decent degree.

Another aspect of marginalisation is the violation of the right to civic amenities. In the time of the Emergency, for example, some Muslims complained not only of being excluded from voting lists, and being ascribed foreign identities like a Bangladeshi, but also of being targeted in the sterilisation campaign. Some of these cases were cited in Tarlo (2003). As an interesting result of the marginalisation of Muslims, the alliance with the Dalits and other backward classes was noted. Within the Muslim communities, there has been a shift away from the concerns of security fostered by the Congress to those of equality, rights and dignity, similar to that of the other backward classes' (OBCs) quests for recognition (Sikand, 2004a). Therefore, they are no longer solely considered a vote bank; they are being transformed into nationwide political communities aiming at full citizenship (Alam, 2001, 2004).

The role of lower-caste Muslim organisations should not be neglected, especially when we note the difference in their mobilisation strategies and articulation of demands. For example, whereas North Indian Muslim elites have fostered and furthered the cause of the Urdu language, Dalit Muslim organisations (*pasmandah*) have clearly delineated this issue not only as insignificant but also as a part of an Ashrafisation project and hence a social mobility ladder. Individuals in these groups stress that Urdu is not their mother language and that the linguistic concern of the elites has been rotating from English to Persian to Urdu, but there are many other problems that are more vital than the decline of Urdu: "We are literally dying, we do not have education, why do I die for Urdu? Why not Hindi since it has even a more empowering national character?", a social activist in Delhi emphasised.

Through these *pasmandah* politics, lower-caste Muslims are articulating demands that are different from the middle-class ones. In the Indian democracy, political representation seems to be circumscribed to upper-caste Muslims, with their different social experience; hence, the dilemmas of low-caste Muslims are not prevalent in the political discourses:

> We are *shudra* first then we are Muslims because if you change your religion, your caste does not change. This garb of religion is not real. Justice should not be limited to one community. In Jamiat Ulama Hind, these *madanis* and *sayeds* are all upper caste. Sons succeed their fathers. Democracy does not work within these organisations.
>
> (NGO activist from UP, September 2010)

> Because 80% of Muslims are low caste, different narratives must be woven. Sachar will tell you it is 45% but it is wrong, it is manipulated statistics. Caste has a distinct political function; democracy of Muslim society is not possible without the movement of lower castes. It is about redistribution of resources, not rituals.
>
> (Lecturer at Jamia, December 2010)

The scenario in Kerala does not differ much. Caste plays a strong social role in the South Indian's everyday life, regardless of their religion. In contemporary society, two apparent low castes appear among the Muslims and are being, to an extent, discriminated against within the community itself. These are the fishermen and the barbers. Inter-caste marriage is a strict taboo, especially for the *Sayyids* or the *Thangals* (the upper classes). The political reflection of caste politics appear in the strong support of the Muslim League, which is dominated by *Thangals* who claim religious and not only political authority and hence manage to mobilise masses from the lower castes.

What could be witnessed in Kerala is a strong affiliation between the lower castes and the Muslims who work together. Different political forces in India have sought to build alliances with other marginalised, deprived or oppressed groups, as partners in political struggles. Interestingly, many Islamists have taken up the cause of the struggles of Dalits, tribal groups and women. Feminist voices have even found space within the publications of some of the Islamist forces – for example, on the pages of the *Madhyamam* weekly magazine, which is affiliated to the Jamaati Islami-i-Hind in Kerala and now among the leading weekly magazines in South India. This magazine is known to publish different views dedicated to issues on Muslims, Dalits and women. Another example is the PDP (People's Democratic Party), established by Madani, which is considered to be the first party in Kerala specifically aimed at allying the Muslim–Dalit–Backward caste fronts by its formulation of "power to the *avarnas* and liberation to the oppressed (*avarnankku athikaram, peeditharkku mochanam*)" (Rowena, 2011).

The ideal of secularism and its predicaments in India

Throughout my fieldwork in India, a recurrent theme emerged as a possibly additional hegemonic discourse – namely, secularism. There is a divergence, however, in the perception of secularism as a hegemonic discourse between the intellectual elite and the common people. During my interviews with university professors, lawyers and even some students, they often made reference to secularism as a tool to either alienate or terrorise Muslims.[16] Secularism as a term does not find a translated equivalent in Urdu (since the transliterated English term is used in written Urdu), hence does not feature in the conversations of the public, but rather in their own everyday practices of coexistence.

Whereas some saw secularism as a hegemonising alien idea, the widespread opinion of the common people regarded the commitment to secularism as the only solution to the threats concerning their livelihood and existence. Significant evidence in the Indian Muslim milieu shows the surprising and strict adherence to the idea of secularism. For example, there is a clear dearth of Islamic militancy and extremist Islamic parties in India (despite the absence of a constitutional ban). Political parties, in general, adopt strategies demonstrating a minor stream of separate Muslim parties; support of other parties; and involvement in public life through participation in debates, community and educational services. Perhaps the exception is the Popular Front of India (based in Kerala) and the attached, newly found political party, the Social Democratic Party of India (SDPI). The refusal to sing *Vande Mataram* is also considered a resistant mechanism to the Hindu national ideal and a desire to adhere to secularism, as Madhu Kishwar argued.[17]

The contemporary political and legal history of India offers many examples of the predicaments facing the application of the ideal of secularism in India. From the critique of Hindu *pūjas* (prayers) being conducted in the inauguration of national projects, such as the new terminal at New Delhi international airport, to complicated election-related political games, such as the government dealing with the Shah Bano case, leading up to more severe practices of the Hindu right, like the demolishment of the Babri Masjid.

The demolishment of the Babri Mosque in 1992 was considered an eye-opener to many Muslims to the bitter reality of a general deterioration of the secular environment. However, many Muslims adopt Imtiaz Ahmad's line of thinking in recognising the difficulty inherent in reconciling hidden intentions that could be at best inferred, and apparent pretexts, which could be ascertained.[18] Therefore, to them, any assessment of the Indian Muslim situation in terms of widely prevalent negative attitudes and perceptions arising out of the deterioration in the secular environment can only make Indian Muslims relapse into empty political rhetoric and is unlikely to be productive of positive results, except when the complaint is collective and large-scale mobilisation against the action can be achieved (Ahmad, 1989, pp. 43–46).

To conclude, regardless of all the criticism evolving around the subject, it remains a considerable fact that Indian Muslims in their official and religious discourses have managed to accommodate and integrate the idea of secularism as an everyday reality. This is a measure that Muslim communities around the globe are still struggling with, be it the majority in Turkey and the Arab world or the minorities in Europe. Shaz, who regarded the Muslim question in India not as a minority issue as much as an interesting dynamic of Islamicness and an understanding of the religious and ideological dimensions of the community, contends:

> Never before in 1400 years long Islamic history, or for that matter, during 1000 years of their positive history in the subcontinent, have Muslims had to readjust themselves with an alien system which openly de-recognised Islam as the guiding principle and yet they, as loyal citizens of free India, were expected to honour the new national creed, the secular democracy.
>
> (Shaz, 2001, p. 9)

Summary

This chapter has demonstrated the life-space in which the majority of Indian Muslims (with an emphasis on North India) practise their citizenship rights and obligations. The hegemonic discourses presented here emerged after a literature review of studies pertaining to contemporary issues of Indian Muslims. These discourses, hence, were divided into three main sections: political, ideological and socio-economic. After conducting one year of fieldwork in India, I tried to compare these discourses with the specific ones emanating from Indian Muslims themselves. This resulted in adding the discourse on secularism.

Despite the democratic nature of the Indian political system, several impediments to the realisation of a sense of equal citizenship emerge. After the appalling events of Babri Masjid, Ayodha and Gujarat, to name but a few, the circle of communal tension, coupled with government inaction as a response, and thus a deep feeling of injustice that prevails among Muslims were reinforced. The consequences of the enactment of the now-repealed Prevention of Terrorist Activities Act in 2002, as well as the enduring problems of delays in giving compensation, the attitude of police and the ghettoisation and shrinking of common spaces are principal facets of these problems. It is widely argued that alienation is the condition that best describes the political sentiments from which the majority of the Muslim minority suffers. This produces citizenship of subjugation that perpetuates cycles of oppression. Hence, concern was towards tackling the issue of inclusive citizenship, and how it links to the situation of Muslims in India as a major minority group facing dilemmas, deprivations and predicaments in the social, economic and political spheres.

Having reviewed these main dilemmas and how they are perceived by Indian Muslims, I turn in the next chapters to look at two case studies: North Indian Muslim youth in Delhi and Muslim female youth in Kerala. The objective of these case studies is to offer a deeper insight into the mechanisms of resistance these youth employ to face the above-mentioned hegemonic discourses. They also highlight the actual concerns of youth, apart from the elite-dominated agenda of political concerns and intentions.

Notes

1 On the concept of life-space, see Hasan (2006).
2 In 2010, Darul Uloom Deoband, the biggest Muslim seminary in India, issued a *fatwa* (edict) condemning women's work. This has received wide coverage by the English media and led to a sense of frustration among Muslims since the media usually neglect many of their more pertinent issues, yet widely focus on a non-essential personal *fatwa*. For details of the *fatwa*, see: http://articles.timesofindia.indiatimes. com/2010-05-12/india/28280924_1_fatwa-muslim-women-darul-uloom-deoband.
3 Ibn Khaldun, in his fourteenth-century *Al-Muqaddimah* (*The Introduction*), wrote that the "[t]he vanquished always wants to imitate the victor in his distinctive mark(s), his dress, his occupation, and all his other conditions and customs". See Khaldun (1427/1981).
4 In an interview, a young married Muslim woman in Kerala complained to me that her name was removed from the electoral rolls after her marriage, although she had not changed her address officially, and she was thus banned from voting both in her family's area and in her husband's. Accordingly, she filed a case to regain her right to have her name listed.
5 It has become extremely hard for Muslims to find accommodation in most urban areas, especially in Gujarat. The example of Juhapura in Ahmedabad is striking as it is considered the biggest Muslim ghetto in Gujarat. It has a population of 2.5 lakh residents, but it suffers from a lack of services such as banks, public transportation, maintained roads, water and garbage pickup. However, the police force is present, but to allegedly control terrorists (Bandukwala, 2006).
6 An example is the banning of Jaswant Singh's book *Jinnah: India, Partition, Independence* in Gujarat due to his remarks on the role of Sardar Patel in the partition of India.
7 Shaheena K. K. is a Keralite Muslim female journalist, who upon investigations in the Madani case (to be explained in the chapter on Kerala), and after interviewing him, was pursued by the Karnataka state police suspected of affiliation to terrorist networks and alleged attempts to threaten witnesses in the Madani case. For more information, see: Ashraf and Rowena (2010), *The Hindu* (2010).
8 Teesta Setalvad argues that extrajudicial killings are being used as tactics by the authorities. The recent cases of Ishrat Jahan and Sohrabuddin as victims of these extrajudicial killings were widely circulated in the Urdu press.
9 *Vande Mataram* is originally a poem written in Bengali and Sanskrit by Bankim Chandra Chattopadhyay in 1882. The first two verses became India's national song and stirred significant agitation among certain Muslim groups who banned its singing due to the veneration of India as a mother, and thus due to the aspect of idolatry.

10 *Qutub Minar* refers to a historical minaret in Delhi and the area surrounding it.
11 Major organisations making up the Hindutva network are the RSS, the BJP, the VHP (Vishva Hindu Parishad), the Bajrang Dal and the Shiv Sena.
12 The *Saraswati Vandana Mantra* is another important Hindu *mantra* linked to the Hindu Goddess of knowledge and wisdom, Saraswati.
13 This is according to the Arabic Dictionaries; an example of it is *al-mu'jam al-waseet*, retrieved on 12 October 2011 from http://kamoos.reefnet.gov.sy/?page=entry&id =286287.
14 In addition to the partition background, there are other historical studies aiming at falsifying theories on Muslim educational backwardness based on ideas of a 'hurt pride' and religious obscurantism by attributing backwardness to discriminatory policies practised by the colonial powers (see, for example, Siddiqui, 1989).
15 As a result, the Muslims in Kerala are entitled to reservations in education and employment to the extent of 50% of their share of the population (Shahabuddin & Wright, 1987, p. 164). This is provided by the right to equality Article 16(4) of the fundamental rights of the Constitution dealing with "the equality of opportunity in matters of public employment" and stating:

> Nothing in this article shall prevent the State from making any provision for the reservation of appointments or posts in favour of any backward class of citizens which, in the opinion of the State, is not adequately represented in the services under the State.

16 Interviews with Zoya Hasan (Professor of Political Science at Jawaharlal Nehru University) and Mustafa Sherwani (a lawyer and head of a regional political party in Lucknow, UP).
17 Madhu Kishwar's talk entitled *The Religious Divide in the Indian Society*, at the conference "Cultural and Religious Pluralism: The Muslim Minority in the Indian Democracy, East–West Comparison", New Delhi, 18–20 October, 2010, at the India Habitat Centre and Jamia Millia Islamia.
18 On a side note, Imtiaz Ahmad, at the conference "Cultural and Religious Pluralism: The Muslim Minority in the Indian Democracy, East–West Comparison" (New Delhi, 18–20 October 2010, India Habitat Centre and Jamia Millia Islamia), in commenting on the High Court ruling in the Babri Masjid dispute, said that the High Court gave a panchayat kind of judgment in the sense of attempting not to hurt anyone.

References

Abdul Rauf, T. (2011). Violence Inflicted on Muslims: Direct, Cultural and Structural. *Economic and Political Weekly*, 46(23), 69–76.
Ahmad, I. (1989). The Problems of Indian Muslims: Methodology for Analysis. In I. Ansari (ed.), *The Muslim Situation in India* (pp. 40–47). New Delhi: Sterling.
Alam, J. (1999). *India: Living with Modernity.* Delhi: Oxford University Press.
Alam, J. (2001). Is Caste Appeal Casteism? Oppressed Castes in Politics. In S. Jodhka (ed.), *Community and Identities: Contemporary Discourses on Culture and Politics in India* (pp. 97–110). Delhi: Sage.
Alam, J. (2004). *Who Wants Democracy.* New Delhi: Orient Longman.
Alam, M. S. (2009). Whither Muslim Politics? *Economic and Political Weekly*, 44(39), 92–95.
Ali, M. (2012, 26 January). *War on Terror: If You Can't Find the Terrorist, Make One.* Retrieved on 27 January 2012, from Two Circles: http://twocircles.net/2012jan26/war_ terror_if_you_can't_find_terrorist_make_one.html.

Almond, G. A., & Verba, S. (1989). *The Civic Culture: Political Attitudes and Democracy in Five Nations.* London: Sage.

Amanullah, A. (2004). Islam as News in Indian Newspapers. *Islam and the Modern Age,* 35(4), 73–92.

Ansari, I. (1989). Muslim Educational Backwardness. In I. Ansari (ed.), *The Muslim Situation in India* (pp. 88–97). New Delhi: Sterling Publisher.

Ansari, I. (2006a). Police Partisanship During Communal Riots: Needs for its Secularization and Pluralization. In A. A. Engineer & A. Narang (eds), *Minorities and Police in India* (pp. 163–175). New Delhi: Manohar.

Ansari, I. (2006b). *Political Representation of Muslims in India 1952–2004.* Delhi: Manak.

Ansari, N. (1999). *Choosing to Stay: Memoirs of an Indian Muslim.* (R. Russel, Trans.). Karachi: City Press.

An-Na'im, A. (2008). *Islam and the Secular State.* Cambridge, MA and London: Harvard University Press.

Asad, T. (2003). *Formations of the Secular: Christianity, Islam, Modernity.* Stanford, CA: Stanford University Press.

Asif, A. U. (1998). Image of Muslims. In A. Asif (ed.), *Media and Muslims in India Since Independence* (pp. 23–33). Delhi: Institute of Objective Studies.

Ashraf, K. and Rowena, J. (2010, 30 November). When Two Muslims Meet: The Media(ted) Case Of Madani And Shahina. Retrieved on 30 July 2012, from www.countercurrents.org/ashraf301110.htm.

Babu, T. (2010, 1–15 May). One Third of Indian Muslims Below Poverty Line: Survey. *The Milli Gazette,* 6.

Bandukwala, J. (2006, 8 April). Indian Muslims: Past, Present and Future. *Economic and Political Weekly,* 41(14), 1341–1344.

Bharatiya Janata Party. (2012). Integral Humanism. Retrieved on 3 January 2012, from www.bjp.org/index.php?option=com_content&view=article&id=134&Itemid=442.

Bourdieu, P. (ed.) (1993). *The Weight of the World: Social Suffering in Contemporary Society* (P. P. Ferguson et al., Trans.). Stanford: Stanford University Press.

Census of India. (2001). Retrieved on 3 July 2012, from www.censusindia.gov.in/Census_Data_2001/Census_data_finder/C_Series/Population_by_religious_communities.htm.

Chakrabarty, D. (1995). Modernity and Ethnicity in India: A History for the Present, *Economic and Political Weekly,* 30, 3373–3380.

Chatterjee, P. (1998). Secularism and Tolerance. In R. Bhargava (ed.), *Secularism and its Critics* (pp. 345–379). New Delhi: Oxford University Press.

Chowdary, T. (2007). A Country with Minorities: Overwhelming Un-Unifiable Majority. In R. Dixit (ed.), *Secularism as Minorityism: Highway to National Harakiri* (pp. 133–147). New Delhi: India First Foundation.

Daechsel, M. (2006). *The Politics of Self-Expression: the Urdu Middle-Class Milieu in Mid-Twentieth-Century India and Pakistan.* London: Routledge.

Das, R. (2004). Encountering (Cultural) Nationalism, Islam and Gender in the Body Politics of India. *Social Identities,* 10(3), 369–398.

Dirks, N. (1997). The Study of State and Society in India. In S. Kaviraj (ed.), *Politics in India* (pp. 159–168). New Delhi: Oxford University Press.

Engineer, A. A. (1985). *Indian Muslims: A Study of the Minority Problem in India.* Delhi: Ajanta.

Engineer, A. A. (1998). Fundamentalism, Traditionalism and Communalism: Challenges to the Indian Polity. In Z. Banu (ed.), *Decline and Fall of Indian Politics* (pp. 138–152). New Delhi: Kanishka.

Engineer, I. (1995). Politics of Muslim Vote Bank. *Economic and Political Weekly*, 30(4), 197–200.

Farouqui, A. (2009). Urdu Press in India. In A. Farouqui (ed.), *Muslims and Media Images: News Versus* Views (pp. 237–252). Delhi: Oxford University Press.

Foucault, M. (2009). *Archaeology of Knowledge* (A. S. Smith, Trans.). London & New York: Routledge Classics (original work published 1969).

Goyal, S. (1990). *Social Background of Indian Administrative Service*. New Delhi: ISID.

Gupta, D. (2005). *Learning to Forget: The Anti-Memoirs of Modernity*. Delhi: Oxford University Press.

Hasan, M. (1980). Communalisation in the Provinces: A Case Study of Bengal and Punjab, 1922–26, *Economic & Political Weekly*, 15(33), 1395–1406.

Hasan, M. (1997). *Legacy of a Divided Nation: Indian's Muslims since Independence*. Delhi: Oxford University Press.

Hasan, M. (2008). *Moderate or Militant: Images of India's Muslims*. New Delhi: Oxford University Press.

Hasan, Q. (1987). *Muslims in India: Attitudes, Adjustments and Reactions*. New Delhi: Northern Book Centre.

Hasan, Q. (2006). Life-Space of Indian Muslims. In N. Hasnain (ed.), *Islam and Muslim Communities in South Asia* (pp. 254–280). New Delhi: Serials Publications.

Hashmi, S. (2012, 30 January). *You Can't Show Light to Those Who Have Chosen Darkness: The Case of Imam Bukhari*. Retrieved on 30 January 2012, from Kafila, http://kafila.org/2012/01/30/you-cant-show-light-to-those-who-have-chosen-darkness-the-case-of-imam-bukhari/.

Indian Muslim Blog. (2012, 13 January). *Saffronisation in Madhya Pradesh: Isn't it BJP's Appeasement of the Majority Community?* Retrieved on 14 January 2012, from An Indian Muslim's Blog, www.anindianmuslim.com/2012/01/saffronisation-in-madhya-pradesh-isnt.html.

Indian Readership Survey. (2012). Retrieved on 1 July 2015, from http://mruc.net/sites/default/files/IRS%202012%20Q4%20Topline%20Findings.pdf.

Jaffrelot, C. (1996). *The Hindu Nationalist Movement in India 1925 to the 1990s*. New Delhi: Viking Penguin India.

Jaffrelot, C. (2007). The 2002 Pogrom in Gujarat: The Post-9/11 Face of Hindu Nationalist Anti-Muslim Violence. In J. R. Hinnells and R. King (eds), *Religion and Violence in South Asia: Theory and Practice* (pp. 164–182). New York: Routledge.

Jaffrelot, C. (2010). Abhinav Bharat, the Malegaon Blast and Hindu Nationalism: Resisting and Emulating Islamist Terrorism. *Economic and Political Weekly*, 45(36), 51–58.

Kaviraj, S. (1992). The Imaginary Institution of India. In P. Chatterjee and G. Pandey (eds), *Subaltern Studies VII* (pp. 1–39). Delhi: Oxford University Press.

Khaldun, I. (1981). *The Muqadimmah, an Introduction to History* (F. Rosenthal, Trans.). Princeton: Princeton University Press (original work written in 1427). Retrieved on 1 July 2015, from www.muslimphilosophy.com/ik/Muqaddimah/Chapter2/Ch_2_22.htm.

Khaliq, A. (2011, 26 November). *Douse Communal Fires*. Retrieved on 11 January 2012, from Tehelka, www.tehelka.com/story_main51.asp?filename=Op261011How.asp.

Khan, A. (2006). Police Prejudice against the Muslims. In A. A. Engineer & A. S. Narang (eds), *Minorities and Police in India* (pp. 143–162). New Delhi: Manohar.

Khan, W. (2009). Muslims and the Press. In A. Farouqui (ed.), *Muslims and Media Images: News Versus Views* (pp. 253–261). Delhi: Oxford University Press.

Kothari, R. (2000). The Decline of the Moderate State. In Z. Hassan (ed.), *Politics and the State in India* (pp. 177–205). New Delhi: Sage.

Kutty, F. (1997). Indian Muslims: Rebuilding a Community. *Journal of Muslim Minority Affairs*, 17(1), 167–177.

Lewin, K. (1951). Field Theory in Social Sciences. In D. Cartwright (ed.) *Selected Theoretical Papers*. New York: Harper & Row.

Madanipour, A. (1998). Social Exclusion and Space. In A. Madanipour, J. Allen & G. Cars (eds), *Social Exclusion in European Cities: Social Experiences, Processes and Responses* (pp. 158–165). London: Routledge.

Mahajan, G. (2005). Indian Exceptionalism or Indian Model: Negotiating Cultural Diversity and Minority Rights in a Democratic Nation-State. In B. He & W. Kymlicka (eds), *Multiculturalism in Asia* (pp. 288–313). Oxford: Oxford University Press.

Mander, H. (2004). *Cry, My Beloved Country: Reflections on the Gujarat Carnage*. Delhi: Rainbow Publishers.

Mayer, P. B. (1981). Tombs and Dark Houses: Ideology, Intellectuals, and Proletarians in the Study of Contemporary Indian Islam. *Journal of Asian Studies*, 25(3), 484–497.

Mehta, P. B. (2004). Secularism and the Identity Trap. In M. Hasan (ed.), *Will Secular India Survive?* (pp. 72–92). Gurgaon: Imprint One.

Mehta, P. B. (2006). Urdu: Between Rights and the Nation. In A. Farouqui (ed.), *Redefining Urdu Politics in India* (pp. 13–31). New Delhi: Oxford University Press.

Mitchell, T. (1990). Everyday Metaphors of Power. *Theory and Society*, 19(5), 545–577.

Mitra, C. (2009). The Print Media and Minority Images. In A. Farouqui (ed.), *Muslims and Media Images: News Versus Views* (pp. 91–99). Delhi: Oxford University Press.

Mitra, S. K. (2003). The Morality of Communal Politics: Paul Brass, Hindu–Muslim Conflict, and the Indian State. *India Review*, 2(4), 15–30.

Mitra, S., & Singh, V. (1999). *Democracy and Social Change: A Cross-sectional Analysis of the National Electorate*. New Delhi: Sage.

Nandy, A. (1975). The Acceptance and Rejection of Democratic Norms in India. *Indian Journal of Psychology*, 50(4), 265–278.

Oommen, T.K. (1995). *Alien Concepts and South Asian Reality: Responses and Reformations*. New Delhi: Sage.

Pandey, G. (1989). The Colonial Construction of Communalism: British Writings on Banaras in the 19th Century. In R. Guha (ed.), *Subaltern Studies VI: Writings on South Asian History and Society* (pp. 132–68). New Delhi: Oxford University Press.

Pandey, G. (2004). *Remembering Partition: Violence, Nationalism and History in India*. Cambridge: Cambridge University Press.

Peer, B. (2011, 22 September). *What Lies Beneath*. Retrieved on 15 February 2012, from Foreign Policy, http://foreignpolicy.com/2011/09/22/what-lies-beneath-2/.

Qasmi, M. K. (2005). *Madrasa Education: Its Strength and Weakness*. Mumbai: MMERC and Manak.

Rab, S. F. (1998). Muslim Polity in India During the Post-Independence Period. In M. Siddiqui, *Muslims in Free India: Their Social Profile and Problems* (pp. 33–66). New Delhi: Institute of Objective Studies.

Registrar of Newspapers for India. (2012). Retrieved from http://rni.nic.in/.

Rahman, T. (2012). *From Hindi to Urdu: A Social and Political History*. Karachi: Oxford University Press.

Rizvi, S. A. (1998). A Classic Example of Disinformation. In A. Asif (ed.), *Media and Muslims in India since Independence* (pp. 41–45). New Delhi: Institute of Objective Studies.

Roy, A. (2002). Community, Women Citizens and a Women's Politics. In S. S. Jodhka (ed.), *Community and Identities: Contemporary Discourses on Culture and Politics in India* (pp. 239–259). New Delhi: Sage.

Rowena, J. (2011, July 26). *Maudani and His Politics*. Retrieved on 1 July 2015, from Fabricated.in: National Campaign Against Fabrication of False cases, http://archive-in. com/page/1819916/2013-04-06/http://fabricated.in/node/139?replytocom=310.

Rumi, R. (2012, 8 February). *Rethinking Urdu Nationalism in Pakistan*. Retrieved on 9 February 2012, from Kafila, http://kafila.org/2012/02/08/rethinking-urdu-nationalism-in-pakistan-raza-rumi/.

Sachar Committee Report. (2006). *Social, Economic and Educational Status of the Muslim Community of India*. Prime Minister's High Level Committee Cabinet Secretariat, Government of India.

Sarkar, T. (2002). Semiotics of Terror: Muslim Children and Women in Hindu Rashtra. *Economic & Political Weekly*, 37(28), 2872–2876.

SDSA. (2008). *State of Democracy in South Asia*. New Delhi: Oxford University Press.

Scott, J. C. (1990). *Domination and the Arts of Resistance*. New Haven and London: Yale University Press.

Setalvad, T. (2010, 10 September). Speech at the Jamia Teachers Solidarity Association's National Convention on The Politics of Terrorism and Suspicion: Two Years after the Batla House Encounter. New Delhi: Jamia Millia Islamia.

Shah, G. (2007). The Condition of Muslims. *Economic and Political Weekly*, 42(10), 836–839.

Shahabuddin, S. and Wright, T. P. Jr (1987). India: Muslim Minority Politics and Society. In J. Esposito (ed.), *Islam in Asia: Religion, Politics and Society* (pp. 152–176). Oxford: Oxford University Press.

Shahid, M. (2006). Muslim Women's Empowerment through Education with Special Reference to Girls' Madrasas in India. *Islam and the Modern Age*, 37(3), 114–126.

Shaz, R. (2001). *Understanding the Muslim Malaise: A Conceptual Approach in the Indian Context*. New Delhi: Milli Publications.

Siddiqui, M. (1989). Muslim Education in Calcutta. In I. Ansari (ed.), *The Muslim Situation in India* (pp. 98–102). New Delhi: Sterling Publisher.

Sikand, Y. (2009, 12 March). *Madhyamam: A Muslim Media Success Story*. Retrieved on 10 January 2012, from Rediff News, http://news.rediff.com/column/2009/mar/12/guest-madhyamam-a-muslim-media-success-story.htm.

Sikand, Y. (2004a). *Islam, Caste and Dalit-Muslim Relations in India*. New Delhi: Global Media Publications.

Sikand, Y. (2004b). *Muslims in India since 1947: Islamic Perspectives on Interfaith Relations*. London: RoutledgeCurzon.

Sikand, Y. (2006). *Muslims in India: Contemporary Social and Political Discourses*. Gurgaon: Hope India.

Singh, K. (2005). India and Islam: The Consolidation of a Composite Culture and the Challenge of Contemporary Politics. *Islam and the Modern Age*, 36(1), 15–28.

South Asian Human Rights Documentation Centre. (2003). Retrieved on 24 April 2012, from www.hrdc.net/sahrdc/hrfeatures/HRF71.htm.

Subramanian, K. S. (2006). Police and the Minorities: A Study of the Role of the Police during Communal Violence in India. In A. A. Engineer & A. S. Narang (eds), *Minorities and Police in India* (pp. 121–139). New Delhi: Manohar.

Subrahmaniam, V. (2011, 5 August). *Investigating the Investigations*. Retrieved on 10 December 2011, from The Hindu: www.thehindu.com/opinion/lead/investigating-the-investigation/article2328403.ece.

Tarlo, E. (2003). *Unsettling Memories: Narratives of the Emergency in Delhi*. London: C. Hurst.

The Hindu (2010, 6 December) Petition Seeks Withdrawal of Case Against Journalist, *The Hindu.*

Upadhya, C. (2001). The Concept of Community in Indian Social Sciences. In S. Jodhka (ed.), *Communities and Identities: Contemporary Discourses on Culture and Politics in India* (pp. 32–58). New Delhi: Sage.

Weiner, M. (1997). Minority Identities. In S. Kaviraj (ed.) *Politics in India* (pp. 241–254). Delhi: Oxford University Press.

Werbner, P. (1997). Essentialising Essentialism, Essentialising Silence: Ambivalence and Multiplicity in the Constructions of Racism and Ethnicity. In P. Werbner & T. Modood (eds) *Debating Cultural Hybridity: Multicultural Identities and the Politics of Anti-Racism* (pp. 226–254). London: Zed Books.

Wilkinson, S. (2002). Putting Gujarat in Perspective. *Economic and Political Weekly,* 37(17), 1579–1583.

Williams, P. (2011). Hindu-Muslim Relations and the 'War on Terror'. In I. Clark-Decès, *A Companion to the Anthropology of India* (pp. 241–259). Malden, MA: Wiley-Blackwell.

Worsley, P. (1984). *The Three Worlds: Culture and World Development.* Chicago: University of Chicago Press.

Vatuk, S. (2005). Muslim Women and Personal Law. In Z. Hasan & R. Menon (eds), *In a Minority: Essays on Muslim Women in India* (pp. 18–68). New Delhi: Oxford University Press.

Zavos, J. (2000). *The Emergence of Hindu Nationalism in India.* New Delhi: Oxford University Press.

4 North Indian Muslim youth and everyday *jihād*

tujhe abaa se apne koi nisbat ho nahin sakti ke tu guftar voh kardar, tu thaabet voh sayyara
You could not be a relation to your ancestors
Because they were active and constantly on the move
While you merely talked and remained stationary.

(Iqbal, 1908)

For forty-five minutes, I had been sitting in the car with two young, bearded Muslim men. In the beginning, they drove along Nadwa road and clearly Muslim-dominated areas, where signs of extreme poverty, several dilapidated tin houses and bathing buffalos were dominant features of the road. Then, we passed by many congested areas outlining the end of the urban scene with *Nawabi* architecture in a dismal state and Hindu- and Muslim-named shops. I wanted to ask whether these areas were mixed or Muslim dominated, but I remained silent for fear of annoying them and burdening them with the sins of hearing a female voice. I sensed it was enough that they felt they had already sinned by being with me in the car: me – a woman whose face showed. At one point, these urban signs started fading away, and we started crossing fields of nothingness, where houses ceased to exist. I could not help wondering what kinds of girls go to this faraway school and how they reach it. I felt this would indeed turn out to be a futile journey. I had little hope in my ability to make the girls I was heading to meet speak and open up their mind and heart to me. Since I had not received any reply to the *Salamu alaikum* greeting I gave to my male companions upon entering the car, my fears grew stronger.

Apart from a bunch of scattered huts and naked children running around, there was no sign of any human settlement or development. Finally, a lonely building appeared, and we stopped in front of a gate that stated the *madrasa*'s name in both English and Arabic scripts. I was guided to the office right next to the gate where two men sat, one around his early thirties and the other in his sixties. The one whose photo shows on the picture gallery on the institution's website said that he was responsible for managing the institution, and that the older man was his senior.

I introduced myself, then they asked me the following questions: where I learned my Urdu, if I had come alone, and whether I was married.

Then I was offered to go to the institution.

The student from Nadwa came along with me, knocked on a door and said that he had a guest; the girls behind did not appear, but just slightly opened the door and let me in alone. We did not exchange any conversation and thus I did not have a chance to ask how long he was going to wait for me outside.

With both their hands, girls who were hiding behind the door shook mine, saying *Salamu alaikum*. I was guided to the principal's office, and after meeting her, I was astonished to realise how men who were extremely conservative tended to be friendlier than this woman. She asked me again what I was doing, whether I came alone, and then asked how come I was walking with my face showing without being covered under a *pardah*. I explained that it was not oblig-atory in Egypt, which led to her disapproving comment of "what kind of Islam was that then?" She then asked her secretary to accompany me to the library.

We passed classes with open doors, where I saw very young girls, around age six or seven, sitting on the ground writing in notebooks and loudly reciting Arabic texts. They were all wearing a *salwar qameez* uniform and covering their head with a white scarf.

After introducing myself to the librarian, she called on many girls who were in fact young teachers. The minute I started introducing both my research and myself, strange exclamation expressions appeared on their faces. They became mute. The librarian did all the talking. When I asked about voting and whether they thought it made a difference, she instantly asked them all to leave. She started replying in a very mechanical way, stressing there was no difference in India between a woman and a man, both can vote and both have equal rights. I told her I knew that, but I was asking another question. Again she mentioned the same thing. At this point, I was sure she was ignoring me. Then she added that, in India, there was no difference between Hindus and Muslims when it came to elections and political rights; it was only about personal law matters. In her own words:

> Voting is our right. We people have the right to choose who will work better for us. There is discrimination though and Muslims feel injustice after Babri Masjid, which rendered them without dignity, shocked and in sorrow. However, there is no risk on Muslims living in India because Allah protects us and we try to build our future ourselves through what Allah has destined for us (*allah ka kismet milta hei*).

I asked her how she answered those who said that education was bad for women. She said:

> It is an obligation on us to learn. Or else there would be no difference between an animal and a human being. It is important to have institutions like this so that the poor can learn. It is also important to learn the Quran.

I asked about the founding of this institution. She said it was by Maulana Rizwan and his wife and was inaugurated by Maulana Abul Hasan Nadwi. It hosted 800 students, from all parts of India, not just UP. They graduate, teach the younger generations and then leave to get married. At the end, she had to leave to catch the school bus to go home. She gave me her number and told me to call her to chat with her about any other questions I had.

Then she wore her *burka*, told me her *salams*, and left. I walked towards the door where I had come from and there the young secretary took me and asked me if she could show me around.

I was taken to a courtyard and walked until we reached the bedroom of two girls: the principal's secretary (I will refer to her as Siddiqa) and her room mate, who was a teacher. Both were nineteen. Plates of food arrived. Sliced fresh fruit, savoury Indian snacks, chocolate cookies and water were offered to me. The girl said there was a power cut and asked, "Do you also have power cuts in Delhi or is the electricity running without problems?" Then she asked one of the students who kept peeping in from the door, asking for permission to come in to greet me, to bring a hand fan. She came into the room and started fanning for us. When I showed unrest with this, Siddiqa took it and did it herself, as if to show me that she is not enslaving her students. Two eighteen-year-old teachers came in: a silent one, and an eloquent girl with the name Mariam Batoul (the Arabic term for the Virgin Mary). As I steered the conversation away from food, we turned to politics. They said they had not voted yet because they were young but they would definitely vote in the coming elections. When I asked them how they decided whom to vote for, they said it depended on what they heard about this person, his family and his background. They were surprised when I asked them if they were going to vote. One of the girls said, "Of course, we live in a country where our chief minister and our president are both women." Although she could not remember the name of the president of India, she emphasised the fact that it was a woman. They stated that voting was their right in India. I asked if they could think of any other rights of being citizens. They could not. They also did not grasp the concept of citizenship. They asked what kind of political system we had in Egypt; they had always thought it was a democracy. When I negated that, they asked if it was like Saudi Arabia; again I said no and then I tried explaining it to them and they were shocked. They were in favour of democracy despite its malfunctioning in India. A great sign of this democratic fault, in their opinion, was the countless encounters of the Batla House type. They spoke strongly, asserting the injustice in these encounters.

On education, they said it was not true that Muslim women were not educated; it depended on whether they wanted to be educated or not: "We wanted to and we told our parents and here we are. It is always a matter of heart, whether one's heart goes towards education or not." One of the girls was waiting for God to send her a suitor so she could get married and leave. The other said she just got accepted to a university in Hyderabad and she could not apply in Lucknow because it is mixed education with boys, while in Hyderabad it is not. One girl explained that she wanted to pursue her education and get a BA in Urdu, Arabic or Islamic studies. They asked me whether I was married or not. Then the *burka* discussion came up. They asked what kind of clothes I wore in Germany and Egypt and if I wore this *salwar qameez* style as I was wearing then. They said some girls in India wore jeans and tops, but they would never wear that. They said they also never show their face in public and this was a matter of tradition and had nothing to do with Islam. According to them, the Quran did not say a woman has to cover her face, and this was why they could understand my position and how I walked with my face uncovered, but to them it was simply a matter of custom and being accustomed to that. Siddiqa kept insisting that I should eat and she offered the two other girls but they refused. Mariam remarked, "It is not time for food." It was obvious how they were disciplined. Even a snack for them seemed out of order, for it was not the proper time. Their reply to the offer was not that they were full, but that it was not the proper time to eat. We went out and they accompanied me all the way to the gate. They hid there so no one would be able to see them and I bid them farewell and good luck in their lives.

The senior man who had welcomed me upon my arrival was waiting for me outside the gate. He asked me if I enjoyed talking to the girls and how I found the institution. He also asked if I had understood them since we were communicating only in Urdu. Another driver was waiting for me – again no word. At that point, I decided to start covering my face with my shawl. This way, the man sitting in the car could feel a bit more liberal in talking to me. He asked me about my thesis topic and where I studied, speaking in Arabic. He talked with a smile. I kept wondering if it was the *burka* making that difference or was it just the different attitude of another human being.

What made these girls different – in my opinion – was that they not only knew what they wanted, but they also had a clear idea of what they did not want. In comparison to the developed world, where individuals have access to almost everything, from excellent health services, to good education, to career opportunities, all in the context of great mobility, these girls in almost prison-like settings managed to acquire a different perspective and a scope for dreaming.

There are many interwoven narratives which we can note from the conversations I had with these girls and their teachers. The most basic one, which I would like to draw attention to, is the emphasis on education and its link to modernisation that directly relates to citizenship and the emergence of the middle class. The issue of Islam, as both a religion and a paradigm of thought and action, plays an additional analytical category (especially due to the fact that almost no religion has an emphasis on education like Islam).[1] There are different actors contributing to the discourse on accommodating religious identity within the secular democratic field: the upper-caste Islamic scholars or the class of the *'ulama*, the urban and rural poor and the youth with their multifarious educational, regional and economic backgrounds.

This chapter concerns the first case study of this book, namely Muslim youth in Delhi, in addition to fieldwork-based reference to Muslim youth in *madrasas* in Uttar Pradesh and Haryana. The focus is directed to educated Muslim youth (both male and female) who belong to the Indian middle class. The attempt is not to generate a representative study of all Indian Muslim youth in general, since, as I noted in the previous chapter, the divisions along regions and classes are utterly overwhelming and preventive of any representative study. It could be thus inferred that the possibility of finding a special class or region which could represent the Indian Muslim is very faint, if not absent. The absence of a pan-Indian Muslim identity, the dearth of leadership, except to an extent in specific regional and local politics, and the lack of homogeneity in the level of education, following Islamic rules, or adherence to the '*ulama* are all reasons for this representation's impossibility.

As I investigated the problem of being a citizen minority or what difference being a Muslim makes in the political Indian field, I realised how the educated middle-class Muslim youth strives to be an active citizen, in a process not divorced at all from the historical idea of composite nationalism. Since frustration and a drive of insecurity overwhelm these youth, their struggle towards the creation of spaces for agency and hence social change should be highlighted. This chapter starts by focusing on significant centres of learning, where the formation of middle-class citizens takes place; this is mainly in minority institutions such as Jamia and *madrasas*.[2] The emphasis on these institutions is central since the present concentration of Muslim students there poses difficulties in the attempt of the construction of a citizen imaginary in India due to the predicaments faced with the police forces and media, fake encounters and the propaganda on *madrasas* as potential centres for terrorism. The next step is demonstrating these Muslim youth's measurable sense of collective action and their stance to political and social indicators, such as their feelings of alienation and discrimination, the terrorism discourse and the increasingly developing gender issues.

The interlinkage between the middle class, citizenship and education

"Would you like to visit the school where I work?" This is a question I have been asked innumerable times whenever I have met teachers in India. For both teachers and students, education was viewed as a duty on account of being Muslims. In a Jamaati Islami primary school in Delhi, on a noticeboard, three goals of education were outlined: self-reform, society's development and the nation and country's welfare. Education, as it will appear in the following pages, is a tool of both reform and resistance in the quest for inclusive citizenship.

The choice to consider the middle class in Delhi stems from several factors. The first is the conviction that the middle class carries a strong belief in education as a social mobility factor and thus realisation of the ideas of citizenship. With speculations on the increasingly differentiated Indian middle class's size swelling by half of its population in the next generation (Rothermund, 2008; Das, 2002),[3] emphasis is duly placed on the role this class plays and the ideals it holds (See: Ahmad & Reifeld, 2001; Bhatia, 1994; Fernandes, 2006; Jaffrelot,

2008; Pandey, 2010; Varma, 2007). Second, most studies have focused on the Hindu middle class and its role in the emergence of Hindu nationalism (Jaffrelot, 2008; Fernandes, 2006), perhaps in a manner reminiscent of the role the middle class played in the rise of fascism in Europe (Fromm, 1941). Very little, however, has been written on the Muslim middle class (Daechsel, 2006; Gill, 2008).

In their edited volume on the middle class in Europe and India, Ahmad and Reifeld (2001) point out the origin of the middle class as a social category and how it differed in India than in Europe where the age of Enlightenment, the Industrial Revolution and the large-scale mechanical production heralded a new social order, distinct from feudalism and bounded on free relations. The middle class, thus, constituted a composite intermediate layer consisting of a wide range of occupational interests but bounded together by a common style of living and behavioural patterns. It stood for certain liberal, democratic values, which it expressed in its social and political conduct, but did not always pursue with the fullest possible commitment.

The situation dramatically differed in India, where the middle class was a by-product of the colonial educational policies (Misra, 1961; Béteille, 2001; Gill, 2008). On the Muslim front, despite the historical emphasis on the class gap between the feudal Ashrafs and the Ajlafs, Mujeeb writes of a different account; of the bourgeoisie Muslim class that existed in medieval India and was com-posed mainly of merchants and financial middle men providing the artisans (Mujeeb, 1967, p. 374). As for independent India, it could be argued that, beside the occupational and the economic background, education and culture came to define the new middle class (Béteille, 2001).

The middle class as a repository of ideals for modernistic nations assumed the momentum of the partition of India and the rise of an idea of nationalism. After the advancement of the professional classes, especially under the system of sepa-rate electorates, a Muslim middle class and leadership arose (Gill, 2008). This was followed by a paradoxical elaboration of a cultural and liberal elite at Aligarh Muslim University who adopted the cause for Pakistan (Bhatia, 1994).

The Indian case is a unique one, where the modern educated elite – mani-fested in the Aligarh movement – chose the nationalistic path based on Islam, and largely ignored the religious scholars, mainly from Deoband and Jamiat-Ulama e Hind, who zealously tried to convince the Muslim masses that there was no such thing as religion-based nationalism, and that the idea of the nation was based on the homeland and not on religion.

How was it possible that the modern idea of citizenship developed in such a unique way among the pro-Pakistan movement? How was the importation of this western concept, which was based on a secular foundation, so deviant in its Indian application? Again we are faced with a case where political processes, when combined with education, do not produce the logical formula. Actually, education in itself does not necessarily politicise individuals. Education is a domain where processes of citizenship are manufactured and produced. The reproduction of citizenship of the educated, as Hansen (2000) argues, is different from what happens at public rallies in slums and villages, where the uneducated masses are addressed through religious legends within a framework enhancing the networks of trust in their community leaders. According to the liberal and republican paradigms (e.g. Arendt 1951), these masses lack the civic virtue of the educated ones and thus could be easily turned, when religiously manipulated, into violent crowds. From another perspective, Kymlicka and Norman (1994) demonstrate the controversial aspect of treating citizenship through education by considering the role played by groups who rely heavily on unquestionable tradition and authority.

A significant by-product of education, which was treated as a variable in this study, is the production of a middle class holding the values of citizenship. In defining and measuring the middle class, characteristics such as different attitudes to women, education, media, usage of information technology and consumption are usually noted. Via these factors, the middle class contributes to two major challenges to the achievement of a citizen society: namely, the reinforcement of exclusion and the establishment of a hegemonic consumer society. The values reflected by the Indian new middle classes often reinforce and recreate caste, religion and gender-based exclusions (Fernandes, 2006). Here, an apparent difference between Hindu and Muslim middle classes' orientations appear; since Muslims are concerned with issues such as Dalit and OBCs' causes, co-housing, co-education and hence overcoming ghettoisation. By this sharing, a conceptualisation of the new common man based on a consumer-citizen model has been developed. Fernandes (2006) argues that this new common man is "victimized both by a corrupt and ineffective political system" and by "the supposedly privileged and protected poor and working classes" (Fernandes, 2006, p. 187). Middle-class Muslims echoed this sentiment in several conversations. For example, in an interview with a middle-class family who were spending some spare time sitting at Jama Masjid, after attending a wedding in Chandni Chowk, the mother told me:

> Although there is one law for the poor and the rich, the poor get everything in this life for free: free education, free books, everything. But the middle class has the highest number of problems and worries and it is a big class, around 50%. On every level, there are problems: occupation, housing and education. But the most important problem is education. Not all the middle class can afford education, and to get admission in a private English-medium school, you must give a large amount of money as a 'donation', otherwise you cannot get admission. Add to this the problem of discrimination. The chances of finding jobs are very thin if you pursue English or medical studies, because of the competition with Hindus. But Arabic or Urdu guarantees them a job quickly after graduation.

Although it should be argued that these were not peculiar 'Muslim' issues, but a general Indian middle-class concern, one additional aspect is discrimination, of which Muslims and Dalits complain. Eventually, corruption has no religion; a rich

Muslim, when bribing an official, can easily strike off a Hindu competitor. The change in the mentality of middle-class Muslims to adopt this conviction of the equality of discrimination has been a contrasting feature in many conversations I have had with Muslims. One of the important reasons for this is Gulf employment – a process facilitating social change through remittances and a belief in the value of education. Another factor is the overburden of political discourses in which Muslims engage in the North. A student from Hyderabad contends that the situation is much better than the North. According to her, in the South, people are more educated and more aware, hence they do not fall victim to the traps of being politicised or, in her own words, are not overburdened by 'political problems' and thus most Muslims in Hyderabad have the chance to go to school.

The phenomenon of Gulf migration has also contributed to the establishment of a consumer society. This means that there is a relationship of 'perpetual unfinishedness' between consumption, politics, middle-class socio-cultural identities and their frustrated ambitions (Baudrillard, 1998; Daechsel, 2006). Somehow the phenomenon of lavish weddings and over-consumption of food, especially *biryani*, in many events celebrated by the Muslims is a clear translation of this argument. Food itself has an exaggerated value in developing societies as a compensatory mechanism for deprivation in other fields and hence as one of the markers of backwardness. In the coming section, I will briefly introduce two educational backgrounds pertaining to North Indian Muslim youth in which dynamics of identity, secularism and citizenship emerge.

Madrasa education and Nadwatul Ulama Lucknow as a case study

> My education in *madrasas* and universities empowered me to go beyond stereotypes. Yes, *'ulama* have a legacy but they fail to interpret it for the younger generation, to make it more palatable and puritanical, and to interact with their people in their projections. But the importance lies in socialising with non-Muslims as a consequence of *da'wah*. When I first came to Jamia, I was exposed to Foucault, Marx and Bourdieu, that is what professors know, but they do not know about the Vedic, traditional, oriental and Islamic education. As a self, I am transcending this border of East and West.
>
> (A Delhi-based Muslim environmental activist, September 2010)

> I went to Rampur, which was so far from Hyderabad because it is so famous. It is exactly like people wanting to go to Oxford or Cambridge. Would not they go all the way from Nigeria or India? It is the same idea with these famous *madrasas*. However, the problem with *madrasas* is that they give excellent education and specialisation in Islamic studies and Urdu and Arabic, but they lack secular subjects since they do not teach any modern sciences and thus students have no chances when pursuing their further education, especially in specific universities and specific subjects.
>
> (A Hyderabadi female PhD student, Delhi, November 2010)

The discourse on *madrasa* education is enmeshed within two general discourses: one relating to backwardness and the other created by media hype over terrorism. Through this discovery of Muslim backwardness (Seth, 2001), modern education became a site for the production of Foucauldian governmentality. *Madrasa* graduates typically find themselves engulfed with a social image as being backward and less modern than their counterparts who were educated in modern schools and colleges. Nevertheless, there have been many cases where the *madrasa* background did not act as a barrier to earning a postgraduate university degree since universities such as Jamia Millia Islamia, Jawaharlal Nehru University and Jamia Hamdard have recognised *madrasa* degrees and thus qualify their holders to join many graduate courses in humanities and social sciences.

Despite the argument that *madrasas* were created as a reaction to the modernity imposed by the colonial powers, it was interesting to see that, in their curricula, there was no rejection of central values such as secularism, which naturally came in this post-Enlightenment package. In fact, *madrasas* had been founded as a dual hegemonic tool employed by the *'ulama* to overcome the colonial powers and the so-called un-Islamic practices found among the converts from the lower castes (Alam, 2008a). This point has been replaced by the increasing media propaganda about *madrasas* being grounds for breeding terrorism (Chatterjee, 2004; Sikand, 2005, 2006a, 2006b).

I started this chapter with a narration of my visit to an institution that is informally linked to Nadwatul Ulama Lucknow, which is considered one of the oldest Islamic schools in South Asia.[4] Although Nadwa is designed exclusively for male education, many of its *'ulama* supervise and teach in girls' *madrasas*.

Together with Darul Uloom Deoband, both *madrasas* occupy a high status among Islamic scholarship in Asia. What differentiates Nadwa from Deoband is the moderate attitude and stream that the scholars choose to adopt and thus differs from the ultra conservative and orthodox Deobandis. The history of Nadwa dates back to the 1890s when a group of *'ulama* called for the implementation of the principle of the middle way, or moderation (*wasat*), which was the interpretation of the verse: "And thus we have made you a just community that you will be witnesses over the people" (The Quran, 2:143).[5] They tried to concentrate on three aspects of the concept of the moderate *Ummah*: the cultural, the intellectual and the social. Culturally, they emphasised the reform of the educational system and developing it according to the needs of time and shaping it on the basis of Quran and *Sunnah*, Islamic *fiqh*, history, Islamic sciences, as well as modern sciences. The intellectual aim was the correction of Islamic conceptions and thought and interpreting religion according to the life of the Prophet through publications, translation and Islamic preaching. The social goal was to unite the Muslims by finding the spirit of tolerance among them and to establish solidarity on all intellectual and sectarian levels.

Nadwa emerged as a public civil association in 1893 AD in a meeting of South Asian Muslim intellectuals in Kanpur, eighty kilometres from Lucknow, to discuss the situation of Muslims under the predicament of colonial rule and western modernity. Their aims were the reform of educational curricula, uniting Muslims and performing *da'wah*, or preaching, in effective means. Eventually, Maulana Muhammad Ali Almongiri, the first general secretary, established a comprehensive school called Darul Uloom of Nadwatul Ulama in Lucknow in 1898. This school was led by Allama Shibli Nomani, who was responsible for the educational department (Al-Nadwi, 2008; Khan, 2004).

Nadwatul Ulama Movement was considered a bridge between Islamic and western cultures, and *'ulama* and modernistic intellectuals. Upon direct influence and interaction with the Arab World (Hartung, 2006), the foundational members' goal was to establish a new school of thought joining "the benevolent tradition (*alqadeem al-saleh*)" and "the useful modern (*aljadeed alnafi'*)" and to find a moderate approach between fixation on sources and goals and flexibility in means and mechanisms (Al-Nadwi, 2005). This vision was thus based on a critique of Sir Syed Khan's educational policy, as carried through the Aligarh movement, which, according to Al-Nadwi (2005), did not adapt the western-based educational system to the nature of the Indian Muslim society.

Nadwa has produced one of the most influential Islamic scholars in modern India: Syed Abul Hasan Nadwi, whose works are being studied and quoted worldwide (see Al-Nadwi, 2002, 2005, 2006, 2010). Abul Hasan Nadwi was known for his opposition to Maududi strategies; although they both agreed on the significance of the creation of the Islamic state, they differed on the means. Nadwi eschewed violence and saw that the establishment of faith has to be pursued through peaceful means, such as reform (*islah*), consultation (*musha-warat*) and wisdom (*hikmat*), making use of all available legitimate spaces, such as literature, public discussions and volunteers, in an attempt for a silent revolution (*khamoshi inquilab*) (Sikand, 2004).

Despite this, the portrayal of the *madrasa* system of Islamic education has been increasingly stigmatised in the previous decade, with negative stereotypes through the discourse on terrorism. It is argued that *madrasas* are becoming terrorist preparation camps, and thus are drawing Indian Muslims away from the national mainstream. The rise of Hindutva politics enhanced this propaganda, in addition to several other factors, including the rise of militancy in Kashmir and the radicalism in Afghanistan and Pakistan. The media is full of examples of RSS and VHP leaders' statements, such as Praveen Togadia's (the general secretary of the VHP) in 1995, in which he claimed, "one hundred thousand *madrasas* in India were all engaged in a sinister plot to train *jihadists* to massacre the Hindus and establish Islamic rule all over the world" (Sikand, 2006a, p. 221). During the Vajpayee government, this tone increased since *madrasas* were labelled centres for militants and the mosques as shelters for ISI agents (Shahabuddin, 2004).[6] There is also Advani's (the former president of BJP) famous call for the intervention in *madrasa* issues due to the foreign funding from Saudi Arabia (Fahimuddin, 2008). The transnational aspect of the scholarship undertaken not only at Nadwa but also at major big *madrasas* in India is an interesting fact. Nadwa, however, maintains stronger relations with the Arab world due to its historical ties with Egypt and Saudi Arabia (earlier Hijaz).

Muslim leaders have brought attention to this matter and realised that this campaign against Islam and *madrasas* could be overcome through the strategic use of mass media, especially since India is a democratic state (Muhammad Raby' Hasan Nadwi, head of the AIMPLB and rector of the Nadwatul Ulama Lucknow, cited in Sikand, 2006a). Other counter-propaganda views stress the difference between the modern and western-educated Al-Qaeda members and how their social profile radically differs from modest *madrasa* students (Qasmi, 2005).

Amidst these discourses, there is a considerable absence of other counter-discourses reporting the reform of the *madrasa* system of education and thus defending it. Yoginder Sikand, a prominent scholar interested in the reform of Muslim education and the dialogue among Muslim and non-Muslim communities in India, is considered one of the few voices that seek to give a different picture of the insides of *madrasas*. Several metanarratives comprise the structural hindrances to the reform. The 'modernisation project', endorsed by the state and developmental paradigms (Metcalf, 2007), clashes with the Islamic theory of knowledge that the *madrasa* system is based upon, most evident in the non-existence of a twofold distinction between the modern and traditional, and the secular and religious. Another hurdle linked to the state is the rise of Hindu nationalism to power and the consolidation of a hegemonic discourse implying that Muslims are out of the 'national mainstream' and need to be brought in. Sikand (2005) in this regard argues that the autonomy of *madrasas* from state surveillance and control acts as a challenge to the "monolithic Indian nationalism [that] is based on Brahminical Hinduism" (pp. 241–242). This is especially significant considering that the majority of *madrasas* are independent bodies free in their administration and syllabus setting (Sikand, 2009). On an internal level, the dividing strife among the *'ulamas* is a persistent feature that impedes reform projects. The debate is dominated by contentious forces among traditional *'ulamas* who are afraid of losing their authority as leaders of the community, if projects of *madrasa* reform are endorsed.

On the other hand, young *madrasa* graduates who joined regular universities for higher education disseminate ideas of reform. Their ideas include spreading awareness concerning international and national affairs; publishing articles and thus contributing to the elimination of silence on the positive examples of *madrasa* students; and encouraging social work and thus playing a role in an active civil society.

The contextual and regional difference gives us an overview of the complexity of the discussion on *madrasas*. There is a significant disparity, for example, between Kerala's and North Indian *madrasas*. Not only do most children in Kerala combine both means of education by going either first to the *madrasas* for two hours at sunrise, then to the modern school, or in the evening after school, but there is also a significant role played by language. The usage of Urdu in the North and to a lesser extent in Hyderabad and Bangalore spurs a debate on an alleged exclusion or mal-integration of Muslims in the social mainstream. This is juxtaposed to the Keralite context, where Malayalam was the medium used in most *madrasas*, albeit with a creative twist: writing it in Arabic script so as not to be alienated from the language of the Quran.[7] In West Bengal, the picture is also different since there is news on *madrasas* with more Hindu students than Muslims.[8] This opens a huge debate on the politicisation of religious identity across different contexts.

There is no specific figure of the number of *madrasas* in India; however, a ten-year-old governmental census accounted for 25,000 fully fledged *madrasas* and 80,000 *maktabs*, which are often located in mosques (Qasmi, 2005). The percentage of *madrasa*-going children as compared to those going to modern schools has been a matter of debate. According to both non-official Muslim citizen testaments and official reports, such as the Sachar Report, this percentage is considerably low.[9] In conversations with North Indian Muslim middle-class families, one mother asserted: "It is not true that religious people send their children to *madrasas* and others to modern schools. Actually, very few school-going children go to *madrasas*, around 5%, while the other 95% go to regular schools." Other interview respondents argued that, in most poor Muslim localities, there are no government schools, not even for primary education and, since the overwhelming majority of Muslims are below the poverty line, they would send their children to *madrasas* where they get food, clothing and education for free. This financial provision comes from the *zakat* given by a great number of Indian Muslims. If it were not for the *madrasas*, these children would be denied basic literacy. I was told that Muslims benefit from the special scheme enacted in Haryana where poor children receive monthly pocket money if they join school, so children would go to the *madrasa* to get free clothes and study materials, as well as to get the pocket money. A *madrasa* teacher in Haryana had expressed to me the change in the mentality of Muslims:

> As for the future of Muslims, thank god, I am optimistic; the Muslims have awaken now because a lot of parents do not leave their children without education, but take them to both Islamic and modern schools, and especially in this village where there are no problems, and Muslims who are around 20% live peacefully with non-Muslims.
>
> (Pipli Mazra *Madrasa*, November 2010)

In an attempt to delineate the role of politics in *madrasa* education, I looked at the curricula and noticed that discussion on the state is clearly absent. Apart from the fact that some *madrasas* concentrate more on *hadith*, and others on the Quran's *tafsīr*, the study of *fiqh* in both groups focuses more on matters of worship and does not extend to political affairs. Looking through the curricula of two of the biggest *madrasas* in India, Darul Uloom Deoband and Nadwatul Ulama Lucknow, there was no mentioning of any course taught on Islamic political thought or on matters related to Islamic governance. The adaptation to the secular and minority setting of the newly independent India was reflected in the socialisation process of *madrasa* education, in which it was deemed that studying the terms of the Islamic state ruled by *shari'ah* was unwarranted. The need for the preservation of the Islamic identity in the face of the wave of Hin-duisation of the Indian society, as Sikand (2006a) argues, was the most funda-mental task facing the *madrasa* system.

Madrasas have additional functions: most importantly as a means of identity formation (Aleaz, 2005; Alam, 2008a, 2008b; Noor, Sikand, & Bruinessen, 2009), as a site for legal guidance and as means for social mobility of students coming from poor families and thus guaranteeing jobs as *imams* or teachers afterwards. The activities of *madrasas* on national holidays is a marker of this accommoda-tion. Kerala presents a unique case that is presented in the next chapter. In North India, important *madrasas* organise functions on the Indian Republic and Inde-pendence Days, unfurl the flag, make the students sing patriotic songs and invite both Muslims and non-Muslim figures to participate and give speeches, especially on the role of *'ulama* in the independence struggle (Sikand, 2006a).

Madrasas are thus clearly significant because of the link between authority and power, on the one hand, and the creation of collective memories of martyrdom of the *'ulama* through their role in nation building, on the other hand. The same *'ulama* who are heads and leaders of today's big *madrasas* are among the most influential political leaders within the Muslim community in India, especially the Muslim Personal Law Board and Jamiatul Ulama-e-Hind, who play a great role in mobilising thousands of Muslims and influencing their polit-ical and social decisions.

Madrasas, and afterwards universities, have a symbolic power as a place of aggregation of students who would be mobilised. *'Ulama* in India are considered strong mobilising agents. In January 2009, hundreds of Muslims from UP arrived on a chartered train christened *The Ulama Express*. Their aim was to protest against the harassment of youth by the police in UP and the encounters, especially the Batla House and the killing of two Muslim youth from Azamgarh (Indian Social Institute, 2009). As this chapter concerns North Indian Muslim youth, I see it necessary to introduce another educational background of which subjects of this study belong.

The role of Jamia Millia Islamia

> This is the home of my yearnings
> This is the land of my dreams
> Here, conscience is the beacon light and guide
> Here is the Mecca of heart where the guiding faith resides
> Ceaseless movement is our faith
> And blasphemy is to stay still
> Here, the destined goal is the march on and on
> Here, the swimming urge seeks
> Newer and newer storms
> Restless wave itself is our resurrected shore
> > (*Muhammad Khaleeq Siddiqui-Jamia Taranah*
> > [Anthem], translated from Urdu)

When I replied that I was a student at Jamia, he said, "Achcha Jamia. Tabhi toh aap aise sawal karte ho. Tum logon ki mentality aisi hoti hai" ("Oh Jamia. That's why you are asking such questions. This is all that you people can think of").

(An administrative official to a student following up a RTI application on the Batla House Encounter, 2010, quoted in Polanki, 2010, p. 7)

During one of my interviews with a Muslim social worker, I noticed a sign on a wall in his office, with a quotation in Arabic taken from a Quranic verse that translates to "And Allah taught the human being what he did not know." I was instantly reminded that this is the same verse inscribed on the logo of Jamia Millia Islamia. As an Arab Muslim myself, I was surprised that, whereas this verse has acquired the popularity that renders it as material for calligraphic art on wooden signs, its significance remained in oblivion to many Arabic-speaking nations (since, for instance, I have never seen it inscribed anywhere in Egypt). Zakir Hussain, one of the founders of Jamia, explicated the symbolism behind the logo. He explained that the star on the top served the role of guidance, its characteristic, as being a star of Allah ("Allah is great" is inscribed on it), "reflects the truth that Allah is the greatest and he who bows his head before Him only, discovers the truth". According to Hussain, this was a reminder to believers of the impossibility and illegitimacy of subjugation to any other power. Beneath this star, one sees an open book (the Holy Quran) with the above-explained inscription in Arabic (*'Allamma al-Insāna Mā lam Ya'lam*). Hussain continues his description of the two palm trees as being:

symbolic of the barren valley in which nothing grew; but it was there that the sapling of *din* (religion) took root. These trees are emblems of hope from a land in which not a leaf or flower could sprout; but wherein suddenly the springs of *hidaya* (guidance) burst forth and drenched the "communities of the heart".... At the very bottom is a tiny silver crescent which reads Jamia Millia Islamia. This crescent is small but just as it expands to become the full moon on the fourteenth night, so also Jamia. Meaning that this is the beginning of our work.

(Zakir Hussain, Jamia Millia Islamia website, accessed in 2012)

Jamia Millia Islamia, or the National Muslim University (a translation of its Urdu name), was created as the counterpart to the Pakistan movement carried out by Aligarh University and was formed as a joint initiative between secular Muslim intellectuals and religious Muslim scholars who were part of the Khilafat movement and the anti-colonial struggle. Hence, the success in overcoming the secular versus Islamic polarisation was evident from Jamia's inception. Muhammad Ali, one of its founders, outlined the character of education in Jamia as combining religious and worldly education. Religious education was enhanced by the stress on the Arabic language in order to understand the Quran and modern education was endorsed in a Gandhian manner to fight colonial subjugation and thus overcoming the shortcomings of Islamic *madrasas*, such as Deoband or Nadwa and English-language-based schools and colleges (Hasan & Jalil, 2006). The preference not just to learn but also to write in Arabic is a symbolic decision and should not be dismissed from the analysis of the socialisation process inherent in the Muslim educational institutions. Founders and supporters envisioned Jamia as upholding the principles of 'good citizenship' – a reference to tolerance. Dr Ansari and Hakim Ajmal Khan, for example, aimed at joining Islamism with ideas of democracy, individual freedom and modernity (Hasan & Jalil, 2006). In 1937, Zakir Hussain noted the basis of these objectives as: "the belief that a true education of their religion will imbibe in Indian Muslims a love for their country, and a passion for national integration, and prepare them to take active part in seeking independence and progress for India" (Hasan & Jalil, 2006, p. 92). In Halidé Edib's words,[10] "the institution has two purposes: First, to train the Muslim youth with definite ideas of their rights and duties as Indian citizens. Second, to co-ordinate Islamic thought and behavior with Hindu[ism]" (ibid., p. 104).

Jamia now has around 17,000 students coming from all over India, but mainly from Delhi, UP and Bihar. It is a whole system of education that starts with a primary school and ends with a doctoral degree. It encompasses different disciplines such as language, Islamic studies, engineering, natural sciences and social sciences (Jamia Millia Islamia, 2011). The following list, though not exhaustive, shows the preferences of the student body: engineering which has the maximum number of students, followed by commerce, architecture, education, political science, economics, Arabic language, mathematics and law (Jamia Millia Islamia, 2012).

Jamia had great significance for my research on youth; politically, since it played a great role in the community as a mechanism of absorbing anger after the Batla House (Setalvad, 2010); and generally, because it encompassed different kinds of students: those with *madrasa* background and those not; those who were bearded and wearing a *kurta-salwar* and those dressed in western clothes.

Liberal versus illiberal spaces: the political stage of traditional and non-traditional political indicators

> One may observe, for example, the overwhelming influence the Islamic Truth still exerts on the people who attend, for example, the Friday congregational prayer and listen to the *khutba* (sermon) of the *imam* in the mosque. In fact, the words of the *imam* would deeply shake the audience in such a manner that we often witness a man completely immersed in his tears. Indeed, the *imam* himself, so much excited, may sometimes be unable to continue his speech!
>
> However, once the prayer is over and once he has returned to his worldly affairs, the Truth which has just shaken the man would rather, unfortunately, be left in the mosque and thus fails to accompany him in his 'public life'.
>
> (Bennabi, 1962/2002)

Through this section, I quickly demonstrate the stage on which the previously mentioned discourses threatening a full sense of citizenship take place. By liberal spaces, I allude to those democratically and constitutionally enabled channels through which Indian Muslims politically act and strive for citizenship. These range from voting, to holding legitimate demonstrations and protests, to actively participating in a process of social change through university education. Illiberal spaces, on the other hand, are manifested in religious spheres, or zones where the practice of Islamic rituals is dominant and authoritarian. These are manifested in the mosque, the *madrasa* and the family.

In the case of *madrasas*, the negotiable feature of the struggle for citizenship is manifested in its independence from the state, which is considered by many religious leaders as a criterion of citizenship rights in the unique political 'secular' settings in India. The majority of *madrasas* are funded through Muslim donations. The rest are aided by state governments and are under their supervision (more details are provided in the Sachar Report). In the past years, there has been a rising debate among Muslim leaders on the issue of the Central Madrasa Board, which aimed at uniting *madrasas* under a governmental scheme. There are already state *madrasa* boards in eight states and some universities recognise their degrees. However, the majority of leaders staunchly rejected the Central Madrasa Board bill. In a letter sent to Sonya Gandhi, Manmohan Singh and Arjun Singh, Maulana Arshad Madani commented:

> We are clearly demonstrating our position before the government: we could contribute with the government to the development of schools, colleges, professional and technical educational institutions, but no interference shall be accepted in the affairs, curriculum and management of the *madrasas* that have been founded for the sake of preserving Muslim identity.
>
> (Madani, 2012, pp. 51–52, my translation)

Ordinary citizens mainly have three options when faced with constraining forces and repressive institutions: comply and show loyalty to the system by joining the mainstream; disengage and surrender their rights to voice concerns and hence exit the political stage; or manage to express their contention loudly and clearly (through being vocal despite being marginal). This is all reflected in Muslim youth's reactions on the Indian political stage through traditional and non-traditional political indicators.

There is a noted low sense of activism among the mainstream Hindu middle class in Northern India, which is anchored by their stratification and the absence of a community gathering unlike the Muslims on Fridays or the Christians on Sundays, where caste, kinship and class gets transcended (Varma, 2001). However, does this mean that the mosque could be considered as a political site? The answer is positively affirmed in many non-secular countries. However, the picture in India is quite complex. There is an ambivalent relationship between accepting the ideal of secularism and activating the mosque as a political arena for mobilisation. Some mosques in India, like the Jama Masjid of Delhi, have acquired a historical status as a political arena. From Azad's famous speech in 1947 to recent and recurrent news on the Imam Bukhari's political appeals in election times:

> The minarets of Jama Masjid want to ask you a question. Where have you lost the glorious pages from your chronicles? Was it only yesterday that on the banks of the Jamuna, your caravans performed *wuzu?* Today, you are afraid of living here!
>
> (Azad's address to Delhi Muslims, 23 October 1947)

Among scholars, there is no consensus whether the political role of the mosque should be maintained. In an interview with Akhtarul Wasey, he contends that

> Mosques are not a centre for political activity and should not be, but I am sorry to say that. Mosques are not used as a centre for creating a social and civic awareness. Mosques are no longer community centres, but generally mosques are used for primary religious education (*maktabs*). Mosques should not be places of political disputes, because people from different political orientations and parties come to pray in the mosque. Otherwise, mosques will become centres of conflict and confrontation. And we should learn something from Hazrat Ali. Why did Hazrat Ali migrate from Medina to Kufa (in Iraq) and shift the political capital of Islam? Just to keep *Madinat-u-nabbi* (the city of the prophet) free from all types of politics, so as to maintain the religious reverence and dignity of that city. So we should follow Hazrat Ali's example and keep the mosque free from political disputes.
>
> (Author interview, September 2010)

Wasey reaffirms his stance by stressing that Hindus and Muslims share, and should keep sharing, spaces in which their voices and protests could be cast. This is a distinct characteristic of India; hence, "in the same areas where Hindu groups stage their processions or events like in Ram Lila Maidan, you find all the rallies by Muslims against Hindutva" (Wasey, author interview, September 2010).

Another Muslim religious site, which has been recently interlinked with politics, is the political *iftār*. An *iftār* is the breaking of the fast by Muslims in Ramadan. Political *iftārs* refer to feasts hosted by politicians who are not necessarily Muslims, but to which influential Muslim leaders are invited. News on these *iftārs* is abundantly available in the Urdu press. For instance, in Mumbai, some organisations asserted that unless the innocent victims of the Malegaon blasts, who have been falsely accused, are released, they would boycott all political *iftārs*. This was considered a recommendable initiative that reflects the political awareness of such Muslim groups (as a letter to the editor carried in *Sahafat*, 11 August 2011). Another Muslim newspaper mentioning a piece of news on a political *iftār* in the *Milli Gazette* reported that Indira Gandhi had used the *iftār* as a political tool to measure the political sentiments among Muslim leaders. The report was on a political *iftār* held by a Muslim BJP Member of Parliament, which Indian Prime Minister Manmohan Singh attended and caused surprise, especially after controversial anti-Congress remarks made by the BJP president (Khan, 2010).

Active, reactive and interactive citizens

Are Muslim youth in India alienated and not active citizens, as the media propagates? Youth worldwide are contributing to the formation of youthscapes, a term coined by Maira and Soep (2005), which refers to a site that is geographic, temporal, social and political, bound up with questions of power and materiality. These contexts, in which youthscapes develop, shape political variables such as the sense of political efficacy, agency, conception of citizenship rights and belief in democracy. Indian Muslim youth differ from other Muslim youth as they actively engage in the secular democratic process. Their 'active citizenship', borrowing Bayat's (2009) term, is not seen as a desperate person's last refuge in constitutional rights, but is surprisingly often emerging out of Islamic incentives. In their own words, their struggle as a citizen minority is one of *jihād*. Self-rule, education and striving for social mobility and patience are all operationalised mechanisms of what *jihād* means for them.

According to Qamar Hasan's study on patterns of political alienation in India, Muslims are less insiders (active and efficacious supporters of the existing political system and politically integrated in the core of the system) or active dissenters, but more outsiders (27.2%) who lack a sense of efficacy (Hasan, 1987, pp. 183–186). Self-efficacy refers to the belief that one is capable of performing in a certain manner to attain certain goals. In a political sense, efficacy refers to a belief in the responsiveness of the government to the desires of the individuals (Easton & Dennis, 1967, cited in Hasan, 1987, p. 201).

Just like the polymorphous perceptions or conceptions of the state, as imagined by Rudolph and Rudolph (1987) in being a third actor, a liberal or citizens' state, capitalist or socialist, the same logic could be applied to the conception of one's citizenship, especially in the Muslim case. Identities related, to citizenship among Muslims could be analysed on three levels: the transcultural where the perception of the *Ummah* is noted; the minority level, where discourses on injustice or *zulm* is dominant; and the legal–civil practice. All these are related to one's sphere of civil and political action.

In a survey I conducted among Muslim students in Delhi, I measured the sense of collectivity through the regular attendance of the Jumaa prayer at the mosque. Of the male students, 91% said they always went, but only 7% of the females did. Another criterion was membership in Islamic associations: 15.2% confirmed they were, and when the figure was broken up into females and males, it accounted for 9.5% and 19%, respectively. Figure 4.1 shows the divisions of Islamic associations to which survey respondents belonged. Although these figures are not representative of North Indian youth, they still show the rising trend in membership of Jamaati Islami among the middle-class students of Jamia.

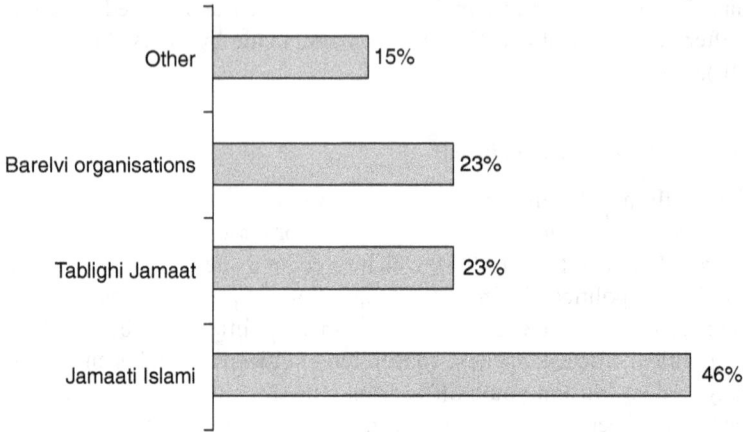

Figure 4.1 Membership of Islamic associations (source: own survey).

The survey showed how the Muslim youth projected a strong and active sense of citizenship, as 55.2% of the respondents said they participated in protests. This remains gendered since the difference between male and female participation is obvious: 29.3% of females participated while 54.7% of males did. What is of significance to the dynamics of identity and citizenship is how the majority of issues (51.4%) that respondents protested about had to do with broader national politics (reservations for Muslims as the principal cause, Kashmir, corruption and the *lokpal* bill, student politics, rise in food prices, private education bill, anti-malaria campaigns, arms control, Dalit issues and land struggles, female infanticide and women's development, human rights, Binayak Sen case, anti POTA), 25.7% of issues had to do with the Muslim community (reservations at university, fake encounters like Batla House, Muslim unity, Jamia minority status) and 22.8% had to do with international concerns (the Palestinian conflict – the top issue among the international concerns, anti-Mubarak, anti-US, Danish cartoons, Indo-US nuclear deals).

This projected sense of citizenship carries an interesting factor as it combines the pan-Islamic perspective. When they were asked whether they would be willing to go on a protest for a Muslim-identity-related cause, 86.8% confirmed, 10.4% said they could not decide and only 2.8% rejected this. It has to be noted that there is no student union in Jamia, and thus there is rarely any political demonstration on campus, apart from the Batla House-related sit-ins organised by the Jamia Teachers Solidarity Association.

Would it have made sense to present an argument linking faith with being political? To try to answer this, I aimed at measuring the level of religiosity among the students. I asked first whether they were a Quran *hafiz* (a person who memorises the whole Quran) or knew parts of it by heart: 77.1% confirmed they did. The second question in this category concerned their reading of the *tafsīr* (interpretation) of the Quran: 71% said they did, but the figure was lower among the female-only sample and amounted to 53.8%. This experiment resulted in finding a correlation between those who protest and the level of religiosity, especially among those going to the Friday prayer.

Discrimination, minority feeling and finding the refuge in the Constitution

> One day a friend told me: thank god there is corruption in India, because at least corruption does not discriminate between a Muslim and a non-Muslim.
>
> (A retired Muslim IAS officer, 2010)

What could be clearly drawn from the Muslim youth's narrations on their present and future is the constant fear or complaint of discrimination. Although the ideal governance model in India is not religion-based, Hindutva politics acts as the trigger to this discrimination. These politics aim at disabling citizenship rights that are enshrined in the Constitution.

Several historical watersheds, like the partition of India and the demolishing of Babri Masjid, make this fear of discrimination valid in numerous cases. Many Muslims claim that they were first confronted with their identity as Muslims in India on 6 December 1992. As a Muslim journalist argues:

> India operates at two levels. The first is the system level, which is unconsciously Hindu and discriminates against others, but much more against Muslims because they are a threat since 1947. They perceive that Muslims have fought for partition and taken their share and thus now they do not have a stake in the system, therefore the system always denies them opportunities; schools and banks do not open in Muslims localities or give them loans, and they are not given health care. The second level is the people level. Indians are culturally and civilisationally the most secular people in the world in their everyday life. On Friday or Eid Namaz, if you come to that area where there are only twenty-five Muslims, you will see how the traffic gets blocked because half of the flyover is taken, but no one objects. You will find hundreds of Muslims visiting Hindu shrines and they do not find it odd. I come from Allahabad. Every Muslim in Allahabad participates in Hindu festivals.
>
> (Author interview, September 2010)

The partition of India has resulted in a culture of demonisation of Muslims and burdening them with an alleged sense of guilt. In addition to this, the construction of the historical narratives of the nineteenth century in a manner portraying Muslims as despotic rulers who subjugated Hindus, forcing them to convert to Islam and demolishing their temples in order to build mosques on their sites, adds up to the establishment of today's reality and the 'othering' mentality that is conducive to discrimination and stereotyping. This is not to say that this 'othering' state of mind is exclusive in the way Muslims are being perceived. Even Muslims themselves contribute to this, especially as a result of the spatial segregation that is found in urban cities such as Delhi and Mumbai.

Several human right activists and scholars regard the penetration of the Hindu right-wing in different institutional bodies as the biggest reason behind discrimination. In an interview, the chairman of an institute in Delhi argued that the *Sangh Parivar* managed to penetrate different levels, in addition to the societal one. The first is the bureaucracy, especially the IAS and the IPS, through establishing in their minds that Muslims are not patriotic and thus cannot be trusted. The second level is of policy makers, where Muslims are dealt with as vote banks rather than participants in policy making. Eventually, these segments kept the Muslims away from the development of their economic environment, educational institutions and social integration.

Despite these accounts, there is a counter-picture manifested in the beliefs of many Muslims. The rise of right-wing Hindu politics led to the rise of the level of consciousness among the young and educated Muslims of their 'Indianness'. Muslims are being assertive now due to several reasons. The first relates to the set of fundamental rights, which was visualised by the framers of the Constitution and are being used as key judicial and political tools. In addition to this, articles such as 29 and 30 of the Constitution give tools to minorities to legally fight for their rights. The constitutional recognition of religion and language is a vital aspect. This ideally transforms the minority-subjugated mentality into one of active citizenship. In Akhtarul Wasey's words:

> Islam is my religion and Urdu is my mother tongue and both are recognised. In this Hindu majority country, I was given the freedom not only to practise but also to preach my religion. Of course there is the Gujarat incident and all sorts of discrimination. But there is a simultaneous picture. There are all types of deprivation in the Hindu community also. Thank god the Indian Muslims are more comfortable in this country than Muslims in any Muslim country. I have said the same to General Musharraf, "Sir, you have Islamabad, but we have Islam." This is the country where a Hindu is not permitted to have a second wife, but Muslims are permitted to have four wives.
>
> (Wasey, author interview, September 2010)

On a collective and political level, this explains the plethora of Muslim political organisations that either run for elections or act as pressure groups on political parties and representatives in an environment which is indicative of a process towards educational and political development in the Muslim community. This is also strengthened by certain legislations, like the right to information act, by the democratic channels allowing strikes and filing petitions, and definitely by the role of the media. In an interview with Shahid Mehdi, the former vice chancellor of Jamia recounts how, in Andhra Pradesh, students who got governmental scholarships were not allowed to receive the money in cash but through banks. However, certain branch managers refused to open bank accounts for Muslims.

When the Hyderabad-based Urdu newspaper *Sisyast* then raised a huge outcry, bank managers were compelled to open the bank accounts (author interview, December 2010). The idea of opportunities granted by the democratic and secular channels and guaranteed to every citizen in India is a recurrent theme in many conversations I had with Indian Muslims, especially from the ones with a lower-middle-class background. In the words of a female PhD student:

> There is an overstress on the discourse of marginalisation. The problems Muslims are facing are on a high level and not on the daily life level because people get a chance to get an education and to have health services. This access is equal to all. There is no discrimination in education but in jobs.
>
> (Delhi, October 2010)

What is striking as we look at the everyday lives of Indian Muslims is the ability to implement the previously mentioned theoretical concepts developed by Islamic jurists, such as composite nationalism or *mithaq al-madina* (treaty of Medina). On secularism, the following excerpts from interviews with Islamic scholars at Lucknow's Nadwatul Ulama provides an insight to the way the *'ulama* perceive the location of the ideal of secularism in their empirical everyday life and their conceptual realm, which is in turn reflected in the youths' psyche through the socialisation process:

> Secularism is the only way of uniting Muslims in India, although it is Islamically rejected, but in India, secularism is not like in Turkey. In India, they accepted secularism with the acceptance of all other religions, and made secularism the formula of governance only. Religion sustained the control of the private sphere. Secularism in fact eases all the problems every sect faces. If any religious institution needs to organise an event or function, then it gets full support from the government and authorities. There is no law against public meetings. Tablighi Jamaat, for example, holds conferences attended by millions of people. Muslims live freely and religiously without any barriers. Such facilitations are not found in other countries. In Arab countries, for example, if a Muslim goes regularly to pray in a mosque, he will end up under surveillance and doubt of the police, same for meetings which are actually banned, and there is no freedom of expression of either emotions or opinions. Magazines and newspapers with a specific religious orientation are banned. But for Muslims in India, there is complete freedom, unparalleled in the rest of the world. However, concerning rights, there is suffering. Rights are not totally achieved in India.

> India is considered *dar al amn* (abode of peace and security) because the Constitution provided security for all citizens. Although we are deprived of basic rights, we do not consider ourselves weak. We feel fulfilled with our religion and our approach and do not consider ourselves less than any Muslim in the Arab world. All Muslim forces including Jamaati Islami and

Tablighi Jamaat are proud of this. We do not suffer from deficiency or inferiority complex. We have intellectual independence. We preserved our identity and we renewed it in the context of India, and we can preserve our
existence. We express our Islamic opinion with a free pen, unrivalled in the
Islamic world where mouths are muffled.

(Lucknow, October 2010)

Despite this, some still acknowledge many of the dilemmas of Muslims, especially the urban middle-class ones. A comment by a Hindu reader on an article
in *The Hindu* titled "A Decade After 9/11, Indian Jihad Still Thrives" reflects
this:

Apart from dealing with terrorism at the political and administrative levels,
there is a strong need to deal with it at the societal and individual levels. We
have to make a conscious effort to bring into the mainstream disgruntled
middle-class and lower-middle-class Muslims who are forced to live in
ghettos because of the 'housing apartheid' and are discriminated against in
jobs. We have to muffle the voices within our families and our circles of
friends that justify the alienation and discrimination.[11]

Seeing that there was a sense of rampant frustration, which is directly linked to
the demolishment of mosques,[12] an attempt to measure the sense of discrimination among the respondents was pivotal. Among both males and females, 35.2%
said they experienced discrimination at their educational institution or a governmental office. When I looked at the female-only percentage, it declined to
23.8%. Concerning the exact places where the students witnessed this discrimination, 50% was at the university, 38.4% at government offices, 7.6% at home
and 3.8% in their place of employment.

There was a consensus that discrimination is witnessed in the national holidays in India, where everyone is expected to celebrate the Hindu ones, whereas
the Muslim festivities are entirely ghettoised. When I asked a group of female
students sitting together if they feel they are a minority, the affirmative answer
surprised their Hindu friend who was among them. One of the Muslim girls then
told me she had actually felt it sometimes even in Jamia:

Here, we are at the centre of India, where there are opportunities, but it
differs if you go anywhere else in India. You will get a very different
picture. So yes I have rights and I feel I am a full citizen because I live in
Delhi, but I do not know if I would be able to say the same thing if I was
living outside Delhi.

The statistics could also be misleading because the majority of the respondents
live in Muslim majority areas and hence the chances of discrimination or experi-
encing being among a minority could be lower than of those living outside the
Muslim ghettos. (Some of the students who did not encounter problems had told

me that they have always lived in places with Muslim majority and probably this is why they had never faced any discrimination. They added that the scenario might be different for other Muslims.) The respondents had a very low level of 'being experienced to reality' because their frictions with real-life situations were minimal; their daily routine includes going to university and staying at a hostel. There was no significant level of interaction with the outside world (be it in other districts or at work). Conversation with the older age groups (between twenty-five and thirty-five) showed how the Muslim name one carries could put one in unfavourable circumstances, such as at work or the airport. The 'coming out' of the safe cocoon of one's village into the bigger world of metropolises such as Mumbai and Delhi was the first encounter these youth faced with discrimination and reminders of their difference, especially once coupled with poverty.

When asked if they feel they are a minority, 76.9% confirmed this feeling. The numerical idea did not dominate their mode of thinking while answering this question. Being empowered was the main driving force to consider oneself as a minority or not. There is a difference, however, in the gender aspect; 84.4% of the males confirmed this, while only 65% of women shared this feeling.

There is also a shared feeling that the lives of Indian Muslims are much better than the lives of Muslims in Pakistan, Bangladesh or the Arab world. Some students complained about the mentality of Indian Muslims themselves. Some said they are fundamentalists; others said that:

> Muslims have better rights to live, to develop and to participate in the mainstream; the problem lies in the sick mentality of *mullahs* and *madrasas*. There is an urgent need to either revise the syllabi of these *madrasas* or simply close them down. The educational system of this country is in a transitional phase and due to recent government's special efforts, Muslims have started taking up higher studies and enjoying better economic status. However, women's freedom is still a major issue.

> The major problem with Indian Muslims is their victim-centred mentality. Look at Japan and Israel, they do not mourn, but are optimistic. The government creates this victimisation. There is also a failure of Indian *madrasas* with their 500-year-old syllabuses. How can you issue *fatwas* if you do not know about world affairs? Muslim '*ulama* are leaders of poorest of poor and the lower middle classes.

> Hindu–Muslim problems emerge from politicians, not people. This is evident in the opportunistic politics (*roti garam karna*). They make use of the sentiments of people to their advantage, which results in too much injustice. This division has detrimental effects on the Muslims; eventually their opponents win with these divide and rule tactics. There is no unity among Muslims, unlike Sikhs, for example, who stuck to their faith in the UK and insisted on wearing the *kirpan* and *turban* till it was legalised for them.

Three things if properly maintained then the issues in India would be reformed; these are the hospital, the police station and the court. The problem is in the *Sangh Parivar*. But they lack authority, and this is why they resort to high voice and violence. A human being has to be honest with oneself first. Three levels are essential: the soul, then the nation (*qawm*) and then the country (*waṭan*).

When asked if they felt that the Indian state had been just to the Muslim community, 33% affirmed it while 56.3% negated it. Here, historical experience plays an influential role in this perception. Taking the Babri Masjid and the stance of the government towards it is an example of what Muslims term as injustice on the part of the state and a breach of the principle of secularism as enshrined in the Constitution. Zafrul Islam Khan, the editor of the English newspaper *Milli Gazette*, comments: "The myth suddenly became a real person and has a guardian (the law). Muslims will not forget it. Hindus will speak with a mentality of ruling. This won't stop here. Many other mosques are on the way" (author interview, October 2010).

When I asked the students if the Ayodhya verdict was fair to the Muslims, 64.7% said no, while 8.8% affirmed it and 26.5% refused to give their opinion or had no opinion. The 'no opinion' answer is a politically burdened one. It was not chosen so as to convey political ignorance or unawareness, but to assert a statement. Students were critical of the question in the first place, since it was not a matter of justice to them; it was rather a matter of common sense. In other cases, students did not want to sound too critical of the High Court since it is deemed unacceptable for an Indian citizen to challenge a court's decision. Again we see an example of practising an act of self-marginalisation to abide by the traditional guidelines of a model citizen. There were also many students who shared the opinion that the Babri verdict was not fair to Muslims but was fair enough to the general public. Another interesting answer was:

This is a monkey's division (*bandar baant*); the Hindus got everything for themselves and gave almost nothing to the Muslims. What was supposed to be done was that it should have been ruled that it should be turned into a secular place. What is wrong in turning it into a hospital or a park? This judgment was simply useless.

(Female student, Delhi, October 2010)

Finally, to see if there is any impact of following *fatwas* on the way their political decisions are perceived, I calculated the percentages of students who always followed *fatwas* and perceived the verdict to be unfair. This showed no significant difference and indicated the rather weak role *fatwas* play in the socialisation and opinion-forming process among the educated youth.

Terrorism and security concerns

Terrorists are fasadis not jihadis.

(A. Khan, 2010)

Many Islamic organisations and independent Muslim scholars have struggled to erase the stigma and propaganda equating terrorism with *jihād*. In one of the resolutions enacted by Jamiat Ulama-i-Hind, it was stated that, while *jihād* was constructive, terrorism was a destructive phenomenon (Indian Social Institute, 2009). The constructivity and creativity of Muslims were outlined in the long liberal and innovative tradition that India held in the field of Islamic studies and economics, for example (Zafrul Islam Khan, author interview, 2010).

In a literary work comprised of a long letter sent by an Indian Muslim to his friend in Pakistan titled "Choosing to Stay: Memoirs of an Indian Muslim", Ansari shows how the Indian Sufi culture has been an antagonistic environment to fundamentalism:

> The average Muslim relies upon his God who conceals man's faults, is forgiving and compassionate. This average person knows how to enjoy the blessings which his God has conferred upon him. The freedom of imagination and expression found in Urdu, Arabic and Persian poetry is unparalleled in any other language. It is obvious that the people who have this colourful temperament cannot be accused of fundamentalism.
>
> (Ansari, 1999, pp. 121–122)

Through these discourses, Muslim scholars and intellectuals project the conceptual underpinnings on which Indian Muslim youth go about in their everyday. However, on the praxis level, there is a widespread feeling of frustration among the Muslim youth in India. This stems from the above-mentioned discrimination discourse and the constant feeling of being doubted and suspected as a terrorist. According to a news report in the Urdu daily *Sahafat*, there are almost 16,000 Muslim young people in Indian jails arrested under suspicion of terrorism (*Sahafat*, 14 August 2011). Having visible features that easily identify members of the Muslim community with their religion (be it the skull cap or the beard) adds up to this climate of suspicion. While starting my research on Indian Muslims, I was trying to map major Muslim social workers and activists working on issues of the community. I started this by typing into Google: 'Muslim NGOs India'. Interestingly, the following 'did you mean?' list emerged:

jobs indian ngos
christian ngo india
indian ngo list
indian terrorist organisations

The terrorism discourse emerges as part of a larger Hindu nationalistic discourse aiming at signalling Muslims as disloyal subjects of the Indian state who have allegiance towards Pakistan. Of the young men I interviewed, 22% confirmed that they had been once accused of being a Pakistani or a non-Indian.

The frequency of police fake encounters in Muslim residential areas and the targeting of Muslim students without sufficient evidence is a serious predicament facing this youth and the ways their perceive their future. There are many famous incidents in which Muslim students were implicated with no evidence. In the 2007 Mecca Masjid blast, around 200 Muslim youth were detained following the attacks, but most of them were released later by the courts as investigations showed that they were innocent and that the bombing was executed by former members of the RSS. However, the release of the rest of these youth, who were subjected to torture, was not prompt. They were branded as terrorists by both the police and the media, which led to agitations of several human rights groups and Muslim political organisations until the Andhra Pradesh Court acquitted them two years later.[13]

The second incident is the previously mentioned Batla House Encounter of 2008. What is significant to report in this regard is the continual targeting of the Batla House area in Okhla until this date. In fact in the months of February and March 2012, there were continuous accounts in both Urdu and English newspapers of police brutality and the recurrent arrests of innocent youth and accusations of being illegal Bangladeshi immigrants and terror suspects. The community showed collective action in refusing this behaviour on the part of the police and their arrest of these youth without a warrant or a judicial order and hence staging protests, including women and even school children, who have been subject to police abuse. Since the police came wearing civilian clothes, the residents themselves in one of these raids, upon hearing the warning call from the local mosque, held the police officers captive until the local police officers came to release their colleagues.[14]

In January 2012, Mohammad Ali was acquitted of terror charges after spending fourteen years in jail. Like many other innocent youth, he was detained with false charges and then released because the prosecution could not produce evidence to prove his involvement in the respective terror cases (Ali, 2012). The activist Shabnam Hashmi from ANHAD (Act Now for Harmony and Democracy) voiced the fatal repercussions of this terrorism-related detention:

> After five to ten years when they are released, there is nobody to say it was a mistake, that this was not right, although in many terror cases, it has been proven that the *Sangh* has done it. Even then, initially, Muslims would be arrested, and for every Muslim boy who has been arrested in a case, they would put against him fifty to sixty cases so when he gets away from one case, there would be another five cases from which he cannot escape.
>
> (Author interview, October 2010)

There has been continuous resistance to this terrorism discourse, which interestingly, instead of taking a physically violent turn, has taken a symbolic one. There is an increasing belief among Muslims that they would be compensated for all the injustices incurred upon them in this world and would be granted heaven, and for them, this is the substitute for armed struggles against their oppressors (Sikand, 2006a). A female Muslim librarian in a *madrasa* on the outskirts of Lucknow told me:

Muslims feel injustice after Babri Masjid; they feel deprived of their dignity, shocked and are in sorrow. However, there is no risk on Muslims living in India because Allah protects us and we try to build our future ourselves through what Allah has destined for us.

Despite all allegations against *madrasas* as terrorist hubs and training centres, Sikand asserts that there is not a single *madrasa* that has called for violence or even armed *jihād* (Sikand, 2006a). In his speech, the vice chancellor of Darul Uloom Deoband, Marghub Ar-Rahman, affirmed that terrorism could never be the means of any struggle of Muslims. In fact, Islam stresses the idea that whoever kills one soul is considered to have murdered all of humanity (Madani, 2012).

Another means of responding to this discourse refers to the sad irony of the overrepresentation of Indian Muslims in Indian prisons as compared to other institutions and governmental bodies in India (according to some of the Muslim university lecturers I interviewed, these are data omitted from the Sachar Report). Mansi Sharma of the human rights group ANHAD recounted details of bomb blasts in various parts of the country that are now known to have been engineered by Hindutva groups. She accused state agencies of delaying the investigations, suppressing vital information and wrongly targeting, arresting and torturing innocent Muslims (Sikand, 2011).

In a conversation in Delhi, one social activist contended that media like the *Times of India* reflect a negative role through reports portraying Jamia Nagar as a terrorist hub, although it is a highly educated area, with its residents comprised of mainly middle-class citizens – the majority of whom believe in secularism. This was echoed in my conversations with Muslim students, 38.5% of whom thought that the media in India portray a negative image of Muslims on a constant basis.

Due to this discourse and the ensuing hate speeches by BJP politicians and the failure of the central and state governments in curbing this, some students claimed that the districts where BJP rules or is a leader became less safe. When asked whether there is any place he would avoid going to, one student said he would not go out on Indian Republic and Independence Days because if any terrorist attack occurred then it might be a problem for him, being part of the Muslim youth who always suffer.

The demand for security, and filling gaps in the sense of citizenship, prompted a deeper analysis of the reasons behind creating enclaves. The reasons for these gaps have proven to be often gender-related and not only emerging from the traditional religious minority discourse. Most respondents actually never go out of the Jamia or Okhla area, which is a predominantly Muslim area (or a ghetto) and this is why their sense of security is relatively high (62.5%), despite the strong fear of crime and police fake encounters.

When asked if there is any place they avoid going for fear of their security, 75% of the female students affirmed this compared with 63.2% of the males. Some stressed that the feeling of insecurity is not dependent on being a Muslim.

The female students stress the increasing crime rate in Delhi, especially in Batla House:

> In every *Eid* there is something wrong with us, last year we had an encounter, the one before there was problems with the police, and this year we have flood. It is the government's fault. Where we are living, the people are not well educated, and who are educated do not have much time to tackle this problem. I do not feel safe where I live; it is less safe compared to the past. Police have to provide security, especially for women.
>
> (Batla House, Delhi, October 2010)

The female variable

> A society can be created where a woman can live a life free from fear and where she can realise her social, economic, political and legal rights. She wants to be treated equally and wants to live a life of respect and dignity.
>
> (Hukook-e-Niswan Federation [Women's Rights Organisation, Mumbai])

Although this chapter deals with Muslim youth in general, the predicaments affecting the practice of their citizenship rights and the way they perceive themselves as citizens and not subjects of the state, separate reference has to be made to gendered differences. Whereas some discourses concern males to a great extent, like terrorism and police brutality (although there are exceptions, like the case of the shooting of Ishrat Jahan in Gujarat), a separation is noted due to the uniqueness of some of the difficulties pertaining to Muslim women and girls. Despite the fact that the majority of these problems are exclusively in the domain of personal laws – the private social sphere – and hence should not be targeted as national political concerns, women's endeavours to legitimise their voice and to appear in the public space are an aspect of citizenship struggle for justice in the public sphere. Young women practise active citizenship not only by acknowledging their problems but also by linking them to the broader quest for citizenship rights. In the words of female students I interviewed:

> If every community has its own rules, then this guarantees justice to the community. Communal violence and corruption erupt when you want to impose others' laws on other people.

> As a Muslim I do not feel the state is just, but as a citizen, yes I feel so.

> It is this secular framework that allows for the oppression of Muslim women through the freedom given to the *'ulama* in providing personal laws.

The struggle towards justice in the public space is preceded in the Indian Muslim women case with a struggle for legitimising their voice to appear in the public space in the first place. Women's access to public spaces has been limited and contingent upon several factors, such as the region where they live, their age, their marital status, their abidance to a specific dress code, their accompaniment of children or others and their level of education. The last factor is particularly significant because it carries the highest potential of emancipatory force. Although the level of literacy of Muslim women in India is considerably low in comparison to other religious groups, as well as to the national average (the National Family Health Survey in 2005–06 indicated it to be 49.5%), it is actually witnessing a serious rise (the first National Family Health Survey of 1992–93 had pointed it out to be 34%). There is a widespread conviction among various Muslim groups and communities all over India, whether orthodox or liberal, of the importance of education, especially among women. In many of my interviews with Muslim scholars and teachers, reference has been made to a statement by Maulana Abul Hasan Ali Nadwi, a famous Islamic scholar and a former rector of Nadwatul Ulama Lucknow: "If we teach one girl, this means we have taught two generations."

Despite the hegemony of patriarchal visions of the role of women and the prevalence of men as gatekeepers for women's education – since, on the one hand, it is usually the father who decides the fate of the children, and on the other hand, the world of the permissible and the non-permissible (in other words *fatwas* or religious edicts) is controlled by male scholars – there are new stirrings in society and evidence of ruptures in these power dynamics. One example is the remarkable breakthrough enacted in a decision by the Nadwatul Ulama to open the door for women to become *muftis*, or jurists, upon completion of a course that has been, historically, limited to male students. This is possible in different *madrasas* in Uttar Pradesh and, precisely, in the cities of Rae Bareli, Azamgarh and Lucknow. In a report by the Indian Social Institute in New Delhi:

> Although history has examples of women *muftis* in the remote past, most of the contemporary Islamic world barred them till 2006 when Syria made a breakthrough and appointed two women *muftis* to work in Damascus and Aleppo. Last year in Lucknow, a Muslim woman priest assumed the role of a *qazi* for a marriage.
>
> (Indian Social Institute, 2009)

Several women's organisations have been active in denouncing restrictive *fatwas* by *'ulama*, especially coming from the ultra-conservative Deoband seminary. Although gender equality is not an intrinsically Islamic principle, women's rights activists in India employ *shari'ah* strategically while simultaneously resorting to the Constitution and the rights enshrined for the Indian woman in general. The all-India women's organisation Bharatiya Muslim Mahila Andolan (BMMA) (the Organisation of Indian Muslim Women), the Mumbai-based Hukook-e-Niswan Federation (the Rights of Women Federation) and Awaaz-e-Niswan (Women's voices) are such examples:

> It is an opportunity for us be to in India, we felt that despite Gujarat, if we look around particularly in South Asia, India is the only place where there is

democracy and thus we have hope to fight for our citizenship rights. We felt that, on the one hand, there is the issue of communalism, violence and discrimination, but on the other hand, the so-called Muslim leadership has totally failed in fulfilling its obligations to the community. So we felt that in 2006 and 2007, if Sachar is saying that the community is lagging behind socially, educationally and economically, this means that we failed to become full citizens in spite of the functional democracy.

(Zakia Soman, BMMA, author interview, December 2010)

Another branch of activists adopt different 'diplomatic' strategies. These aim at minimising the collision with male *'ulama* through talking about women's rights from the *shari'ah* perspective, which is a tactic for earning legitimacy, and is also used to a great extent in the Arab world, where the human rights' perspective has limited institutional channels or support by the system. The proponents of this group argue that they do not need to adopt feminist ideologies because Islam has given full protection and support to women, but the problem lies in the social application or malpractice. Uzma Nahid, a Muslim educational activist and member of the All-Indian Muslim Personal Law Board (AIMPLB), is one example. She had participated in the drafting of a model of conditional *nikahnamah* (marriage contract) that guarantees the rights of women according to *shari'ah*. This *nikahnamah* was adopted as an alternative strategy to the calls for banning triple divorce – a commonly legitimised practice among Indian Muslims. Nahid explains:

The man has the right to divorce by saying it thrice through fax, email or phone. Since most of the Indian Muslims are Hanafi, Indian *'ulama* are saying it is valid and do not want to listen to anything against their verdict. My protest approach was different; it was diplomatic. I told *'ulama* that we have implemented only half *shari'ah* law. What about the punishment of 100 lashes when someone divorces an innocent woman? Since this is not done in India, we should also stop this practice of triple *ṭalāq*. So I never demand any ban on triple *ṭalāq* because then the *'ulama* will use sixty *hadiths* to prove it is as per Islamic law, then with the help of ten people, we drafted a *nikahnamah* on the lines of the work of Maulana Thanvi. We started working in 1994 and, after ten years, the All-India Muslim Personal Law Board issued a conditional one. This is a historic decision; after 400 years the Board has agreed to a conditional *nikahnamah*, which means women can have their conditions at the time of marriage.

(Uzma Nahid, author interview, April 2011)

Mosque entry is another contested debate concerning women's struggle for their presence in the public sphere. Activists cite the reasons why *'ulama* are against women's entry to the mosques as being stuck in the memory of the post-partition India where women's security was at risk. The new life conditions of women and their presence in education and employment necessitated their demand to access mosques. Although women are denied this access in North India and in several mosques in South India, there are many movements emerging now and demanding this right to entry, especially in Andhra Pradesh and Kerala. The Jama masjid in Delhi is an intriguing example where women have simply legitimised their presence and prayer there.

The induction of Muslim women to the public space necessitated another debate on their political roles. The discussion on women's reservations in political bodies was prevalent in both the conversations and the press. The survey I conducted showed no gender gap in favouring reservations for Muslim women. This was indicative of a strong change in the assumedly conservative mentality of Muslims and their approval of women's appearance in public spheres. No statistical correlation was established between following *fatwas* and supporting Muslim women's reservations. This stands paradoxical to the clear stance of *'ulama* on women's reservations and their rejection. However, a deeper look into the reasons why *'ulama* reject reservations for women provides the clue to this statistical result. Being one of the most influential Islamic organisations in North India, the Jamiat Ulama-i-Hind was opposing the Women Reservation Bill on the account that, if it were passed, Muslims would be the most badly affected community from this bill. In an interview in Delhi in 2012, a scholar from the Jamiat asserted that:

> Fifteen general elections have already passed, and the representation of Muslims does not exceed 8%, which accounts for a 50% deprivation level. The situation worsens when we consider the representation of Muslim women in parliament. Since the 1952 elections, only 19 Muslim women were elected. In the current Lok Sabha, there are 59 women; only two of them are Muslim. The way this Women Reservation Bill is devised guarantees that only upper-class women who are linked to corporate or political elites would be elected, which would not serve the general interests of women. A second concern is the status of backward classes and minorities. Since Muslims are not only educationally and economically backward, but also politically (representation-wise), so how would a general women reservation bill do them any good? This is why the Jamiat asks for the amendment of this bill.

When the two discourses of discrimination and security interrelates, the discussion on dress codes emerges. Of the students I interviewed, 56.1% confirmed that the headscarf or the *hijab* gives them a sense of security and sometimes even freedom. When they filled out the survey on their own, it was interesting to see how many men actually decided to answer the question, although it was directly addressed to women. This is why I chose to clearly demarcate the answers of men and women, showing that men's perception of the necessity of the *hijab* is much higher than those who are actually using it, since 76.5% of the males who answered this question gave a positive reply in favour of the *hijab*. This debate is essentially complex because, although some girls confirm that wearing the *burka* enhances their sense of safety, others mention how it makes their identity visible and thus might put them in danger:

> In Delhi, people think that those who wear *burka* or *hijab* are the worse off, but in my opinion this is one of the best things God has provided us. I feel safe in front of God, but not in this area because of my clothing style.

> There is *burka*-related discrimination. At university, there is respect for it, but in common public spaces there is not. Anyway, I do not go alone anywhere because I do not feel safe enough outside the university.

Unlike the media-influenced obsession given to the *pardah* or the *burka* as a means of women's oppression, the *burka* confinements were not projected by the students in any way in this manner. To the contrary, its privacy gave a liberating force to these girls. The major dilemma, however, was the dowry system. As I show in the next chapter, dowry is one of the nightmares in the Indian society that leads to further deterioration of the opportunities girls have. Although it is not as rampant as in the southern states, dowry in North India features as a serious predicament that is rarely addressed by Muslim organisations. To conclude, whereas gendered violence was highlighted in the police attitudes towards male youth and the significant threats this poses to a valid practice of citizenship, females were, to an extent, alleviated from these concerns but suffered from symbolic and cultural violence amplified through their access to the public sphere.

Summary

The idea of *jihād* being a mechanism for social change through education has been emphasised by contemporary Islamic scholars such as Al-Qaradawy (in his earlier studies), who disapproves of a major trend among Muslim youth manifested in abandoning their studies after obtaining progress in majors like engineering or literature or medicine, in pursuit of Islamic studies. According to Al-Qaradawy (2010):

> Such people are ignoring the fact that to pursue knowledge and to excel in a discipline is a collective obligation in Islam. It should also be observed that the competition between Muslims and non-Muslims for mastery of the secular sciences is at its fiercest. When a Muslim seeks to learn, excel, and acquire insight in such sciences for the sake of God he is actually engaging in worship and *jihād*.

(p. 148)

Indian Muslim youth presents us with an alternative image, an image that has understood this message and is applying it. Most of the *madrasa* students I have met started pursuing studies in secular sciences after they had finished their religious education. They realised that education is a means to the betterment of their lives and future generations, in order to fill the gap of the middle class that has been void during partition.

The serious setback that remains in this attempt of social change is the collective memory and sentiment of discrimination and injustice. The space, where ideas of citizenship can flourish, suffers from the presence of an abyss that alienates Muslims and targets them as 'different'. Nevertheless, this research proved that, against intuitive generalisations, Muslims do not succumb to these hurdles, and they attempt to assert their citizenship and their sense of national identity, albeit through alternative mechanisms that endorse 'cultural' or religious aspects through constitutional measures. Before moving on to consider my second case study of Malayalee Muslim women, it would be appropriate to end this chapter with the words of an ordinary woman – a female teacher in a Jamaati Islami school, but in her conviction, a *jihādist*:

> We cannot remain silent, and we cannot get our rights just by sitting. Islam talks about *jihad*. So as per our religion, we are encouraged to get our rights. We, women, go to people's houses and we spread the knowledge of Islam. In *our India*, women are doing a lot about religion; groups have been created to spread Islam. We are not high and low; we are one. These divisions among Muslims are wrong. What is in the *hadith*? Anyone who loves Hussain also loves me. And in *our India*, and in Islam, no one has the right to force someone. They only have the right to speak.
>
> (Delhi, September 2010)

Notes

1 The first word or order that God revealed to the Prophet Muhammad (*pbuh*) via Gabriel, the archangel, was 'Read'. There are also several sayings (*hadith*) by the Prophet Muhammad elevating the importance of knowledge. Among them are the following: "The ink of a man of knowledge is more worthy than the blood of the martyr"; "To spend more time in learning is better than spending more time praying; the support of religion is abstinence. It is better to teach knowledge one hour in the night than to pray all night"; "That person who shall die while he is studying, in order to revive the knowledge of religion, will be only one degree inferior to the prophets"; "The acquisition of knowledge is a duty incumbent on every Muslim, male and female"; "One who covers a way in search of knowledge Allah will lead him to the paradise." There is also considerable reference in the Quran and *hadith* to the importance of *'ulama* and authorities of knowledge: "*'Ulama* are the heirs of the Prophets" and "An A'alim is the trustee of Allah on this earth."

2 Jamia Millia Islamia only acquired the minority institution status in February 2011. This meant that 50% of its seats are reserved for Muslim students.

3 It is difficult to locate a specific size of the Indian middle class; however, Zoya Hasan (2001) points out a study that marks this class as around 20–25% of the population, including 13% of the rural and 42% of the urban households.

4 For a detailed study on the history of Nadwa, see Malik (1997). Other important studies referring to Nadwa are: Hasan (1997, 2002); Noor et al. (2009); Ahmad (2008); Winkelman (2005); Sikand (2006b).

5 As a contemporary scholar, Al-Qaradawy (2010) stresses this aspect of moderation due to the rising extremism among Muslim youth. According to him:

> The Muslim *Ummah* is a nation of justice and moderation which testifies against every deviation from the 'straight path' in this life and in the hereafter. Islamic texts call upon Muslims to exercise moderation and to reject and oppose all kinds of extremism: ghuluw (excessiveness), tanaṭṭu' (nitpicking religiosity) and tashdīd (strictness, austerity). A close examination of such texts shows that Islam emphatically warns against ghuluw. Let us consider the following: "Beware in excessiveness in religion. [People] before you have perished as a result of [such] excessiveness." The people referred to above are the people of other religions, "particularly people of the Book", namely, Jews and Christians, and most notably the Christians.
>
> (p. 9)

6 ISI refers to the Inter-Services Intelligence of Pakistan.
7 Reformist or Mujahid-related schools offer Islamic classes in Arabic and Malayalam as part of an integrated educational system.
8 The news on this *madrasa* in West Bengal is quoted from the *Indian Express*, 19 January 2009, in Indian Social Institute (2009).
9 The Sachar Report had also stated that statistical data seem to counter the commonly held perceptions that Muslims prefer religious education in *madrasas* since only about 3% of all Muslim students of the school-going age group are enrolled in *madrasas* at the all-India level (Sachar Committee Report, 2006).
10 A Turkish female scholar who delivered lectures at Jamia in 1935.
11 www.thehindu.com/opinion/letters/article2444845.ece (accessed 12 September 2011).
12 In January 2011, a thirty-year-old mosque was demolished in Delhi near Nizamuddin area by the government because, according to a Court decision, it had stood on government land. The Muslim authorities claimed that it was *waqf* land, but that they had lost the case in court due to inadequate legal defence, and had argued that the government could have at least offered to sell the area instead of demolishing the mosques (*HT*, 13 January 2011, www.hindustantimes.com/India-news/NewDelhi/Will-allow-prayers-at-mosque-site/Article1-650075.aspx).
13 Accounts of these victims are available in the National Commission of Minorities Report, available at http://ncm.nic.in/pdf/Mecca_Masjid.pdf (accessed 12 August 2012).
14 *Times of India*, Batla Cries Police Brutality, Shuts Down, 29 February 2012, http://timesofindia.indiatimes.com/city/delhi/Batla-cries-police-brutality-shuts-down/article show/12076197.cms; *The Sunday Guardian*, Jamia Residents Come Together Against Police Raids, 28 February 2012, www.sunday-guardian.com/news/jamia-residents-come-together-against-police-raids; *The Sunday Guardian*, Jamia Nagar Lives in Fear After a Series of Police Raids, 26 February 2012, www.sunday-guardian.com/investigation/jamia-nagar-lives-in-fear-after-a-series-of-police-raids#.T0yPvYMYow0.twitter.

References

Ahmad, I. (2008). Power, Purity and the Vanguard: Educational Ideology of the Jama'at-i Islami of India. In J. Malik (ed.), *Madrasas in Asia: Teaching Terror?* (pp. 142–164). London: Routledge.

Ahmad, I., & Reifeld, H. (2001). *Middle Class Values in India and Western Europe*. New Delhi: Social Science Press.

Al-Nadwi, A. A. A. (2002). *Qimat Al-Ummah Al-Islāmiyyah: Munjizātiha wa waq'ha almu'āssir (The Value of the Muslim Ummah: Its Achievements and Contemporary Reality)*, Second Edition. Lucknow: Almajma' Al-lslami Al-'ilmi.

Al-Nadwi, A. A. A. (2005). *Al-Sirā' Baina Al-fikrah Al-Islāmiyyah wal fikrah al-gharbiyyah fil aqtār al-islāmiyyah (Conflict: Between Islamic and Western Thought in Muslim Regions)*, Fourth Edition. Lucknow: Almajma Al'ilmy (first published 1965).

Al-Nadwi, A. A. A. (2006). *Al-Muslimūn fil Hind (Muslims in India)*, Third Edition. Lucknow: Almajma' Al-lslami Al-'ilmi.

Al-Nadwi, A. A. A. (2010) *Matha khasar al'ālam bi inhitāt almuslimīn (What Did the World Lose by the Deterioration of Muslims?)*, Eighth Edition. Lucknow: Almajma' Al-lslami Al-'ilmi.

Al-Nadwi, M. A.-r. (2008). *Nadtwatul Ulama: Al-mafhūm wal iqtirāb (Nadwatul Ulama: Its Concept and Approach)*, Third Edition. Lucknow: Almajma Al'ilmy.

Al-Qaradawy, Y. (2010). *Islamic Awakening Between Rejection and Extremism.* Kuala Lumpur: Islamic Book Trust.

Alam, A. (2008a). Beyond Rhetoric: Understanding Contemporary Madrasas. In N. Hasnain (ed.), *Beyond Textual Islam* (pp. 282–295). New Delhi: Serials.

Alam, A. (2008b). Making Muslims: Identity and Difference in Indian Madrasas. In J. Malik (ed.), *Madrasas in South Asia: Teaching Terror* (pp. 45–60). London: Routledge.

Aleaz, B. (2005). Madrasa Education, State and Community Consciousness: Muslims in West Bengal. *Economic and Political Weekly*, 40(6), 555–564.

Ali, M. (2012, 26 January). *War on Terror: If you Can't Find the Terrorist, Make One.* Retrieved on 27 January 2012, from Two Circles: http://twocircles.net/2012jan26/war_terror_if_you_can't_find_terrorist_make_one.html.

Ansari, N. (1999). *Choosing to Stay: Memoirs of an Indian Muslim* (R. Russel, Trans.). Karachi: City Press.

Arendt, H. (1951). *The Origins of Totalitarianism.* New York: Harcourt, Brace and Co.

Baudrillard, J. (1998). *The Consumer Society: Myths and Structures.* London: Sage Publications.

Bayat, A. (2009). *Life as Politics: How Ordinary People Change the Middle East.* Cairo: The American University in Cairo Press.

Bennabi, M. (2002). *On the Origins of Human Society: The Social Relations Network* (M. E.-T. El-Mesawi, Trans.). Kuala Lumpur: Islamic Book Trust (first published 1962).

Béteille, A. (2001). The Social Character of the Indian Middle Class. In I. Ahmad & H. Reifeld (eds), *Middle Class Values in India and Western Europe* (pp. 73–85). New Delhi: Social Science Press.

Bhatia, B. M. (1994). *India's Middle Class Role in Nation Building.* New Delhi: Konark.

Chatterjee, P. (2004). *The Politics of the Governed: Reflections on Popular Politics in Most of the World.* Delhi: Permanent Black.

Daechsel, M. (2006). *The Politics of Self-Expression: The Urdu Middle-Class Milieu in Mid-Twentieth-Century India and Pakistan.* London: Routledge.

Das, G. (2002). *India Unbound: From Independence to the Global Information Age.* New Delhi: Penguin.

Fahimuddin. (2008). Rationale of Modernization of Madrasa Education in India. In N. Hasnain (ed.), *Beyond Textual Islam* (pp. 298–323). New Delhi: Serials.

Fernandes, L. (2006). *India's New Middle Class: Democratic Politics in an Era of Economic Reform.* Minneapolis: University of Minnesota Press.

Fromm, E. (1941). *Escape from Freedom.* New York: Farrar and Rinehart.

Gill, S. (2008). *Islam and the Muslims of India: Exploring History, Faith and Dogma.* New Delhi: Penguin.

Hansen, T. B. (2000). Predicaments of Secularism: Muslim Identities and Politics in Mumbai. *Journal of the Royal Anthropological Institute*, 6(2), 255–272.

Hartung, J.-P. (2006). The Nadwat al-'ulama: Chief Patron of Madrasa Education and a Turntable to the Arab World. In J.-P. Hartung & H. Reifeld (eds), *Islamic Education, Diversity, And National Identity: Dini Madaris in India Post 9/11* (pp. 135–157). New Delhi: Sage.

Hasan, M. (1997). *Legacy of a Divided Nation: India's Muslims Since Independence.* Delhi: Oxford University Press.

Hasan, M. (2002). *Islam in the Subcontinent: Muslims in a Plural Society.* Delhi: Manohar.

Hasan, M., & Jalil, R. (2006). *Partners in Freedom: Jamia Millia Islamia.* New Delhi: Nyogi Books.

Hasan, Q. (1987). *Muslims in India: Attitudes, Adjustments and Reactions.* New Delhi: Northern Book Centre.

Hasan, Z. (2001). Changing Political Orientations of the Middle Classes in India. In I. Ahmad & H. Reifeld (eds), *Middle Class Values in India and Western Europe* (pp. 152–170). New Delhi: Social Science Press.

Indian Social Institute. (2009). *Minorities: Muslims 2009 – Human Rights Documenta-tion.* Retrieved on 10 January 2012, from www.isidelhi.org.in/hrnews/isidownload/Muslim/Muslims-2009.pdf.

Iqbal (1908/1990). *Kulliyyaat-i-Iqbal* (Urdu). Lahore: Iqbal Academy Pakistan.

Jaffrelot, C. (2008). Why Should We Vote?: The Indian Muddle Class and the Function-ing of the World's Largest Democracy. In C. Jaffrelot & P. Van der Veer (eds), *Pat-terns of Middle Class Consumption in India and China* (pp. 35–54). London: Sage.

Jamia Millia Islamia. (2011). *Annual Report.* New Delhi: Jamia Millia Islamia.

Jamia Millia Islamia. (2012). *Statistical Data Fact Sheet.* New Delhi: Jamia Millia Islamia.

Khan, A. M. (2010). *Text and Context: Quran and Contemporary Challenges.* New Delhi: Rupa and Co.

Khan, G. A. (2004). *History of Islamic Education in India and Nadvat Ul-'Ulama.* New Delhi: Kitab Bhavan.

Khan, M. N. (2010, 1–15 September) Congress and BJP Hand-in-Hand in Political Iftar. *The Milli Gazette*, p. 1.

Kymlicka, W., & Norman, W. (1994). Return of the Citizen: A Survey of Recent Work on Citizenship Theory. *Ethics*, 104(2), 352–381.

Madani, A. (2012). *Jamiatulama e hind ki khadamāt (The Services of Jamiat Ulama e Hind).* New Delhi: Jamiat Ulama e Hind Publications.

Maira, S., & Soep, E. (eds) (2005). *Youthscapes: The Popular, the National, the Global.* Philadelphia: University of Pennsylvania Press.

Malik, J. (1997). *Islamische Gelehrtenkultur in Nordindien: Entwicklungsgeschichte und Tendenzen am Beispiel von Lucknow.* Leiden: Brill.

Metcalf, B. (2007). Madrasas and Minorities in Secular India. In R. W. Hefner & M. Q. Zaman (eds), *Schooling Islam: The Culture and Politics of Modern Muslim Education* (pp. 87–106). Princeton and Oxford: Princeton University Press.

Misra, B. B. (1961). *The Indian Middle Classes: Their Growth in Modern Times.* London: Oxford University Press.

Mujeeb, M. (1967). *The Indian Muslims.* London: George Allen and Unwin.

National Family Health Survey. (2005–06). International Institute for Population Sciences Deonar, Mumbai.

Noor, F. A., Sikand, Y., & van Bruinessen, M. (eds) (2009). *The Madrasa in Asia: Polit-ical Activism and Transnational Linkages.* Amsterdam: Amsterdam University Press.

Pandey, M. T. (2010). *Globalization and the Indian Urban Middle Class: The Emerging Trend.* Delhi: Uppal Publishing House.

Polanki, P. (2010, 1–15 May). Afroz Alam Sahil – the RTI Maverick. *The Milli Gazette,* p. 7

Qasmi, M. K. (2005). *Madrasa Education: Its Strength and Weakness.* Mumbai: MMERC and Manak.

Rothermund, D. (2008). *India: The Rise of an Asian Giant.* New Haven and London: Yale University Press.

Rudolph, S., & Rudolph, H. (1987). *The Modernity of Tradition: Political Development in India.* Chicago: University of Chicago Press.

Sachar Committee Report. (2006). *Social, Economic and Educational Status of the Muslim Community of India.* Prime Minister's High Level Committee Cabinet Secretariat, Government of India.

Setalvad, T. (2010, 10 September). Speech at the Jamia Teachers Solidarity Association's National Convention on The Politics of Terrorism and Suspicion: Two Years after the Batla House Encounter. Jamia Millia Islamia, New Delhi.

Seth, S. (2001). Constituting the 'Backward but Proud Muslim': Pedagogy, Governmentality and Identity in Colonial India. In M. Hasan & N. Nakazato (eds), *The Unfinished Agenda: Nation Building in South Asia* (pp. 129–149). New Delhi: Manohar.

Shahabuddin, S. (2004, 16 December). *The Muslim Face of the BJP.* Retrieved on 11 November 2009, from The Milli Gazette, www.milligazette.com/Archives/2004/16-31Dec04-Print-Edition/163112200450.htm.

Sikand, Y. (2004). *Muslims in India Since 1947: Islamic Perspectives on Interfaith Relations.* London: RoutledgeCurzon.

Sikand, Y. (2005). The Indian Madrassahs and the Agenda of Reform. *Journal of Muslim Minority Affairs,* 25(2), 219–248.

Sikand, Y. (2006a). Indian Madrasas and 'Terrorism': Myths, Realities and Responses. In N. Hasnain (ed.), *Aspects of Islam and Muslim Societies* (pp. 211–240). New Delhi: Serials.

Sikand, Y. (2006b). Sayyed Abul Hasan 'Ali Nadwi and Contemporary Islamic Thought in India. In I. Abu-Rabi' (ed.), *The Blackwell Companion to Contemporary Islamic Thought* (pp. 88–104). Oxford: Blackwell.

Sikand, Y. (2009). Voices for Reform in the Indian Madrasas. In F. A. Noor, Y. Sikand & M. van Bruinessen (eds), *The Madrasa in Asia: Political Activism and Transnational Linkages* (pp. 31–65). Amsterdam: Amsterdam University Press.

Sikand, Y. (2011, 3 February). *Human Rights Activists Denounce Hindutva Terror.* Retrieved on 4 February 2011, from New Age Islam, http://NewAgeIslam.com/current-affairs/human-rights-activists-denounce-hindutva-terror/d/4052.

Varma, P. (2001). Middle-Class Values and The Creation of a Civil Society. In I. Ahmad & R. Helmut (eds), *Middle Class Values in India and Western Europe* (pp. 86–92). New Delhi: Social Science Press.

Varma, P. (2007). *The Great Indian Middle Class.* New Delhi: Penguin Books India.

Winkelman, M. J. (2005). *'From Behind the Curtain': A Study of a Girls' Madrasa in India.* Amsterdam: Amsterdam University Press.

5 Argumentative *jihād* and Muslim women in Kerala

One day in Kerala, I got the following mobile text message from a Malayalee female student: "An Afghani woman was asked why she felt it necessary to walk five feet behind her husband. She answered: 'Landmines'."

Although the setting is Afghanistan, the inherent message crosses borders as women caricature the prevalent discourses on backwardness. Both the creator and the sender of the text message apparently intended to resist the ways Muslim women are portrayed. I searched for this joke on the internet trying to locate its origins and, most interestingly, I found an older variation of it. The context was post-Gulf War Kuwait in 1991. In the older joke, a journalist had noticed that, before the war, women used to walk behind their husband; after the war, however, it was the men who walked ten feet behind their wives. When the journalist asked one of the women how they managed to create this change, the woman simply replied, "Landmines". Just as this joke reflects a paradox in gender roles and how historically there has been an ebb-and-tide-like liberalisation, configuration and misconfiguration of gender roles, this chapter deals with the paradoxes in the lives of Muslim women in Kerala (the female Malayalee). In this chapter, I start by presenting the inherent differences between the political culture and history of Kerala and North India. Then I refer to the characteristics and the paradoxes of the Kerala model, and eventually I highlight the most significant collective actors in shaping the conceptual and contextual frameworks of *jihād*, citizenship and women's agency, in which Islam is a clear ingredient of the plot for protest and social change.

The Kerala model

> You will find monuments of Muslims in North India, but you will find Islam in Kerala.
>
> (Interview with a lecturer and youth activist in the ISM [itihadul shubanul mujahideen, Union for Mujahid Youth] in Kozhikode)

Being the most south-western region in India, Kerala had direct access to the Arab world via the Arabian Sea. This culminated in a trade-based history that goes back, in certain accounts, even before the time of the emergence of Islam in the Arabian Peninsula in the seventh century. The six northern districts of what is today known as Kerala comprise the historical area named Malabar, which is now dominantly populated by Muslims. This chapter focuses on fieldwork undertaken in two districts of Malabar, namely Malappuram and Kozhikode (also known as Calicut, but Malayalees use the original name Kozhikode).

Kerala has a population of 33,387,677 (Census, 2011) and, according to the 2001 census, the religion-based divisions were as follows: Hindu (56.2%), Muslim (24.7%) and Christian (19%). Muslim Sufi saints and missionaries among the Arab settlers contributed to the consolidation of Islam in Kerala. The growth of the coastal town of Ponnani, 'the little Mecca of Malabar', for example, as a Muslim centre, is related to the Sufi Saint Ibn Abdul Qadir Jilani (1077–166) (Abdul Samad, 1998, p. 9). In its small area of twenty-seven square kilometres, there are eighty-six mosques. It is argued that people lived in the same way as they did in Mecca earlier, and Islamic studies were taught in mosques and affiliated *madrasas* (Abdulrahmankutty, author interview, March 2011).[1]

The elaboration of a different political culture

If you are able to forget the dirt and the squalor for the time being, a memorable experience is awaiting you there. You will see some of the unique examples of medieval Kerala architecture in the mosques and big residential houses. You cannot find these Kerala types of mosques anywhere else in India or anywhere in the world, because they resemble Hindu temples though they were built as mosques. They are neither entirely Muslim nor entirely Hindu in character. It can only be described as 'Medieval Kerala' style, as it is common to Hindu, Muslim and Christian places of worship and residence.

(Narayanan, 2006)

This distinctive historical context resulted in the elaboration of a different political culture in Kerala. The Mughal Empire, for example, did not appear in the history of Kerala and hence did not impact on the collective memory of Mappilas as it did with the North Indian Muslims. In this section, I summarise the main points of difference in the political culture. It has to be noted first that different schools of Islamic thought and jurisprudence left their impact on the way Malayalees perceive their identity and establish global routes to it. In Kerala, Muslims historically belonged to the Shafi' branch of Sunni Islam, while the rest of the Indian Muslims are Hanafi. Since the Hanafi school had more influence in the Mughal Empire, Islamic treaties in this part were written in Persian. However, the Shafi' school has direct links to the Arab world and language, and this explains the emphasis on learning Arabic among the Malayalees, which is not equally stressed among the Urdu-speaking Muslims.

Language thus played a crucial role in the distinction of identity. Whereas the literary heritage of North Indian Muslims was carried through Urdu, Kerala's Muslims developed a unique language called Arabi-Malayalam, which is still in use today.[2] Arabi-Malayalam was also a reason why Kerala witnessed cultural integration between Hindus and Muslims as the Muslims spoke the same language but developed Arabi-Malayalam as a strategy to strike a balance between their Islamic identity and their nationalist drive against the colonial powers.

There is a geographical paradox contributing to the understanding of Kerala's complex political culture. It is often argued that the sea on one side and the mountain range on the other were the reason that Kerala was difficult to conquer during wars and led to its isolation (A. Ahsan, author interview, April 2011), and hence the preservation of Mappila culture and language. On the other hand, Kerala's openness on the western side to the sea has resulted in the reception of influences from many parts of the world, especially the Arab one it is facing. Judaism, Christianity and Islam, hence, came to Kerala via the sea (Miller, 1976).

The different ways Keralites interacted with the Muslims who came as traders via the sea precipitated in a different Islamic culture. Historical narratives account for how Kerala rulers welcomed the Muslim and Jewish traders who came for the spice trade. Hence, the Keralite culture was shaped by this interaction between diverse people coming peacefully in sailing boats from different communities, speaking different languages, belonging to different religions; and the competition in hospitality and reception of these foreigners. Although foreigners are usually an unwelcome category in global historical records, in Kerala they were regarded with utmost hospitality due to their economic value and the precious goods they came with to trade for spices. The host versus guest relationship characterised the cultural history of Kerala. This ease in mixing with others eventually led to two results: first, the current phenomenon of an increase in the rate of migration; second, the absence of a strong base of popularity of right-wing political parties. Neither the Hindu right-wing, the BJP, nor the Muslim right-wing, the People's Democratic Party (PDP) or the Social Democratic Party of India (SDPI), managed to secure seats in Kerala. Upon commenting on the high number of posters plastered on the walls in the streets of Ponnani just before the Legislative Assembly Elections, I was told that the PDP and SDPI exist only on the walls of Kerala but not in people's hearts. The same, to a certain extent, is valid for the BJP.

> The BJP has not managed to win a single seat until now in the Legislative Assembly in Kerala, although they rule the neighbouring state. The reason for that is the history of Kerala. Since the time of Solomon there were cultural and trade relations with others. In the poem of Imru' Al-Qais,[3] he mentions the Indian black pepper, so this is a proof that even before Islam, there were relations between the Arab world and India, and traders always require a peaceful atmosphere for the trade to flourish. The Zamorin Kings have encouraged the spread of Islam among the fishermen by stipulating that at least one member of each family should be a Muslim. This was to encourage trade and sailing away from India because according to Hindu beliefs, crossing the Indian Ocean is against Hinduism.
>
> (K. M. Mohammad, author interview, February 2011)

Despite these different historical legacies, both Gandhi's non-cooperation movement and the Khilafat movement found strong resonance in Malabar. Although *'ulama* played equally significant roles in the freedom and anti-colonial struggle, the collective memory of martyrdom evolves in the Keralite context more vividly than in the North Indian context. Qasmi (2005) refers to the fact that the word *Maulavi* became synonymous with rebel in the British dictionary, since 51,200 out of 200,000 martyrs during the Delhi massacre that followed the 1857 rebellion were *'ulama* (p. 26). However, these *'ulama* were not properly registered in Muslim historical records. Contrary to this, in Kerala, the *'ulama* who participated in the Moplah rebellion were revered as martyrs and their graves have been turned into shrines in different parts of Malabar.[4]

The roles these *'ulama* played in the freedom struggle have been recorded in many historical studies both in English and in Malayalam (see, for example, Abdul Samad, 1998; Dale, 1980; Engineer, 1995; Kunju, 1989; Kurup & Ismail, 2008; Miller, 1976; Randathani, 2007). Wood (1987), in his study of the Moplah rebellion, reiterates how *'ulama*, or 'Moplah divines' as he calls them, endorsed sanctioning the rebellion by "blessing combatants, weapons, forays and in fact almost any activity the rebels chose to undertake in the name of 'Islam'" (p. 198). In other words, the *'ulama* were "the legitimisers of an act of revolt which was the instrument of the ambition of the Ernad Moplah community at large for the creation of an 'Islamic' Raj of justice" (ibid., p. 199).

This interesting hybridisation of Islam and nationalism was also manifested in other forms. Ottappilakkool (2007), in his PhD thesis, found records of Muslim nationalists emphasising that only *Khadi* dress would be worn for *Eidulfitr*.[5] The following is an excerpt from the speech of the secretary of the Kerala Vidyarti Sangham, addressing the Muslims:

> Revered Muslim brothers and sisters, are not we enjoined to abide by the principles laid down by the majority opinions of the *'ulama* of the particular period? And wearing Khadi is a matter unanimously exhorted by all the famous *'ulama* of India. If we examine many other factors too, wearing Khadi is a must even for a Muslim baby now.... Allah the Almighty has asked us not to help and support in sinful and anti-Islamic activities, therefore, wearing Khadi is part of Islamic duties brothers and sisters. This Eid is a good chance for you too to exhibit your true faith. Please do not waste this golden chance. Please do not be deceived.
>
> (Reproduced from P. P. Mohammad Koya, Parappil, Kozhikotte Muslimkalude Charitram [in Malayalam], 1997, quoted in Ottappilakkool, 2007)

Another form of how Islamic principles were employed in the freedom struggle is exemplified in the *jihād*-based mobilisation. In the fight against the Portuguese, an important treatise titled *Tuhfatul Mujahideen*[6], written by Sheikh Zainuddin Makhdoum, is considered the first historical account by a Mappila historian in Arabic, in which he narrated the caste-oriented communities of

Kerala, the beginning of Mappila settlements and their encounters against the Portuguese in a form of *jihād*. This work still has great relevance in promoting an anti-imperialist ideology since it is still taught in Islamic colleges in Kerala.

The *jihād* initiated by the Mappilas against the Portuguese was not initiated to "convert a Darul Harb into Darul Islam but to strengthen the authority of a Hindu ruler" (Kurup, 2006, p. 14). Kerala's history has multiple examples of the support and allegiance Muslims showed towards their non-Muslim rulers. In the years between 1579 and 1607, Qazi Muhammad Abdul Aziz composed the *Fathul Mubin* poem that gave an account of the war between the Portuguese and the Zamorin supported by the Mappilas and showed the strong loyalty Muslims carried to the Zamorin ruler.

Eventually, with the advent of British colonialism, the *'ulama* again raised the call for *jihād* against the British. The rebels secured their blessings and were considered martyrs (*shahīd*) once dead, "for them, the fight against the British was both a holy one and a struggle for existence" (Abdul Samad, 1998, p. 17).

The different role of *'ulama* led to another type of political consciousness among the Muslims in Kerala. Being historically grouped into different organisations, Muslim masses could clearly identify the political orientations of each group. What has been obvious is how these groups have been static in their political choices, unlike their northern counterparts whose allegiance differs with every election. Some Malayalees refer to the difference in literacy rates among Muslims and hence in Kerala; Muslims are thus able to read the Quran and their reliance on the *'ulama* is not as high as in the North. Therefore, they could not be used as vote banks and are not easily politically mobilised.

The picture is nevertheless not as straightforward as this. In an interview, sociologist Hafiz Mohamed asserted how Muslims in Kerala are generally divided into three groups according to their attitudes to Muslim issues. The first group contains those with an organisational background. They have conditioned ideas and do not spur any agitation against their own leaders or criticism of their own policies; they are the most powerful group and are also numerically strong. Having their own media, organisational platforms and sources of funding are other factors of their political strength. The second group could be termed the liberal Muslims, who are not associated with any group and who share a background of Indian nationalism. Their opinions are influenced by nationalists like Azad and Mohammad Abdurahman Sahib from the INC. They are usually shunned socially and are unable to go against the fort-like organisational ideas. Finally, there are the naturally quiet or non-affiliated Muslims who share an indifferent attitude and would not cast reactive responses that involve going against the general will of Muslims.

The educational level of Muslim women was seen as both a reason and a result of the differences between the North and South. In a speech by the president of the Muslim Educational Society in Kerala (MES), Fazal Ghafoor, a reference made to women's social roles was significant. He remarked that, in Kerala, there was no culture of dancers or courtesans like in North India; there is not a single Muslim female actress from Kerala. He boasts the fact that in

Kerala, in all educational institutions, Muslim girls outnumber boys both quantitatively and qualitatively in grades. Jokingly, he comments, "We are actually thinking of converting this college into a men's college."[7]

The backwardness of women educationally, politically, socially and economically in North India was, in the opinion of many interview respondents, a result of these different roles played by the *'ulama*. In the North, *'ulama* prohibited (and are still prohibiting) the mixing of the sexes in public spaces. This was the case historically in Kerala where women's roles have been limited, to a large extent, to the kitchen, and they could neither learn English nor their local language.[8] As would be shown, the reformists in Kerala, or the Mujahids as they are commonly known, were the first to call for women to come out of their homes and into the schools. This movement was started in Malappuram in Areecode in the 1940s by Shaikh Abdulsalam Maulvi, the founder of *jamiat ulmujahideen*. He called for at least one woman from every family to be sent to school. This resulted in 90% of women being educated and working in all fields (I. P. Abdul Salam, ISM, author interview, January 2011).

What was noticeable in Kerala was the strong relevance of social capital and solidarity. The Keralite society is a rural one in which community ties are very strong; there is the *Kudumbasree* (the micro finance system), the *imam* coming to each house for a day in the month to have his meals and give the family his blessings, the marriage broker who anchors the circle of arranged early marriage, the police superintendent who has friendly relations with everyone and where matters function informally.[9] The higher standard of living supported by Gulf money led to more opportunities where social work envisioned in charity and establishing orphanages flourished. There are many institutions in Kerala, especially in Kozhikode, that have orphanages for Gujarati and Kashmiri Muslim children.[10]

On the contemporary political level, Kerala's political culture has been historically characterised with the history of communist parties and the resulting political activation in a strike culture and high voting turnouts. In Heller's (2000) analysis, democracy works better in Kerala to a large extent due to multiple factors concerning literacy, informed participation, civil society and unionisation.

In Malabar, and specifically in Kozhikode and Malappuram districts, the Indian Union Muslim League party is a unique feature.[11] The involvement of Muslims in government and local politics, regardless of their party affiliation, was another reason for the difference. Being visible as ministers and involved in decision-making gave a sense of empowerment and efficacy that is absent from the North Indian case.

The integration of the different religious groups in Kerala was the most apparent reason for the difference in political culture. According to Kurup and Ismail (2008), this was evident in the following themes. First, social practices were associated with matrilineality, especially in inheritance (which is contrary to Islamic *shari'ah*) and matrilocal residence, where the husband moves to live in his in-laws' house. This is, however, limited to the northern area of Kerala, and specifically in Kannur district and an area in Kozhikode city. A second theme features in Hindu customs, such as the tying of *Tali* in connection with marriage celebrations and the observance of harvest festivals like *Onam* and *Puthari*. The observance of *Nerchas* and offerings to saints and divines seeking blessings is a clear impact of this cultural integration.

The mosque architecture also reflects the Mappila community's integration in Kerala since the artisans and craftsmen who built these mosques were Hindu and thus employed the knowledge they had of how to build Hindu temples (Kurup & Ismail, 2008). One sees how the mosques and temples are discrete in the sense that they blend with the housing architectural style, and one cannot easily discern the difference between a *palli*[12] and a house. This is, however, true in the case of small villages and historical towns like Ponnani, but as one goes to the semi-urban centres, one sees the dominating Persian structure of mosques.[13] The new feature is the establishment and transformation of already established mosques into an Indo-Saracen style of architecture. This is due to the flow of Gulf money. The rise of the Babri Masjid disputes and the recent claims that some of the mosques used to be Hindu temples have also led to the revivalist movement in the Islamisation of mosque architecture in Kerala.

There is an apparent process of utilising religion differently by Muslim leaders in India. While reading about the history of the controversy concerning *Vande Mataram*, I asked the housewife whom I live with if she knew this song. She answered:

> Of course! At school in the morning they sing it and in the afternoon they sing *Jana Gana Mana*. There are three important songs, which we all know: *Jana Gana Mana*, *Vande Mataram* and *Sari Jahan*. All these are associated with the Constituent Assembly and are all-India songs.

When I told her that in North India, some Muslims say that singing the *Vande Mataram* is *harām*, she looked at me puzzled, and said, "But it is not a Hindu song, it is for all of India."

Arif Khan (2010) mentions how it was Jinnah and the Muslim League that had started opposing this song because of the opposition to the idea of *swaraj* and not that of being anti-Islamic. Seeing this housewife's reaction confirms the fact that partition-related history has little resonance in Keralite society. We cannot consider any factor of unawareness since this same woman is well aware of the position of Muslim *'ulama* on many issues like television, education and marriage. But it also proves that, in Kerala, the Muslim *'ulama* refrain from giving their opinion on political issues.

Dress habits are another feature of difference. Although now it has radically changed due to the introduction of the *pardah* among the majority of Muslim women, Malayalees in general wear a *sari* on their official and festive occasions.[14] This is, however, a superficial outlook to the reality of dress-based differentiation.[15] One sees clear identity markers starting from schools where Muslim girls differ in dressing style from non-Muslims and are always required to wear a headscarf. This is enhanced in private schools with Muslim management, where both boys and girls are differentiated. The following is an example of the guidelines of a school uniform: White cap is obligatory for Muslim boys, while for girls it differs according to their age. From the age of one till ten, it is a *salwar qameez* suit. Above ten it is a *pardah* with a headscarf.

Whereas the Babri Masjid controversy occupied a huge space in North Indians' socio-political psyche, it had a minor impact on the actions of Muslims (a majority of whom had repeatedly emphasised the role of the Muslim League in containing the anger). In addition to this, there is a fascinating hybrid manifestation of the unique political identity Keralite Muslims possess. During my fieldwork, I went to a celebration of the Indian Republic Day in a *madrasa*. The *madrasa* had organised an evening programme on this occasion and included folklore Muslim dancing and chanting of Muslim Sufi poetry praising the Prophet. Figure 5.1 is a photo taken of one of these performances depicting a hybrid form of martial art called *kolkali*.[16] Just as these forms of art reflect the long history of accommodation with a different culture and religion, it is argued that the Muslim Keralites have sustained a hybrid political identity in which secularism is interestingly mingled with a distinct religious identity.

However, this strengthened sense of an acceptance of secular democracy is currently being challenged on account of the rising war against terrorism. As I was once told, "Malappuram now is the Kashmir of Kerala." This was in reference to the recent arrests of Muslim youth as terror suspects who are being targeted through the RSS-related process of anti-national branding. This discourse

Figure 5.1 Kolkali performance at a *madrasa* in Malappuram district on the Indian Republic Day (source: photo taken by author).

had a strong resonance among the Muslim youth in Kerala, to the extent that a hip-hop song and video was created on this topic by a group of Muslim students and was internationally circulated via YouTube.[17] With the victory of BJP and the coming to power of Modi, several Malayalees have raised their concerns over the involvement of right-wing politics in Keralite society. The arrest of a Muslim youth who did not stand up during the national anthem in a cinema hall in Trivandrum is a recent example.[18]

The transformation from aversion to secular education

Questioning the idea that modern education is the milestone of progress has been a recurrent theme in Muslim scholarship. As I showed in the previous chapter, Islamic education has been a correlative factor of social change in North India. The history of the southern state of Kerala is another testimony to the impact of Muslim scholars and education. Jeffrey (1992) comments that social change has been greater for Kerala's Mappilas than for any other community. Their literacy rates have risen dramatically, from less than 5% in 1931 to 48% in the 1970s, with almost all children attending school (pp. 110–111).

Defining literacy in the historical context of Kerala is complicated, since even today one may find women who are able to read and write only Arabic and hence Arabi-Malayalam. After the Mappila Revolt, the destiny of Arabi-Malayalam was its overnight semi-death. A backwardness discourse erupted when modern education took over violently, and Muslims were called illiterate overnight. The Muslims' ignorance of the English language pulled them back from modernisation (Abdul Samad, 1998).

In an interview, the Malayalam professor Shamshad Hussain recounts how Arabi-Malayalam emerged as a progressive language when the '*ulama* had stood against studying Malayalam (for being the language of the Hindus) and English (for being the language of the colonial power). The first novel in Kerala was in fact written in Arabi-Malayalam. For Hussain, publication of novels is a key indicator of the modernity of a language. In other communities in Kerala, while Brahmin women and Dalits were not allowed to study, Muslims had always been studying. Many magazines were written in Arabi-Malayalam. There were even women's magazines like *Nisa ul Islam*. Vakkom Moulavi, who was a nationalist freedom fighter, ran a newspaper titled *Al-Muslim* and led this movement. Modern historical records suffer from a sporadic selection of what is to be included. Hussain refers to Haleema Bibi,[19] the first female publisher, who wrote in the 1930s in the Muslim *Vaneetha*, and who is absent from the history of the renaissance of Kerala. At the age of eighteen, Heleema Bibi organised a conference on Muslim girls' education in Kerala in 1938 and stated the following:

> Surely, it is mothers who must raise children up to be citizens. When we see that the truth is that no other women are under such bondage as are women of our community, we feel ashamed about the culture of the Muslims. We should not allow ourselves to subsist on others' labour anymore, our

womanliness devastated, and remain in chains, restricted, to disfigure our community and our brothers. It is but the truth that a woman can work much more effectively for the betterment of the community than a man can.

(Haleema Beevi, 1938, cited in Devika, 2005, p. 169)[20]

Such an event is considered a vigorous attempt in an age where Muslim women could not appear in any public space. Just around ten years before Haleema Bibi spoke, learning both the Quran and Malayalam was prohibited for women. The efforts that had resulted in her speech in 1938 were basically engineered and put forward by the Muslim reformist *'ulama*. In 2011, one can see the most apparent result of their attempts, since 43.8% of the young women I interviewed (their ages ranging from sixteen to thirty-two) knew significant parts of the Quran by heart; 91.4% read the *tafsīr* or interpretation of the Quran; 25.9% went to the Jumaa prayer in the mosque on a permanent basis; and 17.5% were members of Islamic student or youth organisations.

Since this chapter focuses more on the impact of the high educational level of Kerala on women, the aspect of mobility and marriage has to be emphasised. Despite the social significance given to education, the idea of female Malayalees travelling outside of Kerala is still considered a taboo to a large extent. Upon delivering a lecture in an Arabic college in Malappuram district, one girl told me:

For Muslim girls, there are so many limitations on their mobility, we cannot travel anywhere without a male family member, we are puzzled to see you here alone, I want to know how you managed to overcome these limitations.

For them, to know that another world existed must have been painful, because then their fight would be more meaningful and stronger. When I compare them to their northern comrades, I think that North Indian girls are luckier. Their lack of education and the prison-like social control enacted upon their lives prevents them from witnessing or planning any different lives. However, these girls are subject to a different type of social control; they are well educated, well read, they know a lot about the world and the problems in their lives and, to some extent, they have the ability to bargain and negotiate. It is significant to note the way they smile so vehemently when I ask if they are married, and they shake their heads and hands negatively to assert that they won this battle; they are twenty years old and had managed to postpone the confinements of early marriage until they finish their education.

Whereas women's problems in India generally revolve around low literacy rates or malnourishment, their predicaments in Kerala relate to different and non-conventional issues, such as violence against women, low decision-making capacities from the home level to the district and state level, and hence the gender disparities in private and public spheres. A social worker, employed in the *Kerala Mahila Samakhya Society*'s (Women Equality Society) development programmes in Nilambur municipality in Malappuram district,[21] told me that women's problems were usually related to mental health, mobility and decision-making capacity. This is why they develop awareness programmes especially in legal aspects, since the power lies in the hands of the father or the husband. There is a big difference between reality and statistics. Among women, regardless of caste, enrolment in professional courses is low. Their emphasis is always on teaching or medicine. And even after completing the course, a small minority of them are allowed to pursue work. This is the case not only in the professional arena, but there are also very few women who are allowed to work in shops or agricultural fields.

During my fieldwork, I noticed that in non-Arabic or non-Islamic colleges in Malabar, the ratio of employed Muslim females to males or non-Muslim females is extremely low. For example at the MES women's college in Kozhikode, of approximately thirty teachers, only two were Muslim females. When an official was asked about this, he said that Muslim women simply do not apply.[22]

Paradoxes in the Kerala model

Whereas the Arab world was historically dependent on trade with Malabar, con-temporarily, the cultural and economic ties are reversed. Since the oil boom in the 1970s, the economical links between India and the Arab world have become dependent on labour migration to build up the newly developing Gulf states. Kerala is considered the main source of Indian labour to the Gulf and hence Kerala's economy has become reliant on remittances from Gulf migration. Since job opportunities are scarce in Kerala due to the low industrial level and the rural nature of the state, emigration seems to be the main option. However, emigration is heavily directed towards the Gulf and not towards other states of India. High levels of income that match the high consumption levels of Keralites are not the only reason for this orientation. Another major factor is the cheap daily direct flights to the Gulf, implying it is more accessible than going to Delhi (almost everyone I spoke with who was living in the Gulf had never been to Delhi).

A consideration of the facts and figures of Malappuram district is intriguing on account of having the highest Muslim population, amounting to 68.5%, and outnumbering the rest of the districts of Kerala in emigration (17.5% of emig-rants from Kerala are from Malappuram) but not in return emigration. In Kerala, 52.5% of Muslim households have one or more non-resident Keralite. In Malap-puram, 71% of the households have either an emigrant or a return emigrant. The largest amount of remittances in 2007 was received by Malappuram district, amounting to Rs.4.6 thousand crores, or 19% of the state's total. Around 50% of the remittances to the state were received by the Muslim community, which forms around 24% of the total population of the state. Malayalee Muslim resi-dents in the Gulf amount to 1.6 million. This resulted in a phenomenon, as 22.9% of married Muslim women are Gulf wives (whose husbands live and work in one of the Gulf states) (Zachariah & Rajan, 2007). One of the results of this migration is that the highest wage in India is in Kerala: 400 rupees/day (Gangadharan, author interview, January 2011). The physical quality of life index brought Kerala to the attention of development discourses as it "had anom-alously high PQLI[23] and low per capita income" (Jeffrey, 1992, p. 8).

Kerala is considered to be the land of contradictions. In comparison with other states of India, on the one hand, it has the highest levels of literacy, human development, life expectancy and income. On the other hand, it suffers from the highest levels of alcoholism, suicide, crimes and dowry. On a less formal note, while it is propagated by the Indian Tourism Authority as God's own country, a lot of teenage respondents claimed it is rather crime's and insects' own country, and God's own social paradox.[24]

On a positive note, it has the highest human development index and literacy rate in India. It is also the least corrupt state, according to Transparency International (Indian Corruption Study, 2005). Kerala also differs from other states in the appearance of Muslim women in all public spaces without the confines of localities or *burqa*. It is one of the few states in India, in addition to Tamil Nadu and Karnataka, where you can see female bus conductors and petrol station workers. However, in my visits around India, Kerala was not the only state where I saw a Muslim female bus conductor, but this was in the Muslim-majority-populated district of Malappuram. Unlike the overall sex ratio in India of 940 females per 1000 males in 2011, Kerala has the highest female ratio of 1084 females, and Malappuram has an even higher one (1098 females) due to male migration. Kerala's literacy rate is 93.91%. In Malappuram, it is 93.57%, and in Kozhikode it is 96.80%.

Several Gulf-influenced trends are central to the analysis of social change initiated in Kerala. Not only did historical trade relations result in an exchange of material goods, such as spices and wood, but the impact of trade was witnessed in the cultural goods that came, first, in artistic and literary forms (hybrid language and folklore) and then diverted to social aspects (inter-religious marriages, conversions and later women's education and dress code). In today's times and after the oil boom, this cultural exchange is not only one-sided but also consumerist to a great extent. Goods, dressing and eating styles came in a one-dimensional manner. The improving standard of living led to the proliferation of what the Malayalees call 'Gulf goods', which are mainly imported smart phones, computers, and kitchen and cooking devices.

These consumerist trends resulted in significant social changes due to the enlargement of the middle class in Kerala and extended to private healthcare and education services, induced by the Gulf remittances. Although Kerala scores high on the PQLI and Human Development Index, the privatisation of

Table 5.1 Gender statistics obtained from the Census of India and UNDP reports

Factor	Malappuram	Kerala	India
Literacy, 2011	93.57%	93.91%	74.04%
Sex ratio, 2011, per 1000 males	1098	1084	940
Female work participation rate, 2001	6.6%	15.4%	25.6%
Life expectancy (in years)	–	76	63.5
Human Development Index, 2011	–	0.920	0.547

these services ushers in serious challenges to the sustainability of the Kerala model if variables such as inequality and poverty are involved (Oommen, 2008; Wilson, 2010).

Building new houses is another trend found amongst the families of emigrants. Perhaps what is most significant about this trend is that women's agency and autonomy appear unrivalled to any other situation. Usually it is the women who are the recipients of money which their husbands send through bank transfers or Western Union, and hence are often solely responsible for all the paperwork concerning obtaining construction permits from the municipality, choosing a design for the house and managing all construction-related steps. In a survey conducted by Zachariah and Rajan in 2007, the role of the wife in managing the finances of the household was highly apparent (60% of respondents managed on their own and 69% had their own bank accounts).

During my fieldwork, I met an agent who had an authorised money-wiring office and I asked him to whom the money was usually sent. He confirmed that in 90% of the situations it is the wife. In my visits to municipality offices in Malappuram district, I often saw young women in their twenties going around with papers. I was introduced to one who was waiting to have some paperwork done, as she was the only person present there who was conversant in English. She was twenty-one, with a college degree in mathematics, a Gulf wife, and unemployed. She was doing all the paperwork for obtaining a house construction permit. Although her mother-in-law was accompanying her, it was obvious that, due to her education, she was being treated with the highest respect and was more competent than the mother-in-law.

Migration had a strong impact on the socio-cultural lives of Malayalees. Education was accorded an overriding status because there was a strong realisation that a strong educational background secures one a prestigious and highly salaried job in the Gulf. Since most of the Muslim migrants to the Gulf were traders and either low or unskilled labourers, they could easily discern the comparative advantage of their Christian and Hindu neighbours with a higher educational profile and thus a better job.

Gulf money not only led to higher rates of consumerist behaviour in Malabar, but also to higher levels of literacy and education. This is most obvious through a comparative observation of the rapid change in literacy rates over the years. Malappuram witnessed a trend of improvement in female literacy, from 86.26% in 2001 to 91.55% in 201 (higher for males: 95.78%), and in Kozhikode it was higher: from 88.62% in 2001 to 93.16% in 2011 (and 97.57% for males).

Interestingly, Malappuram was the most successful district in achieving the 'Total Literacy Campaign' launched in Kerala in 1991. Aysha, who was a newly literate Muslim woman, was selected to declare Kerala the first literate state in India (Siddique, 2005). Nilambur municipality in Malappuram was also declared the first literate village in India (at that time it had village status), with a 100% literacy rate. However, these figures hide the reality. In fact, the overall average of the Malabar area (the six northern districts) amounts to 89.22% and thus lags behind the state's average. Literacy of Muslim women in Malappuram district is only 86.3%.

A final impact of Gulf money and the networking skills of the non-resident Keralites in the Gulf was the flourishing of Islamic traditional and reformist organisations. Gulf money, whether in the form of donations from the wealthy states or from the Keralite devoted workers, is used to build mosques and organise welfare programmes and conferences, in addition to both religious and secular colleges. It is considered the backbone of all the religious organisations in Kerala. It is argued that, if this flow of money were stopped, these organisations would collapse (Hafiz Mohamed, author interview, March 2011).

The gender paradox

Look at the international day for women, there was a photo in the Manorama newspaper about a conference on that day. The front seats were empty; the women chose to sit in the back seats because they were shy. This is our problem in India; women are too shy to demand their own rights and to come to the front seats. Women are underdeveloped in India and they are under men's control, especially because of domestic violence.

(A female student at a paramedical college in Malappuram district, responding to my question on problems in Kerala, March 2011)

Kerala's model of development is associated with a gender paradox. This paradox refers to the notable absence of women, especially Muslim women, from public spheres in Kerala. The same population, which has incredibly high rates of literacy, suffers from under-representativeness, unemployment, caste oppression, religious restrictions, and sexual and domestic violence (Siddique, 2005). Interestingly, in this cited edited volume about writings on Muslim women in India (Hassan & Menon, 2005), unlike all the articles, the only article written on Kerala is written by a male. This is symbolic of the situation in Kerala, where the scope for structural opportunities for women is, to a large extent, absent.

In my conversations with women and girls in villages, I tried to identify their priorities by asking them to choose what is most crucial for them: education, marriage or physical security. The answers were mostly contradictory. Although security was the dominant answer, education came second. It seemed paradoxical that, in the only state in India where women outnumber men, their main quest is security. And in the opinion of many, it is a quest that precedes freedom.

Shamshad Hussain points out the role of female tutors who were teaching Islamic studies to children (known as *Lebacci*) until the *madrasa* system took over and women lost their educating role. She warns how the *'ulama* try to erase this fact from history to assume full responsibility and deny the role of women in the writing of the history of Kerala's renaissance (S. Hussain, author interview, December 2010).

The interlocking between marriage and education plays a strong role in the predicaments of women. My ethnographic fieldwork revealed many perspectives on this topic, which, when brought together, would offer a semi-complete picture to understand local dynamics of women dilemmas. Having had the opportunity to be educated, young women grieve their inability to continue it further and the forestalments to their career. I heard a story of a Muslim mother who cried at a school's parents' meeting upon seeing her classmate become an English teacher. She cried because, while her life had changed course and she had been forced to quit school, and hence never pursued her dreams, she saw how her classmate had achieved what she was deprived of. In one of the focus groups of young mothers in a village in Malappuram district, as soon as the question of the level of education came up, a twenty-year-old burst into tears. Her friend explained that she was the top student in her class and she wanted to go to college, but her father took her out of school and got her married; hence whenever anyone mentioned school to her, she started crying.

Apart from escaping the payment of a high dowry, another reason for this widespread phenomenon of early marriage, as explained by a Muslim female psychologist and social activist, is the inability to tolerate adolescent problems on the part of the parents, and especially for a Gulf wife taking sole care of her children. This inability to take responsibility for teens results in passing the burden onto the future husband instead. According to J. Devika, what educated unemployed women end up doing is a sort of child crafting to compensate the loss of decision-making capacity in their lives. This is a result of a growing sense of individuation (author interview, February 2011). According to a Muslim female lawyer, high levels of women's education granted women self-confidence and individuality, which complicated traditional family settings in Kerala. Most of her clients were actually men suffering from domestic problems. She said that women and not men are usually the reason for any family problem. Interestingly, she asserted that men usually give freedom to their wives, but it is the mother-in-law or sister-in-law who starts creating problems between the couple.

As these observations demonstrate, female literacy among Muslims is not a panacea for the dilemmas of women's agency. The results of the survey I conducted among Muslim students in Kerala prove this. When asked if they perceive that they enjoy equal rights as Indian citizens, 27.6% confirmed that this is how they always feel, 51.3% said it is not always the case and 13.2% simply rejected this claim. This 51% figure is the quantitative translation of the gender paradox in my opinion.

The level of employment among women in Kerala and especially Muslims is very low, as only 8.9% of Muslim women are employed (Census of India, 2001). The percentage of women in the workforce in 1991 was 15.8% (below the national average of 22.3%). Surprisingly, in 2001 the figure decreased to 15.4% while the national average increased to 25.6%. In Malappuram district, the figure is dismally low: 8.7% (Siddique, 2005). Despite this, Gulf migration has altered the traditional employment paths set for women, which were mainly in the educational field. Young women in India are transforming this through being career-oriented. When I asked students in a paramedical college, where surprisingly everyone showed a desire to be employed, whether they would search for employment opportunities in India or the Gulf, the majority opted for the Gulf, and all of them chose their subject of study because of job opportunities. When I asked them how they would deal with their husband if they wanted to go to the Gulf, they smiled and said: "We take him with us and he gets a job there."

The severity of the absence of women in public bodies called on the affirmative action of seat reservation. This was manifested in the decision in 2009 to reserve half of the seats for women in local governmental bodies. Shockingly, not a single Muslim Malayalee woman was ever elected to the Lok Sabha. Only 6.4% of the elected members of the Legislative Assembly (MLAs) were women. Despite this, there are aspects of change. The 2011 Kerala Assembly witnessed the election of seven female MLAs; two of them were Muslims belonging to the Communist Party of India (Marxist) and the Janata Dal, since the IUML did not present any female candidate, while Congress only presented three – one of them was a Muslim but did not make it. In the 2014 elections, only one Muslim lady was nominated by the CPI (M).

The Muslim Keralite context is also plagued with the tradition of dowry, which is considered by many as the biggest problem facing women in Kerala. Originating as a Hindu tradition, the custom was copied by the Muslims. The older the girl is, the more dowry her family is supposed to provide. This is usually in the form of gold and, in some cases, additional cash as well. The girl is supposed to retain the gold, but often she surrenders it to the husband's family. Cash goes automatically to the husband, as well as any other gifts, such as cars, electric appliances or even expensive watches. The patriarchal nature of the Keralite society is the basic incentive behind the continuity of this custom, since males are attributed higher significance. The fact that the girl is educated does not significantly change the scenario because her family will have to pay a higher dowry to the also well-educated boy.

In one of the focus groups in a college, I asked an eloquent girl which age she thought was most suitable for marriage, and she said, "Twenty". When I asked her if she would be able to convince her parents of that if they insisted on making her marry before the age of twenty, she answered:

> My parents' opinion is my opinion, you see because of our economic condition; I cannot insist on marrying late, my father does not afford a high dowry. Here men in Malabar want to marry young girls, so although I think twenty is a better age for marriage, if my family tells me to marry now, I will agree.

Violence against women is another element of the gender paradox in Kerala. According to police records from 2007 until 2013, Malappuram appears constantly as the district with the highest rate of violence against women. This is due to reported domestic violence or cruelty by the husband or relatives. In a survey I conducted among Muslim students in Malappuram and Kozhikode, 71.1% of the female students said they did not feel safe where they lived.

Reform through *jihād*

> Allah at the end of each century will bring forwards one who will revive the faith of this *Ummah*.
>
> (A Prophet's *hadith* [Sunnan Abu Dawood])

> In India although Muslims are closer theologically to ahl-i kitab, Muslims gave *fatwa* to support Hindus against the Portuguese. This was probably the first *ijtihād* of this kind in the world.
>
> (Mujeeburahman, editor of the Mujahid *Shabab Weekly* magazine, 2011)

According to the reformist leader Husain Madavoor, the meaning of *jihād* ranges from the recital of Quranic messages to the unbelievers, to the mass movements aimed at establishing social justice and freedom of faith, and culminating in the highest form, which is the individual's effort to restrain the self. In a *hadith* by the Prophet answering his wife's question as to whether a woman has to perform *jihād*, he stated that, for women, *jihād* is free of combat; it is only via intellectual debates, with the self, with her money and through performing pilgrimage (*ḥaj*).

The word *jihād* has strong significance in the Keralite context but in an interestingly different manner. In 2009, there was strong media hype concerning alleged plots of the Popular Front of India and Muslim extremists to convert Hindu and Christian girls in Kerala and Karnataka to Islam by luring them into marriage and thus increasing the percentage of Muslims within the states. Hindu right-wing organisations like VHP and RSS termed this as 'love *jihād*'. In 2010 and 2011, the issue was renewed in Kerala with a new term '*penne* (women) *jihād*', in which gender roles were reversed, and Muslim girls were allegedly seducing Hindu boys to make them convert and marry them. In addition to Muslim organisations, which have denied these allegations and regarded them as violations of basic justice, the Karnataka High Court had also ruled against one of these cases. During my fieldwork, the Muslim youth I interviewed always referred to this media hype as a Hindu right-wing conspiracy, and in an interview with a female student activist, she asserted that India is a democracy, and girls should have the freedom to choose their partner. She later referred to the endless efforts of RSS to stain the Muslim community, especially by attacking the activist female Muslim youth and claiming they practise *jihād* against the Hindus.[25]

The less-featured Muslim narratives actually give us a different picture. One of the most pressing problems in India – which the Jamaati Islami, for example, identifies – is what they call the moral degradation among the youth. According to Jamaati Islami, not only is there an increasing rate of crime, alcohol and narcotic consumption, but also a large number of Muslim girls are getting married to non-Muslims, hence ignoring Islamic rules. Secular media's influence was the reason behind this phenomenon:

> You see, for example, the issue of love *jihād*, they claimed that around four thousand non-Muslim girls converted and were kidnapped by Muslim boys.

In fact, there are more than five thousand Muslim girls who get kidnapped by non-Muslim boys. But we cannot discuss this or project it the way they do.

(Author interview with a Jamaati Islami leader, February 2011)

There are cited media reports on the response of Muslim leaders and mosque preachers in Kerala to this love *jihād* topic. They have exhorted the community not to believe in such allegations since love cannot be a means of *jihād* and pre-marital relationships are considered sinful activities (Indian Social Institute, 2009). What is interesting in this regard is this usage of the space of the mosque to counter the allegations, discouraging conversion activities, and even repri-manding them.

What I aim to achieve through this chapter is a limited twist to this imagina-tion by portraying young women as *jihādist* or initiators of some form of agency (to put it into mainstream sociological terminology). I call the Muslim young women in Kerala *jihādist* because they struggle against problems such as dowry, early marriage and thus discontinuation of education, the 'Gulf wife' syndrome and limited mobility. Just as *jihād* is considered a typical Islamic ritual, I put forward the claim that, in their struggles, several rituals appear. These rituals include first going to the mosque, employing their Islamic education from the *madrasas* and colleges to resist male-dominated authority and dealing with the ritual of segregation they have experienced since puberty.

Another term related etymologically to *jihād* is *ijtihād*, meaning independent reasoning. *Ijtihād*, as a process, opens the space for agency and stresses the human element of change; here *ijtihād* becomes the bridge on which *jihād* as a struggle is translated into meaningful action to reach the goal. Jalal (2008) describes writing her book as an intellectual *jihād* in the sense of a constant struggle based on the rigorous exercise of *ijtihād*. When a young woman, or a twenty-year-old girl, tells me that she has learnt Arabic, and she can read both the original text of the Quran and its translation, then she can decide for herself what is *harām* and what is *halāl*, and thus does not need the *fatwa* or the *mul-lah*'s version of truth – this is called *ijtihād*, and on her part, it leads to having better opportunities in life, through education, marital life, career or simply self-contentment and peace of mind.

Vatuk (2008) focuses on the emerging phenomenon of 'a new breed of Muslim women scholar activists' who are critically studying the foundational texts of their religion in order to challenge received wisdom. Although there is obvious preference for the authority of the Quran in their struggle to assert their rights, still the Indian Constitution as a basis of reference is not ignored. Thus, although Vatuk tends to belittle the reference to the Constitution, my ethno-graphic material in Kerala proves otherwise. In many conversations with female Muslim students, they often asked me whether there are constitutional guaran-tees for Christians in Egypt, as they enjoy such guarantees in India. In a more critically reflective pause, a student showed surprise at my interest in Indian democracy; to her: "This democracy gives equal citizenship to all. However, it diminishes citizenship for Muslim women. This freedom is for men to limit the freedom of women through the Muslim Personal Law."

Before I delve into how Muslim women in Kerala reconstruct their roles and agencies, it is necessary to stress that the Muslim community in Kerala is far from homogenous. Hence, the position of Muslim women varies according to the dealings with each group. In general, apart from small groups such as the Tablighi Jamaat and Ahmadiyyah, there are three major Islamic groups in Kerala.[26] The first is the most widely spread Sufi group, or *Ahlu-Sunnat wal-jamaat*, called Sunnis. It is claimed that around 70% of the Muslim community in Kerala follow this group. In popularity, Kerala Nadwatul Mujahideen (KNM) or the Mujahids follow, with around 20%.[27] The third small, yet powerful, group is the Jamaati Islami-Hind's Kerala Chapter, with just under 10% of the Muslim population.[28]

Whereas the KNM's role is circumscribed to social issues, Jamaati Islami is gaining increasing ground in the social spectrum as a progressive and politically Islamist force. Two points of similarities arise between these two groups – the first relates to their urban power. Whereas the Sunnis dominate the villages, Mujahids and Jamaati have strong power-holds in urban centres, especially in Kozhikode city. The second, more intrinsic similarity is that both groups are termed revivalist or *mujaddīdeen* in Arabic. Both believe in the following Prophet's saying: "Allah at the end of each century will bring forwards one who will revive the faith of this *Ummah*." They believe that, as revivalists, their function is to "cleanse Islam of all the ungodly elements, present it and make it flourish in its original pure form" (Maududi, quoted in Abdul Samad, 1998, p. 25).

Sunni/Sufi organisations

Being the organisation with the widest support base, the Samastha Kerala Jamiyyathul Ulama leads the Muslim organisational scene in Kerala. The formation of Samastha came as a response of the *'ulama* to the conditions of post-1921 in which Kerala's Muslim community witnessed a radical shift from individual leadership to the grouping of Muslims under organisations. The *'ulama* founding Samastha identified several dangers or trends that the Muslim community was facing. On the one hand, there was the colonial and imperialistic attack after the 1920s Mappila rebellion. On the other hand, modernisation forces among Muslims coming from the Arab world were advancing. The latter forces are identified by the Samastha as "the fundamental and puritanical views of Muhammad bin Abdul Wahhab (1702–93), Salafism of Rashid Rida (1865–1935), Islamic modernism of Muhammad Abduh (1819–1905), pan-Islamism of Jamaluddin Afghani (1897–1939) and the Tahreek-e-Mujahedeen in North India" (Samastha Brochure in Arabic, 2011, my translation).

The Samastha is traditionally the authoritative religious body that holds momentous influence over Muslims. It has supervised the traditional *madrasa* education for eighty-five years (Bahauddin, principal of Darul Huda Islamic University, author interview, April 2011). Now around 9000 *madrasas* in India and the Gulf are run by this organisation, with a student population of 1.2 million taught by around 100,000 teachers (Al-Qasmi, 2000).

Part of the strength of the hold of Samastha is linked to the *mohalla* influence. Demographically, Muslim populations are divided in Kerala into *mohalla* units. A *mohalla* is the division of people living around a single mosque. So every *mohalla* has a local committee (*palli* committee or the mosque committee). The *mohalla* system is a strong one, which governs Muslim populations in Kerala and has been an indicator of the Sunnis' authority. Each *mohalla* consists of an *imam* and a committee that runs the mosque and the executive board. Its responsibility is not only the maintenance of the mosque but marriages and all social activities in the *mohalla* (P. Aboobakr, author interview, February, 2011). Unlike in countries like Egypt, there are no independent mosques in Kerala, which are not under the *waqf* board. They all belong to different organisations and are the same for the *madrasas*.[29]

In these *mohallas*, public spaces are regularly occupied by student-led protests. In fact, a dominant feature of Kerala is the street parades organised by political parties and their youth wings or nominally non-political bodies like the student organisations affiliated to the Sunni groups and Mujahids. The main goal behind these parades is a display of symbolic power; this visibility is an important factor in the assessment of student power. Figure 5.2 shows an

Figure 5.2 A common street march by the Sunni Students' Federation (SSF) (source: photo taken by author).

example of a street march by the Sunni Students' Federation (SSF) in a protest against the *Endosulfan* case, in which news had spread of people who developed cancer caused by governmental pesticides. The banner they were carrying referred to a *hadith* by the Prophet that my interpreter, who was accompanying me, translated as "the wolf would not eat those who are in a group".[30] Being a recurrent event, among different political and religious organisations in Kerala, one notices how these parades are incorporated into the everyday scene. Mechanisms of self-policing are developed as a result of the long history of democracy and protest politics in Kerala. These manifestations reflect many remarkable dynamics at hand, especially due to the impact of Gulf money on the expansion of the organisations and its activities.[31]

Due to political differences, the Sunni organisations split into another faction currently led by AP Aboobacker Musliar. In 1978, Sheikh Aboobacker Ahmed Alias founded the Jamia Markazu Saqafathi Sunniyya (Sunni Islamic Cultural Centre) in Kozhikode. The Markaz is a socio-cultural foundation in the field of both Islamic and modern education, which includes different schools, colleges and institutions: faculties of *shari'ah*, Arabic language, fundamentals of religion, Arabic and Islamic studies, arts and commerce, Urdu; preparatory and secondary institutes, a computer training institute, an institute of vocational training, an orphanage for boys, and another for girls, with a separate house for orphans and poor children from Kashmir, *madrasas* all over Kerala and even modern private schools. It has over 9000 students. Its faculties' degrees are accredited by Al-Azhar University in Egypt (similar to the other Sunni sect's main university). Apart from education, it has activities in the realm of solidarity and peaceful coexistence, as well as relief and charity. Some of the students I interviewed, both male and female, volunteered in these orphanages as a form of social work.

Other projects the Sunnis endorse are marriages of the poor. Unlike the reformist organisations that fight dowry, the Sunnis encourage the practice. In one of the brochures of the Markaz, the gold is placed with a strong visual message affirming its integral context in the marriage deal, which is a clear violation of Islamic principles. When I asked about this photo as proof indicting the Sunnis, a Sunni student told me, "They give this gold to the girl, this gold stays with the girl, it is our custom, and the father is embarrassed to send off his daughter without any gold."

As I will be showing, the major difference between the traditional Sunni or Sufi organisations and the reformists is the emphasis on *ijtihād* and accommodation of Islam in the contemporary age. In a conversation with a Sunni student from the Markaz, he justified why the Jumaa speech was in Arabic by stating that the Quran, the *Adhaan* (call to prayer) and all devotional acts like prayers and the invocation of God (*dhikr*) are all in Arabic and, according to him, religion is not about using the mind but about blind following and copying *(aldeen naql wa laysa 'aql)*.

What is remarkable here is the comparison with the Arab world. Just as in North India, the emergence of reformist organisations and their consolidation in Kerala was a direct result of transcultural flows of ideas that came from Egypt and travelled to India. Vakkom Maulvi was deeply influenced by Rashid Rida and had translated his *al-Manar* magazine from Arabic to Arabi-Malayalam. Although they are also called *salafis*, there are stark differences between them and their Arab counterparts who appear to be more fundamentalist, to be involved in politics and to place more stress on outside appearances. They also differ by allocating serious importance to the Arabic language and the applied understanding of the Quran. Whereas *ijtihād* is endorsed by many Mujahids, it is considered a taboo for many Arab Salafis, who deem it confined to a narrow circle of scholars and not open for the common man to endorse.

One last remark to be made on the Sunni organisations is their political affiliation. The Samastha group holds allegiance to the Muslim League and the authority it enjoys is inseparable from the IUML power. Leaders of IUML are also deemed as not only political but also spiritual leaders. The allegiance to the Muslim League on the part of the Samastha contributes eventually to the perpetuation of caste-based politics. Among the Sunnis, the former leader of IUML, the late Shehab Thangal, is widely revered by the common people in Malabar.[32] This linkage is criticised by middle- and lower-class Muslims in Kerala on two grounds. The first is the perception that the League discriminates against communities such as the fishermen and the barbers as they are of lower caste, while the league leaders are *Thangals*. The second point of difference is that *Thangals* should not be involved in politics because they are religious leaders and not common people (interview with a Muslim fisherman, Malappuram district, March 2011).

Contrary to this, the other Sunni group, known as the A. P. Sunnis, oscillates its political affiliation with different parties. It appears impossible, therefore, to build political generalisations on the interplay of religion and Muslim politics. The pragmatic options adopted by Muslim leaders that are fuelled by pure personal objectives are the determining factors in the dynamics of political organisations in Kerala.

Kerala Nadwatul Mujahideen (the Mujahids)

Reformist organisations among the Muslim community started to appear in the early twentieth century after the Malabar Rebellion when religious leaders (*'ulama*) started facing the deteriorated conditions of Muslims, especially in the educational field. The contemporary remnant of these reformist organisations is known as 'Kerala Nadwatul Mujahideen'. In Kerala, these reformers influenced the emergence of what is known as the Islahi (Reformist) movement. The role of Sayyid Sanaullah Makhti Tangal, who called for education among the Muslims, is one example. He asserted that if one does not study Malayalam, one loses one's faith (*imān*), since the meaning of the Quran would not be understood. He started by questioning the false and established notion that Malayalam is a language of Hindus.

Chalilakattu Kunjahmad Haji, also known as the Sir Sayyed of Kerala, instructed students to read newspapers, and called for the education of Muslim women and the modernisation of the Arabi-Malayalam language. Hamdani Sheikh, a Sufi scholar, emphasised education for men and women through establishing *madrasas* on all levels. Vakkom Moulavi, also considered the father of the Muslim renaissance in Kerala, through his efforts, allowed Muslims to start entering the threshold of modern education, religious redemption, political regeneration and intellectual achievement (Abdul Samad, 1998; Kurup & Ismail, 2008).[33]

The Mujahids are considered the Kerala equivalent of the *Ahl-hadith* of North India, whose centre is in Delhi and who do not adhere to a specific school of jurisprudence (*fiqh*). In the mosque, the upper floor is usually reserved for women. The Jumaa speech is always in Malayalam. There are around 1000 Mujahid-affiliated mosques in Kerala.[34] Their main emphasis is on the principle of monotheism or *tawḥīd*. The name *nadwatul mujahedeen* comes as an emphasis on the *jihād* against backwardness and poverty (H. Madavoor, principal and leader of the Mujahids, author interview, January 2011). For the Mujahids, education is the most important path to social change. This is embodied in the founding of around twelve Arabic colleges, such as Rouzathul Uloom and Jamia Nadwiyya.

Mujahids assign great significance to the Friday *khutba*. Traditionally, cultural change had been initiated from the *khutba*, which is the strongest tool, in the opinion of many intellectuals, since religion was always taught from the pulpit (*minbar*). In order to exemplify what the Mujahids call for, I am presenting an excerpt from one of the Malayalam *khutbas* in the Mujahid Mosque of Feroke College:

> It is a fact that we do not live forever. We are able to live with so many facilities, but in the after life, no one would be there to help you. There are people who are worrying about what happens to their wife, children, organisation, and so forth after their death. But the basic thought should not be this. We should be preoccupied of what would happen to ourselves after death. If you were corrupt, got dowry, committed all bad deeds, then you would see one approaching who is ugly and horrible. It would tell you, "I am your work." People think that Allah would forgive them all, but this is not going to save them. So all the time, Allah and the Prophet reminded us of that fact of death. In order to get peace in the Day of Judgment and ensure a place in heaven, we should give whatever we have. Whoever is straightforward, whoever prays to god alone, whoever does '*ibadat* (worship) properly, this is the one who would be sure of passing in the experiment at the Day of Judgment. We should start doing our *karmadharma* (work and ethics). When we see the very famous and powerful people like Qaddafi and Mubarak, we want to copy them, or whoever is popular and strong in order to make use of them but the best person whom we should be close to is Allah. We have advice from the Prophet (peace be upon him) not to take from but to give dowry to women.
>
> (*Jumaa Khutba*, 4 March 2011, Feroke College Mosque,
> translated by my interpreter)

Contemporarily, the Mujahids typically cast their votes for the UDF alliance (either the Muslim League or Congress) and refrain from voting for the Communist Party, due to perceived ideological differences between communism and the Muslim identity. The hostile relationship between the Mujahids and the communists was emphasised in a battle that took place symbolically in school textbooks. According to Mujahid Arabic professors I interviewed, the Communist Party gradually instilled in books anti-Islamic principles of atheism and wanted to destroy Islam. The names one found in schoolbooks were always Hindu and never Muslim. They emphasised that when the communist-led coalition government (referred to as LDF) stopped Arabic classes in order to withdraw the Arabic language from schools, they struggled and submitted petitions to the Ministry of Education. In 1980, clashes between the police and Muslim youth protesting against the anti-Arabic laws led to deadly consequences (Muslim Youth League official website, 2014). Thus, in their own words, Kerala became the only place in the world with Arabic language martyrs.[35]

Although the Mujahids are not politically engaged or oriented, since their efforts focus on the social and spiritual sphere, it would not be correct to describe them as alienated either. In many conversations with Mujahids, their need to exclude Islam from politics is attached to a belief in the corruption of the political sphere, on the one hand, and a belief that extremism breeds further extremism, on the other hand. One Mujahid female lecturer told me:

> BJP has no foot in Kerala. Twenty years ago we never heard of it, but now it is appearing with RSS because of NDF. Those extremists among the Muslims are the reason for the emergence of RSS here. With the partition, the powerful Muslims left to Pakistan. India was not supposed to be a Hindu nation, but now it is. We are a small number compared to the Hindus, and they can easily eradicate us. This is why we should remain silent and not give such speeches like those of PFI or NDF against Hindus. We have always lived like brothers and sisters, but because of RSS now, in order to be safe, we must remain silent.

When I asked her son about the popularity of PFI (Popular Front of India), he affirmed they are popular among young men: "Even I, when I listen to their speeches, I get emotionally affected. Everyone gets emotional. You know (*smiling*), there was a teacher in our school who tried to recruit some boys." So I asked, "And what happened?" He smiled: "Nothing. It is funny, people laughed at his attempts. They took it as a joke."

The youth wing of the Mujahid group is called the ISM or Ittihadul Shabab Ulmujahideen (translated as the Union of the Mujahid Youth). Unlike the Sunnis, the Mujahids have a girls group, or rather a movement called the MGM (Mujahid Girls Movement), who are comprised of college female students focusing on both religious and social issues.

Jamaati Islami Hind Kerala Chapter

On 12 February 2011, I received the following text message from an Indian student: "Sixty two years ago, Hasan Al-Banna's blood was shed in the street of Cairo. On this day itself, Cairo realises the decline of dictatorship. Yes, Banna, your blood has not gone in vain. Allah is great." The Egyptian Muslim Brotherhood founder, Hasan Al-Banna, and the Jamaati Islami forefather, Abul Alaa Maududi, had profoundly influenced each other. Their ideas travelled from South Asia to Egypt interchangeably, and Maududi established Jamaati Islami as a model of the Muslim Brotherhood in Egypt.[36]

The lack of unity in the political views of Muslims in India and their division between the Congress and the Muslim League were incentives that shaped Maududi's aspiration for a different political set-up: "one in which the writ of Islam would be supreme" (Abdul Samad, 1998, p. 121). In Kerala, Islahi scholars like V. P. Muhammad Ali of Edayur, who later founded the Jamaat in Kerala, and K. M. Moulavi disseminated Maududi's ideas and the youth associated with the Islahi movement were attracted to these notions.

To counter the attacks on it, Jamaati Islami still tries to shun any allegations of it being an extremist organisation, in fact it is not conceived as part of the extremist political groups in Kerala, who are mainly referred to as NDF (National Development Front) and are essentially the PFI and the PDP. In an interview with a Jamaati-affiliated professor, he recalled that a well-known worker of Jamaati Islami went in solidarity to donate blood to the Christian teacher whose hand was cut by the PFI-affiliated persons.

Since the Jamaati sanctions political means as conducive to its aims, group voting is a tactic it endorses.[37] Their choice is based on the merit of candidates. Before the launching of its own party, the *Shura* council or the consultation leaders' council had usually convened and announced support for a specific group of nominated candidates. Their aims were to first defeat the BJP and Hindu communalism; and second to vote for the candidate who would fit their needs. Jamaati followers would then all vote for this list. In an interview with one of the Jamaati leaders in Kerala, he asserted that one of the Jamaati's goals was to ensure the benevolence of the Indian democratic system since democracy usually brought criminals to power. In his words:

> In our parliament, there are at least 150 criminals and 300 billionaires. How could these come to power if not through buying votes? After the Bombay blasts, a joke was transmitted through SMS. It said, "You can conquer terrorists who come by boats, but you cannot conquer criminals who come by votes." This uncontrolled democracy has become a mockery. Suppose Omar Ibn Al-Khattab comes back and contests in elections against a criminal. You know what will happen? The criminal will easily succeed.[38]

Another goal of the Jamaati Islami is to set up priorities and to enlighten Muslims. The *amīr*, or the president, however, gives policy and guidelines but

not *fatwas*. By their conception of enlightenment, they include a progressive attitude towards Muslim women and how they should 'rise'. The noticeable disappearance of women from the Muslim League's list of twenty-five candidates
contesting in the last Legislative Assembly elections of 2011 was emphasised.
The denial of education for women on the part of the *'ulama* for decades has
been one of the reasons for women's status today. It was only recently that the
'ulama changed their minds, started colleges for girls and softened their stance.
The increasing number of Sunni girls admitted to Calicut University is an indicator of this change.

Jamaati has three youth wings: a male student wing called the Students'
Islamic Organisation (SIO), an open youth movement (which is predominantly
male) called Solidarity and a girls' wing called the Girls' Islamic Organisation
(GIO). The SIO has 2000 members in addition to 10,000 workers. They are most
effective in Kerala, Hyderabad, Maharashtra and Delhi. It is also recognised by
UNESCO. Unlike other organisations, there are several criteria for membership.
First, there is an interview in which the level of commitment to the principles of
SIO is judged, and also the level of reading and writing. The majority of the
members are from middle-class backgrounds, so funding is not a problem. They
have branches in all the Gulf countries under different names. According to the
president of SIO Kerala, the difference between SIO Delhi and Kerala is that in
Delhi the youth are exhausted, not active enough and do not read. In Kerala, on

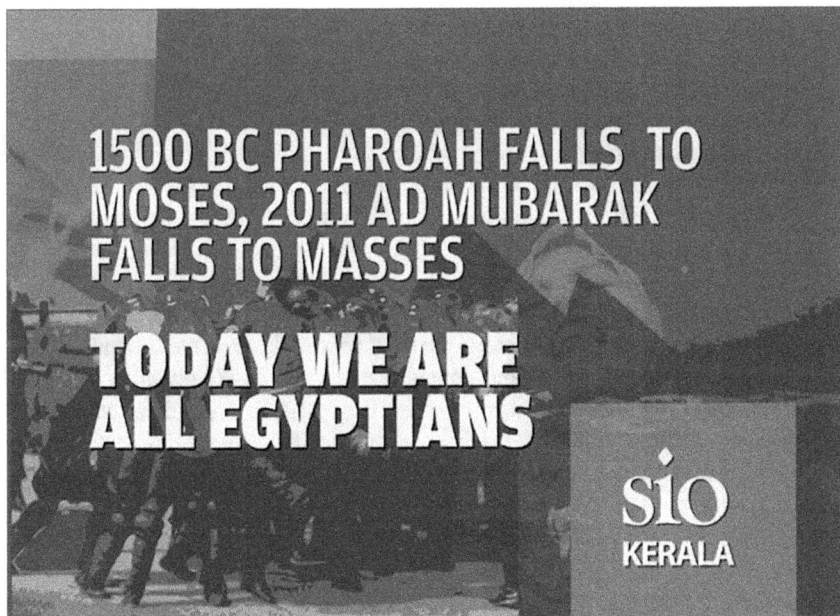

Figure 5.3 SIO poster during the revolution in Egypt, February 2011 (source: author's
own collection).

the contrary, due to the historical effect of maritime trade, a process of cultivation of the minds of Malabaris has been witnessed. This is shown through multiple magazines (religious, political, for women, for children, in addition to the Jamaati-affiliated *Madhyamam* newspaper and its publications). For Jamaati youth wings, focus is cast on service, study, *jihād* and dialogue.

What is also interesting about Jamaati is their engagement with events in the Arab world. Traditionally, the Palestinian issue occupied their stalwart attention. With the popular uprisings occurring in the Arab world at the beginning of 2011, Jamaati dedicated a lot of its attention to the events and organised solidarity protests and events such as talks and broadcasting of revolutionary songs. By the ousting of the Muslim Brotherhood regime in 2013, Jamaati's events took a radical turn by emulating the *rab'aa* sit-in staged by the Muslim Brotherhood supporters in Cairo through holding an overnight protest in Ernakulam in August 2013.

Activism is not confined to the male students, but is equally observable through the GIO, which was established in 1984 and has 1000 members. According to a brochure defining it:

> GIO as well as JIH realises the potential of womenfolk in moulding the society's future, GIO intends to uplift the girls and enhance their power of action and reaction. GIO realises that it is from the girls themselves that the voices for safety and security should arise.

What GIO envisages is:

> A world where girls can travel more freely from the Himalayas to Cape Camorin with their heads straight and thoughts high. GIO aims at the assurance of justice and prosperity without any discrimination of religion and caste, finding a solution for the problems affecting girls in the sociopolitical, moral and cultural zones, and refining the girls as value conscious.
>
> (GIO Brochure, 2011)

According to GIO, its mode of action is "to function girls on the grounds of Islam". This is done within an atmosphere encouraging creative talents of girls by running camps, campaigns and contests. Special focus is given to the campuses. GIO tries to uplift the educational levels of girls, to strengthen them orally and to boost up their talents through its activities. Their activities include protests – for example, on the Shahina case in 2010, when they protested on the highway with muffled mouths. One of their other considerable protests was against the fashion parade in Kozhikode. They also hold writing competitions, quizzes and exposés.

In one of my visits to a Jamaati Islami-affiliated college in Kozhikode district, a twenty-year-old girl came to the principal's office where I was sitting to ask him for something. He introduced her and told me that she contested for the panchayat elections but had lost. She came to the office because she was planning for a sports event at the college. I noticed how that Jamaati college was different from other colleges I went to because they encouraged the sense of independence and initiative for girls; they had sports, drama and media watch sections. Although the sports events for boys and girls were separate, it was considered the first Arabic college in Kerala to have such an event organised solely by female students.

I saw another noticeable difference at this college when I was asked to deliver a lecture on Islamic movements in Egypt and a girl came to the podium to recite the Quran. This was against what I was accustomed to as it was always a boy asked to recite the Quran in the inauguration of any programme or event.

In my conversations with these girls, many imparted that, as a citizen, they had no problems, but as a woman, they were limited; they could not freely express themselves and could not conduct programmes spontaneously like the boys; they always needed permission. Also at home, there was no equality between boys and girls. They could not travel alone; they suffered harassment on the buses. When they heard about the contrasting dowry situation in Egypt where men give the gold to the bride, they jokingly expressed their desire to come and migrate to Egypt. One girl even remarked that if she studied hard enough, she might get a scholarship and go to Egypt. In their perception, problems in their lives came from the family and not from the *'ulama*. *'Ulama*, according to these girls, had no influence socially or politically on their lives; *'ulama* appeared only in marriages or divorce. However, one girl said if a girl joined a drama class at her school, she would be expelled from the *madrasa*. They followed *fatwas* sometimes if they were acceptable to them. However, in their own words:

> Sometimes the *fatwas* are sound, but people do not follow them. For example, there were *fatwas* calling people to limit their expenditures on wedding parties, but people do not listen to it and they still spend a lot. Then there was another *fatwa* concerning banning loud music in weddings because it annoys other people, but still the rich continue doing it. Mostly the rich do not listen, but the others follow.
>
> (Inputs from female students at the Jamaati Islami-affiliated Irshadiyya College, January 2011)

Gender limitations were greatly manifested in the variable of safety. Some seemed to be convinced that abiding by an 'Islamic' dress seemed to be the solution to the lack of physical security. One of the most important programmes of GIO is the training on self-safety and security in order to overcome 'Kerala's molesting society', as one activist put it. They try to teach them that, if they respond and slap back, the molesters would stop. In the words of a GIO-affiliated student:

> Society is mouldable and so are girls. The society simply nurtures girls to be married off. They are not considered human. GIO teaches them to be conscious

of their self. It promotes reading and writing through competitions, it shows that they have a space, at least in GIO. The best access to girls is usually in campus. The strongest difficulty GIO faces is in the organisational level because those who would be responsible for this are usually in the marriage age and thus the membership is fragile and contingent on single girls. Even Hindus participate in the programmes.

[...]

As a citizen of India, I do not want to close my eyes especially to problems of girls. This is why I joined GIO four years ago after joining Calicut University. Females are exploited by the male community. Society decided how women should walk and talk. Women are not aware of this fact; there should be self-confidence of their abilities. They have no time for reading because of domestic duties. The Sunday programme of GIO is to make them socially aware. This year our focus was on academic studies of women. There was also a programme we conducted where we focused on a colony in Calicut notorious for prostitutes and drugs. We conducted health awareness programmes for women there. Those who attended this meeting were all women. Imagine! In this area! No other men participated except for the cameraman!

(Female student, Calicut University, February 2011)

Reformists and women

A great paradox of the reformist agenda appears. Not only do the reformist *'ulama* allow women to go to mosques, but they also encourage them to do so, unlike the prevalent and dominant attitude of the Sunnis. Mujahids and Jamaati Islami reformers place stress on education for girls and women (both secular and religious). Their social, cultural and educational activities are always intermingled (both sexes are in the same classrooms and same conference venues) without any physical barrier separating them. Girls are given spaces to voice their opinions through GIO and MGM. However, all this is performed while a strict dress code is followed.

Choosing what to teach, choosing which experience to write about and choosing whom to talk about are mostly in the hands of men (especially through the media). It was interesting for me to see that the role of women in anti-colonial struggles of the Arab world was totally invisible in all of the publications, curricula and topics of research. Many girls had the same topic of studying Bint Alshati',[39] but none dealt with political feminist figures. There was a perplexing and noticeable gap between women's roles in the Middle East in deploying charity organisations as spaces for assertion of their public role and the non-existence of this in a developed state like Kerala. GIO and MGM's activities remain limited and usually end with the marriage of students. One of the established social realities in Kerala that these reformist organisations are trying to break is that a married woman does not venture into any public action affair.

There is an emerging discourse on responsibility and how Muslim women are the bearers of the biggest share of burdens due to early marriage. To some, it signifies missed opportunities, especially when it has to do with the desire for higher education. And thus, it is always a source of stress. I met several female Muslim psychologists in Malappuram; they all agreed that the biggest psychological problem of girls is stress and anxiety over their future because of early marriage. Marriage, at the age of eighteen, means that these girls are not practically able to pursue their studies, and if they do, then they would not be able to excel or at least retain their level of academic performance. This is due to the expectation that wives do all the house chores. Once married, the girl moves to the extended family house of the husband and is expected to take up housekeeping and cooking chores for the rest of the family.

Aside from marriage, there is a close link between the reformists' agendas and women. Women are regarded as the incumbents of reform since they are responsible for the socialisation process of their children. In contemporary Kerala, educating women appears as an obligation on all Islamic progressive reformers, since, according to them, educating one woman would result in educating at least five persons. In a society historically fused with Hindu culture and alien cultural ingredients to orthodox Saudi-style Islam, Mujahids see women as responsible for the annihilation of these alien factors. Gold accessories for boys are an example for this. In Islam, gold is banned for males, thus Mujahids teach people not to buy or adorn their male children with any gold. In order to differentiate between Sunni and Mujahid children, all one needs to do is look at a child up to the age of three and see if he is wearing any golden accessory. Women exercise some agency in the decision to follow this *fatwa*. Before I knew about this custom of accessorising boys with golden anklets, I confused a baby boy for a girl. Then the mother laughed and remarked, "Ah, you must be a Mujahid. We know that it is *harām* for boys to wear gold." I was impressed by their attitude. It was obvious that their knowledge of the prohibition of this custom did not deter them from going ahead with it. Here, basing the missionary ideals of the Mujahids on the assumed ignorance of rural women of the basic tenets of Islam was ridiculed by this woman's assertion.

The concept of agency is often trapped between conformity (as a pragmatic solution) and domestic agency (as a realistic manifestation of the conceptual boundaries). However, with education and class or caste differences, the employment of the concept deeply varies. Educated girls prove their ability to make rational compromises and decisions. When I asked female informants if they follow *fatwas* issued by *'ulama*, 37.5% confirmed they always do, 40.3% said they do not necessarily follow them, and it is up to them to choose what does and does not sound rational and acceptable, and 22.2% said they do not specifically follow *fatwas* of *'ulama* but they resort to what they conceive as right or wrong.

The initial imaginary of Muslim scholars of women's roles was that they should be "the mistresses of private Islamic space, key transmitters of Islamic values, the symbols of Muslim identity, and guardians of millions of domestic

Islamic shrines" (Robinson, 2006, p. 27). Hence, Maududi and other Islamists emphasised the need for Muslim women to acquire the same knowledge of Islam as the Maulvis: "They were to be the rulers of domestic space, sealed off from all those elements of kufr which polluted public space" (ibid.). Today this is being dismantled by political and economic liberalisation that led to the expansion of communicative spaces and thus the appearance of the public woman.

In the last panchayat elections, women won more than 50% of the seats. Although Jamaati Islami presented many female candidates, none got elected, as they got very few votes. The Muslim League, being the majority party, found itself in a dilemma. It had to find Muslim women to pose for 50% of the seats. This was initially met by resistance from the *'ulama*. The *hadith* on women that bans their participation in politics was well circulated in public debates. Later on, this was subverted by the introduction of *fatwas* for Muslim women to run for the panchayat elections. However, the *fatwa* came with dress code restrictions and instructions such as a curfew to return home before 5 p.m. The *fatwa* even mentioned feminism in a derogatory manner. What is interesting is women's reactions and how they are negotiating these ideas. Many women iterated the following:

> Since we are Muslim women, we are not allowed to participate in the political system. But with strong faith and while being well dressed and since it is a democratic country not an Islamic one, then we can be involved in politics.
> (Shamshad Hussain, author interview, December 2010)

There are contradictory results of both the strong sense of agency and the actual opportunities open to young women. On the one hand, educated and employed women are strong victims of violence (whether physical through sexual harassment or receiving threat letters, or symbolic through rumours). Hence, they easily become victims of mental illnesses, such as individuation, stress and depression. Many informants, including psychologists, asserted how women in Malappuram district suffer from mental disorders and ill health. When I asked a postgraduate student working on this topic what the most prevalent psychological problems in Kerala were, she told me stress and worrying about the future. I heard many stories of women suffering from depression and other psychological diseases, and I met several PhD students who were working on this topic. I was told that the percentage of Muslim women going to hospitals is higher than those from other religions: "They mostly complain of body pain, however, there are no pathological reasons; it is all psychological effects."

On the other hand, women are free from other stress factors related to the fact that they are not duly politicised. Muslim youth in general suffers from the stigma of terrorism and hence every young Muslim feels that he/she is forced to prove they are not a terrorist. Luckily, females in Kerala are not loaded as much with this burden. One of my interviewees, a medical doctor by practice, shares this perception. In his words:

You can be ghettoised even if it is only mentally. Everyone is worried about his future and job opportunities and how to deal with the fact that he carries a Muslim name. Not being aware of this, girls are freed from such worries and thus can concentrate better on their studies, and this is actually one of the reasons they are doing well in education compared to boys. Girls do not fall victim to the terrorism discourse, which is distressing and stressing youth.

The gender paradox is slowly being dismantled. Although women's lives are heavily designed by men in the social sphere, politically it is not, since female voters outnumber the males, and thus it could actually be argued that they determine the political destinies of the male candidates.[40] Women's political awareness and sense of political efficacy are quite high. According to my survey, 63% voted in elections, and the remainder could not vote because they had not reached the suitable age at election time; 78.8% perceived their vote to be important; 84% were able to name the Members of Parliament and Legislative Assembly representing them; 10.9% had contacted them when they needed or faced a problem; 100% read newspapers daily; and 17.9% participated in protests and demonstrations. The most frequently cited causes for protest or campaigns were either education-related or alcohol ban-related; the majority participated in national causes, most prominently supporting a state-based call against alcohol, the communist government, smoking and plastic, and calling for Dalit and minority reservations, AIDS awareness, blood donation campaigns, and college and education improvement. This is in addition to participation in Muslim identity-based campaigns, such as those concerning the Aligarh campus in Kerala, correction of anti-Islamic elements in school textbooks, protests against beauty contests, prostitution and the Danish cartoons controversy.

Perhaps the only difference is that girls, unlike boys, do not participate in election campaigns of Congress and IUML (UDF), which remain mostly male-dominated zones. Women participate separately in the women's wing of the IUML, although it does not translate in any recruitment. There are many women whose husbands are not in IUML and who are interested in politics; two female lawyers I interviewed proved this point. One of them told me that she chose her career as a means to protest against social problems in Kerala. Although IUML in the 2011 Legislative Assembly elections did not nominate a single woman, she had gone to the community leaders and did her best to convince them to nominate a reputed Muslim female teacher who had been a social and political activist. But, according to her, they were not ready to accept a successful woman.

The fact that the Sunnis are the largest group comprising membership in the IUML explains the aversion to recruit women in public positions. The Sunni organisations hold many meetings and organise numerous rallies all year long with exclusively male participants. This has been brought to an end with the initiation of the Muslim Student Federation (MSF) Campus Conference in Calicut University in February 2011, as it was the first Muslim student programme among the Sunnis with women participating.

Apart from MSF and the Sunnis in general, and not as a complementary group as in the Sunnis' activities, girls appear active in the framework of their own Mujahid and Jamaati organisations – MGM and GIO, respectively. In these organisations, protest has become a ritualised activity. While goals change, methods remain the same. These means are manifested in creating human chains along highways, screening movies, holding talks and discussion groups, arranging conferences and workshops, and even joining demonstrations with male youth (as in the case of the anti-Mubarak protests organised by Jamaati youth organisation Solidarity in Calicut in February 2011).

Muslim girls are subject to a strong dress code. All Muslim women in Kerala are compelled to cover their hair. Of course some choose not to, but the majority succumb to it without considerable reflection. Covering the hair became a ritual in the sense that it is performed as an identity marker in an automatic manner. This is greatly contrasted to the situation in the rest of the Muslim world where covering the hair remains an arbitrary decision of the individual or the family, but not a community-wise accepted moral code.

Despite the educational and economic uplifting of the community, especially of women, the reformists assumed a role of responsibility in policing women's moral conduct. They considered themselves responsible in front of God not just to educate women and be financially responsible for them, but also to ensure their decency and their compliance with their own version of divine rules of decency. Interestingly, not only Muslim women were subject to this mentality, but all Malayalee women in general (the upper-caste Namboodiri Brahmins or the lower-caste Ezhavas). Devika and Hussain share my opinion by calling this process 're-forming women'. They point to two constant and contemporary pressures on Muslim women in Kerala: the pressure on the young woman to "conform to norms of dressing found desirable by certain elements claiming to represent community interest" and the pressure under the threat to life (Hussain & Devika, 2010).

Devika (2007) also mentions the process of individualisation as a result of women's education in Kerala. She quotes the following from *A Textbook for the Instruction of Young Girls* (*Streevidya Griha Pathavali*), written in 1914 by Pillai and Ramayyan: "If women were educated, then beyond any doubt, knowledge would itself act as the guardian of chastity and violation of chastity would not occur" (p. 42). The idea was that, through education, self-regulation of the mind was possible, and thus an inhibition of any tendency to adopt deviant ideas or ideas that do not fall within the mainstream attitudes. Control here is enacted with internality without the need to resort to external forms of control. An analogy could be further made between this and education as a precursor for both liberation of women and their subjectivity.

Unfortunately, for those who do not wish to conform, there could be serious repercussions. In 2010, there was the famous case of Rayana, a Muslim college student in her twenties, who received death threats from individuals affiliated with the Popular Front of India who wanted her to shift to wearing the *purdah*. It was obvious that there was inadequate support from the media and religious and feminist organisations, as well as the police, to seriously condemn the pressure to conformity (Hussain & Devika, 2010). Dress has assumed a hegemonic role in Northern Kerala, to the extent that female politicians had to change their dressing style, or fear the loss of votes.[41]

Out of personal experience, in addition to opting to fully cover my hair in order to be granted easy access to my informants and to avoid being labelled a heretic or an undesirable Muslim, it was impossible for me to find private single accommodation in Kozhikode or Malappuram district. When I wanted to move out of the university campus, all those who were trying to help me find accommodation told me that no single women stay on their own in the northern parts of Kerala.

It would be crucial to resort to Bourdieu's concept of 'symbolic violence' to understand the case of Malayalee females, since to Bourdieu, symbolic violence is the "violence which is exercised upon a social agent with his or her complicity" (Bourdieu & Wacquant, 1992, p. 167). In the case of Keralite youth, their choices and their living contexts oblige them to undertake an attitude that balances their opportunities and their abilities. To Bourdieu, it is futile to analyse domination via a dichotomous alternative between freedom and constraint, but it should be processed through an agreement between objective and cognitive structures (ibid., p. 168). For the case of educated women, it is more complicated:

> Intellectuals are often among those in the least favorable position to discover or to become aware of symbolic violence, especially that wielded by the school system, given that they have been subjected to it more intensively than the average person and that they continue to contribute to its exercise.
>
> (Ibid., p. 70)

Emergence of 'public women' and the fight for citizenship in new public spaces

New spaces and BlackBerry jihād

> Alice in Wonderland
> I want to be Alice in Wonderland
> If I had a rebirth
> Like her I want to play in
> Garden with squirrels
> But I have no vast garden
> Our garden is road and
> The squirrels are vehicles
> They are not kind as squirrels
> They are passing me by roaring
> I wish to play with butterflies
> But they do not like plastic flowers

I like to play in earth using stones
But our yard is concreted and tiled
I want to lie under a tree
By smelling the fragrance of flowers
But I have only the foul smell
Coming out from the nearest drainage
I want the hugs and kisses of mother
But she was very busy with
Office and household works
I want to hear stories
But my grandmother is in an old age home
I want to cry loudly
But tears are not coming from the eyes
They are also frozen like
The two-week-old chicken in refrigerator
(A poem written by Fathima Riya,
seventh standard, Malappuram)

Life within a specific insulated community problematises the relation between public space and gender. The portrayal of the 'outside' as different and unsafe zones where one has to constantly negotiate and bargain disturbs this sense of cosiness and perfection of the intricate community network – the family, the mosque, the *madrasa* and the *mohalla*, where everything is traditionally organised and free from politically challenging modes. For women, the street and the public space are considered dangerous zones and hence female spaces are confined to the private sphere where it is 'traditionally' thought that they have everything they 'traditionally' needed: the coconut trees around, the fish seller coming, the husband bringing the ingredients for cooking. Life seems complete and convenient. However, the private mingles with the public to the extent that there is no private any more.

In the Keralite case, this is not just limited to an inter-community context but also to an intra-community one. The division of the community into adherents of different religious organisations – Sunni, Mujahid, Jamaati and, to a lesser extent, Tablighi and Ahmadiyya – led to the curtailment of 'liberal space'. By liberal space, I mean the space for contention and revolt. As one university professor informed me:

The Keralites suffer from the psychological problem of 'conditioning', as their individual opinion is erased and they become conditioned to display the general opinion of the organisation. This results from membership in any political party or Islamic organisation. This eventually leads to hypocrisy. When we see their declared opinion, and we compare them with how they live and deal in their private lives, we see the high level of hypocrisy, which is evident, for example, in the dowry system, respect for women, getting financial aid from the Gulf, claiming that their institution is directed

for the upliftment of Muslim society whereas they take money from teachers or students to give them a job or a seat.

(Kozhikode district, March 2011)

Having seen how the gender paradox was being fractured in Kerala, I point out
the main phenomenon arising from this fracture: the emergence of public women
through new public spaces. In addition to the street as a traditional space for
protest, there is a witnessed emergence of new public spaces created by new
media, especially the internet. Political rituals create contact zones between the
private and the public, and the secular and the religious. These rituals are performed by youth who are located at the periphery of modernity and globality.

Gender usually problematises public spaces, since they are often unsafe for
women who perceive their security to be fragile or at risk. With migration and
education coupled with youth enthusiasm, the fixity of the elder generations was
staggered. Public space was transformed. The media had a great impact on trans-
ferring images from other 'Muslim' societies like the Arab world, where the plot
for gender roles and social change differ. In a speech by the president of the
Muslim Education Society (MES), images of women protesting in the Arab
states, facing the police, sitting in mosques aiding the injured and praying were
emphasised to a big audience of Muslim Malayalee students. He further mentioned how a young Egyptian woman was the guide to the Indian group all over
Cairo.

In Kerala, the GIO played a great role in the transformation of the negative
perception of public spaces as unsafe for women. This started with the first
women's conference in Kerala in 1993, organised by GIO. The organisation
itself was first launched from Kerala in 1984 (Jamaati Islami website, accessed
on 6 May 2012). In 2010, GIO organised a large-scale conference in Northern
Kerala on the theme 'Woman Power for Social Revolution', in which reservations for women, codification for Muslim Personal Law and combating dowry
were the main issues discussed.[42]

The Iranian sociologist Bayat's (2009) notion of 'social non-movements'
brings women as public actors who, through an art of presence, acquire the
ability to use marginal spaces. In addition to the urban poor and women, youth is
another element of these non-movements. Youth embodies a collective challenge
of extending youth habitus (overcoming anxiety over the future, sense of adventure, lightness). Since youth, as a social category, is essentially modern and
urban, youth consciousness is easily generated among atomised individuals by
mass media, shopping malls, youth organisations and urban localities. Identities
are created through the recognition of commonalities and mediated either
through the gaze in public spaces or through mass media. Youth politics is not
just about politics of protest but politics of presence and practice in the public
space. The activism of youth in Kerala has reached a state where it has become a
ritual and an everyday experience. It overcomes activism's classical definition as
an extraordinary activity. Bayat argues that the advantage of such a ritualised
practice is that it becomes exceedingly difficult to suppress it.

The strong teledensity of Kerala and the 1.7 million figure of telephone users contributes to this dismantling. Smart phones are used for multiple purposes: logging on to Facebook and Twitter, downloading examination exercises, applying for jobs online, and matrimonial websites and services. Through these phones, new virtual spaces emerge just like Appadurai's 'technoscapes'. They offer paradoxical instances of freedom and boldness of young women. In an interview, a Muslim college teacher, who is also a social activist, narrated how girls are getting more spaces now, from his daughter who joined the soccer team at school, to girls with iPads and Blackberries. He told me how some of his female students find it very liberal to discuss issues like homosexuality or Islam with him via text messages. It had become 'usual' for him to exchange BBMs (BlackBerry messages) or text messages with female students who either start intellectual debates with him on the phone or dare to ask his opinion in matters pertaining to politics and social problems. It was obvious that these girls with iPads and BlackBerry smart phones, or even simple mobile phones, had managed to create more spaces for themselves and indulged in free and open discussions on sexuality, marriage and their future.

In addition to the emerging spaces created by electronic media, Kerala has an interesting history in regards to its reading culture. Circulation of newspapers and magazines increases every year, with a notable increase in the number of readers. It is a fact asserted by many that everyone in Kerala reads newspapers. The state is characterised by a specifically strong reading culture that dates back to the idea of reading rooms (Bavakutty, 1982).

The proliferation of new media led to the reduction of asymmetry between senders and receivers, producers and consumers (Eickelman & Anderson, 1999) by mingling the participation in secular and religious discourses. In religious spheres, it is obvious in the Jamaati and Mujahid mosques, where there is often a screen in the women's praying area so they can see the preacher or the speaker in the *Jumaa Khutba* (Figure 5.4).

The means extend from the traditional religious spheres to the so-called 'secular' and public spaces. New forms are replacing the traditional media carrying messages of how to lead an Islamic life, or how to deal with the problems faced in everyday life, in an Islamic manner. Traditionally, *fatwas* or religious edicts by Muslim scholars were the sole means to get religious advice. Gradually, *fatwas* started being circulated on audiocassettes, then visual media, and in print books, as well. Apart from these traditional and direct means, *fatwas* found a passage through entertainment and performative media. Comic books and magazines were one way. Another modern way, and somewhat unique in Kerala, is the 'home cinema'. 'Home cinema' refers to independent movies in Kerala made with a small budget, and always revolves around a Muslim family and themes related to Muslims. The main reason for the proliferation of these movies is the rigidly conservative stance of Muslim scholars against cinema halls, or more precisely against intermingling between boys and girls in cinema halls, and against movies that carry either anti-Islamic ideas or indecency. The idea behind 'home cinema' is that people buy the DVDs and watch them at their own homes

Figure 5.4 Lu'Lu' Masjid in Kozhikode, Jumaa speech, February 2011 (source: photo taken by author).

with their families. I asked many teachers and scholars about this phenomenon and whether it has anything to do with an attack on the mainstream movie indus-try in India and the way Muslims are portrayed through it. They answered that they doubt it has anything to do with this issue, and that the spreading of home cinemas carries mainly symbolic weight of consumerist trends, especially with the widening middle class due to Gulf migration. Such enterprises give space to women to occupy new roles, traditionally tabooed or signified as inappropriate. The new spaces are not emerging just in home cinema, with Muslim actresses, but in songs and music videos.

Mappila Muslim music (*Mappillapattu*), which is a traditional and folklore genre of vocalised music in Kerala, is dominated by Muslim women, who are in most cases housewives or young teens. The act of singing these songs could be regarded as a ritual that symbolises the strong popular or folkloric Islamic sense in Kerala. The songs always carry religious and historical themes and are divided into various categories. Among these categories are the wedding songs (*kalyana paattu*), those praising prophets and saints (*madh paattu*), and war songs.

I had an experience with my neighbour, a Gulf wife with two children, living with her mother and sister-in-law (another Gulf wife). Not only does she write and compose songs, but also with the help of both her Saudi-based brother and her husband, she had been able to cooperate with a producer and director to produce her songs in a video form. Fascinatingly, the same housewives who were initially shy to speak with me, because their English and Arabic (they studied Arabic at college) were not so strong, performed in the videos by singing and dancing.[43]

The case of Malayalee youth shows us a re-structuring of traditional roles of women; a counter ritual of females going to the mosque on a weekly basis has broken the traditional ritual of men going to the mosques and confining this space to males. The Friday sermon as a ritual was utilised to prove the agency of women. The authoritative use of Islam is being challenged in Kerala, unlike North India, where educational levels have led to a different culture of dealing with Islam in a more symbolic way. High levels of education among women in Kerala and the process of reform have initiated a change in the way Muslims deal with Islamic texts and how they accommodate Islamic rituals and traditions into their local customs (gold for boys, for example, or women's entry to the mosques).

Argumentative jihād

Japanese proverb: If one can do it, you too can do it. If no one can do it, you must do it.
Indian version: If one can do it, let him do it. If no one can do it, leave it.
Kerala version: If one can do it, stop him from doing it. If no one can do it, make a harthal against it.

(A piece written by a Muslim Malayalee girl in tenth standard, Malappuram district)

Robinson (2000) identifies Quentin Skinner's contribution to the role of ideas in political action through this phrase: "men in pursuing their interests are limited by the range of concepts available to legitimise their actions and that this range of concepts is in turn limited by the prevailing morality of society" (pp. 180–181). This statement carries strong significance in the Keralite context, especially upon looking from a female perspective on the discourse on citizenship, and hence substituting 'men' with 'women'.

The paths shown to women to practise their citizenship were controlled by men to a great extent. In fact, concepts were emptied from their original baggage to fit different moulds and power holders' desires. If we start with the existential meaning of women, this conceptual ambivalence will become clear. In a study on the role of reason in Islam, the anthropology of marriage is a key to understand the means by which men acquired authority in the modern Muslim world. The key to power is argued to have resided in the subjugation of women and thus the establishment of despotism. Despite the ideas concerning Eve's name (in Arabic, it is *Hawaa*', which means container, and hence the container of life), modern contracts of marriage were designed in a manner resembling property ownership (Khalil, 1993).

What Indian Muslim women, and not only feminists, are engaged in now-adays is this readjustment of the understanding of concepts of citizenship and their societal status based on the utilisation of Islam and the Constitution as weaponry in their struggles. V. P. Suhra, for example, a women rights activist in Kozhikode and a self-built woman who does not belong to the academic circles, points out the dynamics of how women are coming to the forefront and reveal-ing the contradictions prevalent in both national and religious histories. To her, political forces are working in Kerala in order to oppose women's full citizen-ship rights (V. P. Suhra, author interview, December 2010).

The biggest hurdle to this struggle lies in the nature of the Muslim Personal Law and its relations with power holders. Unlike, for example, the Dalits' struggle against the caste system, Muslim women's struggle is muffled because their authority is questionable since their weapons are designed by the powerful groups. As the political leaders' power is intertwined with the religious, any crit-icism is destined to be muted with the charges of either heresy or interference in Muslim issues. This is where education comes into place, especially a religious one, and offers women opportunities to readjust their status and roles in society.

Interestingly, although calls for women's representation feature as a com-monly mentioned goal in minority reports and petitions, many women them-selves are sceptical of the new reservations for women in local bodies. This is evident in a common phrase I heard from students: "Now we do not only have to bear the politicians, but we have to bear their wives as well." As I interviewed several of the newly elected Muslim League female panchayat members, a huge difference appeared between them and their counterparts who had been politi-cally active before this decision was enacted. In one 'failed' attempt to interview a panchayat member in Malappuram district, we were accompanied by a male lawyer, who took me to the village, my interpreter and this woman's husband. After each question I asked, the lawyer would reiterate it and try to instil his own answer in the question. She would then, instead of giving answers or making statements, reply in a question form addressed to her husband. The same inci-dent was repeated in other interviews. It became obvious how men were always trying to limit or frame their answers according to their male opinions; in my infuriated interpreter's words, "it became an indirect movement against women's representations".

The MSF Calicut University Campus Conference of 2011 is an example of the changing atmosphere in Kerala triggered by girls' education. As I mentioned earlier, this conference was the first Muslim student programme among the Sunnis with women participating. Around 500 girls participated, as well as two female speakers: one was the Tamil Muslim Leaguer Fatima Muzafar. Despite this, the male-dominated atmosphere was starkly relevant. As I got to know about this conference from one of the students, I decided to join the ranks of female students who were seated in the back rows. Gradually, I started to realise that the whole empowerment discourse one hears of or reads as a title on a pro-gramme or event schedule is a façade to the reality of patriarchy. Since I could not speak Malayalam, I came to the conference when Fatima Muzafar was scheduled to speak. However, as I sat down for two hours, I realised that her talk was postponed and she was to speak after all the political male leaders and *Thangals* had finished. By 4.30 p.m., most of the girls were leaving, with only a few teachers who lived on campus staying. They had to go because they were supposed to be home by 5 p.m.

As usual, the Sunni girls in the conference I talked to were interested in asking me similar questions to those posed by their Jamaati and Mujahid counterparts; they inquired about early marriage, walking freely at night in Egypt, freedom of speech and working opportunities for women. They told me, "Here freedom of expression exists in newspapers. Media is the only freedom we get, but you in Egypt get all the individual freedoms that we do not get in India."

The widespread phenomenon of young women organising conferences, workshops and parades can be looked upon as a form of social performance, which is symbolic and perceived as both a ritual and a strategy of protest and fight for agency. The Arabic college girls represent strong threats to the symbolic *Thangal* power holder or upper-class Muslim men. This is due to breaking the wall of estrangement created by the Muslim *'ulama* through deciphering the codes and thus revealing the reality behind superstitions and myths of healing rituals. This rendered great resistance on the part of the *Thangals* who waged attacks against women's presence in the public space. On the side of the women, this led to higher rates of religiosity, especially manifested through dress to counter any arguments of heresy or immorality. Islam is a moving and live religion, as a Muslim female scholar wrote. This statement proves how hard it is to disentangle Islamic rituals, from everyday social rituals. And as Muslim women acquire more powers through getting hold of the interpretive authority, then we would be witnessing a new order where the practice of rituals gives spaces to new forces and actors.

In their performances, it is important to see the distribution of power among the actors and the performers and, in Alexander's (2006) words, whether social power would manage to eliminate specific parts of a cultural text. Despite the fact that capitalist modes of consumption led to the emphasis on individual will and rational choice, participation in these performances is highly contingent on established hierarchies of gender relations and community politics. So we have a case in Kerala where the teledensity and the increasing dispersion of internet-enabled smart phones, in addition to high literacy rates, led to unbalancing these established keys of entry to the social performative field of power relations. The privileged access to the sacred text, as Alexander (2006) argues, stands in defiance of the impact of literacy. In Kerala, however, increasing numbers of girls are getting access to the Arabic language, mastering it and hence breaking this denial of access and dominance of the *'ulama* authority.

The ability to employ the knowledge acquired in their religious education and to transform this into a tool of argumentation that is applicable to the ways they manage their lives is characteristic of Keralite Muslim girls. It is intriguing to witness the methods by which they project their sense of agency. Two spheres of struggle are relevant here: their fight against dowry and their ability to stress their desire to work. Here is an example of the conversations I had with female students on the latter issue:

ME: In North India, there was a *fatwa* concerning banning women from working along with men. It is the opinion of *'ulama*, what do you think of it? I mean if there were a *palli committee man* telling you not to work with men, what would you say?

STUDENT: I would tell him this is against the Quran.

ME: Some people say that there should never be a woman ruling a country. What do you think?

STUDENT: Where men could not do what was required of them, women proved capable of doing it; that is what Indira Gandhi did. She proved it. She proved what men could not prove.

ME: But religious people mention a *hadith* against this.

STUDENT: Maybe there are certain restrictions for certain jobs, but still we can prove ourselves. And still so many people suffer due to many religious things. This is the main issue with India, there is always a religious problem and one cannot stop this.

For the women I interviewed, the problem of dowry emerged as almost the single predicament in response to my question of what the major problem in Kerala is. I am hence presenting this issue and the way they fight it or respond to it as an example of argumentative *jihād* waged against a tradition enforced by male power holders that has resulted in women's commodification.

As a success story of the fight against dowry, the situation in the Nilambur municipality in Malappuram district is demonstrated, although it should be noted that women were not essentially the leaders of this initiative, but were active agents in the process of change. According to the municipality chairman, Aryadan Shoukath, in Nilambur, like in most villages in Malappuram district, there are thirty-year-old grandmothers, since 80% of the marriages involve girls below the age of eighteen. This is correlated to the fact that 80% of Muslims belong to the Sunni group. Nilambur has a population of 45,000; 40% are Muslim. Of the Muslims, 60% are below the poverty line (BPL). Every week, there are approximately ten marriages, particularly in BPL families. Eight out of ten marriages are dowry marriages with a minimum of 1–1.5 lakh rupees and 4 lakh Gold.

Nilambur had a two-year programme called the thousand-home project, from which 800 homeless people benefitted. After conducting the survey and finding that the number of the homeless was 800, and after giving them houses, the municipality received more applications. Upon enquiry, the applicants said that, at the time of the survey, they were not homeless, but were after they sold their houses to get dowry for their daughters. Every year, 50–75 houses are sold for dowry. Other means of getting the money is through collecting it, borrowing from banks by mortgaging their house or borrowing money from local financiers (*marvari*).

Dowry is spent in multiple ways. The most common way is to spend it to get a visa to the Gulf. The second option, especially for unskilled men, is to buy an auto rickshaw. A major part of it is usually spent on food, feasts and house renovations. Also, in some cases, the dowry would be usurped from the wife for a second marriage.

According to a survey report conducted by the Nilambur municipality, 80% of women have paid dowry. Accordingly, the panchayat in cooperation with the *Kerala Mahila Samakhya Society* undertook an initiative called 'The Dowry Free Village Campaign' to fight this practice. The initiative was fought through two kinds of action: campaigns via street plays and seminars; and capacity building programmes through a community college and free coaching. The idea behind having a community college is to overcome the ramifications of early marriage, which result in the discontinuation of girls' education and thus rendering them fragile in case of divorce or abuse by the husband, since they are totally financially dependent on him due to their lack of skills. The aim is to make girls get educated and find a job, and thus overcome the dowry system.

In addition to this, *Kudumbasree*, or the micro-finance units organised by women in every village, have positively impacted women by enhancing their sense of initiative, decision-making and entry into the public sphere. These local self-help programmes are one of the main sources of women's income. These are neighbourhood programmes, supported by the local government. In Nilambur, in 2011, there were 328 neighbourhood groups, and every BPL family had one member coming under it. In Kerala, 50% BPL came under this. In Nilambur, the figure was much higher: 95%.

After endless questions to every *imam* or Sunni scholar I met about the dowry and why they do not call against it, and after not being able to get satisfying or logical answers, I met a student who wrote his MPhil thesis on dowry in Kerala and told me that what he has found is that the Sunni scholars in the *palli* committee actually take a share from the dowry, and this is how their functions and expenses are covered. On other double standards employed by the traditional *ustādhs*, he laughed and told me how they ban TV for others, but their own kids watch TV more than any others.

In one of my visits to a Mujahid Islamic college, this impact of education was most evident, at least in the perceptive capacities of the girls. When I asked them what their problems in India were, they answered, "Child marriage and the inverted (*ūlta*) dowry". They used the Hindi word *ūlta*, referring to dowry as *ūlta mahr*. This was the first time I heard it used to describe the Indian dowry system. Due to their education, they became aware of the fact that it is inverted and hence abnormal.

After my talk, which extended to a large discussion, or a strong trial on my part to make them overcome their barrier of fear, a girl came to sing a song. She was singing a poem in Arabic. The poem read as follows:

Oh mother, you were joyful with my conception and carriage,
But the minute I was born, I became miserable

Why is it that people treat girls as the lowest of creatures?
Aren't they the gifts of heaven?

When I asked who wrote this poem, I was told it was the grandmother of one of the students, who knew Arabic, and poetry was her hobby.

Summary

I started the previous chapter with a narrative from my fieldwork but I will end this one with another narrative from Kerala: The *imams* (or as they are called, the *ustādh*) of the nearby mosque of the village where I lived in Kerala come every third day of the month to have dinner. In the morning, a boy from the *madrasa* is sent with empty lunch boxes that are filled with very carefully prepared vegetable *korma*, *appam* (a type of rice-flour bread) and tea. The same happens with lunch, but at dinner, he comes in person, eats with the men of the house, while the housewife, Rajiyath, serves without being seen, hides in the kitchen waiting for them to finish, and then he sits out with the other men in the living room, divided from the dining table with a stained glass wall, she sits on the dining table, the *ustādh* reads out *du'ā* (a prayer) and everyone says *amen* after him. From behind this wall, Rajiyath does the same. Interestingly, it is only Rajiyath who understands the meaning of the prayers, due to her knowledge of Arabic from the *madrasa* where she had studied in her childhood.

So on that day in the morning, Rajiyath told me enthusiastically, "The *ustādh* is coming tonight; this is a good chance for you, why don't you interview him?" When she said this to her husband, Mr Abubakr, he replied, "But how can she speak to him? They do not speak to women and she does not know Malayalam." "Well, he speaks Arabic, it will be fine. And she can write down the questions and you give it to him", she answered. I explained to her that the *madrasa ustādhs* definitely did not speak good Arabic because I had just tried to interview an *ustādh* two weeks ago and I needed a ten-year-old child to interpret and translate my questions from English to Malayalam. She was surprised. "Really? They do not know Arabic? But they claim to be masters in this language", she exclaimed. I smiled back at her instant recognition of the questionable authority on the text that religious scholars claim. I wrote the questions and, later that night, I gave them to Mr Abubakr. I wore my *pardah* and went out to sit with his wife and listen to the prayer. After the prayer, he tried to read the questions but my handwriting was not very legible. He called me and from behind the wall I read them out to him. Then he called me to come and introduce me to the *imams*. It was quite strange that in one second the wall vanished, and the two *imams* looked like very ordinary men, talking and addressing me normally. My first question was whether the Muslim *'ulama* and *ustādh* there felt that they were different from their North Indian counterparts. The *imam* replied that the difference lay in them following the Shafi' tradition, whereas the North Indians followed the Hanafi one. In addition to this, the *khuṭba* is in Arabic. In North India, they depend on the *hadith* before issuing the *fatwa*, whereas the South Indians depend first on the Shafi' *fiqh* before proclaiming a *fatwa*. When I asked them what their role in solving social problems was, he did not seem to identify on his own what the social problems I referred to were. So I gave an example of the dowry system. He explained further that the Arabs propagated Islam in Kerala, and when Indians converted, they gave ornaments to the Arabs who were going to marry them. This is how the custom started and it was not essentially very negative in their point of view. However, because of the social malpractices associated to it now, all *'ulama* in his opinion are against dowry, but people keep on practising it. When I asked him if he thought that since people did not totally follow what they preached then this might have indicated that their power was not so strong, he answered that people did not necessarily follow *fatwas*, espe-cially those with strong financial powers. Then I asked about political *fatwas*. He said they never intervened in politics, but if there was a big issue, they usually read and referred to what the Egyptian scholar Yusuf Al-Qaradawy wrote. The Jumaa speech is not part of this since it is in Arabic and thus does not serve as a tool to address socio-political problems. The *imams*, however, play a role in solving social problems because people come to them first before resorting to either the courts or the police.

What is evident through the dynamics outlined in this chapter is the politics of youth, which is to a great extent politics of metaphor. These young women manage to disguise a rebellion within a framework of a dominant culture. Although their struggle seems to be one of 'the ordinary', in reality it is a revolu-tionary struggle for presence and denial of their absence.

What I have tried to show is the heterogeneity of the spaces and contexts in which youth project their active sense of citizenship. Kerala in fact, regardless of the religious variable, is known to be a place where multiple opinions are formed and nurtured; there is a famous saying that holds, "When a Malayalee stays alone, he becomes a poet. When he stays with another one, both form different contending organisations."

Most of these youth are struggling through different conflicting contexts in their life-spaces; they have to deal daily with the societal pressure to be a 'good Muslim' and at the same time, while being influenced by theories of political Islam, they are confronted with the modern democratic secular framework they live in guarantee-ing many rights and liberties. This framework has influenced their upbringing and has led to their realisation of possibilities of different opportunities. This is perhaps in a manner reminiscent to an advertisement for a private school that I once saw in a street in Kerala that said: "Peace Public School: Excellent Secular Education in an Islamic Environment". However, the ability to conform to the hegemonising stream of thought as directed by the political socialisation process, whether at secular or Islamic schools, is not always present for every individual. This is expressed in the words of a young Muslim lecturer:

> Sometimes I am unable to identify myself as a secular Indian citizen because what I learnt from my school about India and its rulers (like Gandhi and Nehru) was met later with the realisation that what I learned is wrong, so

something has to be changed in my own concepts and in the concepts of society and the community I belong to. I believe that every member of Muslim youth in India is going through these crises of religious, social and political identity. The minority is forced to be in the majority and to carry the opinion of the majority in India through the media. They are forcing themselves to be part of this democracy. They should have their own spaces and own ideas, only then would democracy flourish. The community I belong to and also lower castes in India are struggling with their identity.

Notes

1 Literature on the history of Ponnani is scarcely found in English since the majority is in Malayalam. For a brief history of the development of Muslim religious education that started from Ponnani, see Pasha (1995).
2 This is Malayalam written in Arabic script. Arabi-Malayalam refers not only to a script but also to a genre of literature that originated in the ninth or tenth century. One of its famous writers is the satirist philosopher Kunhayin Musaliyar of Tellicherry (Kurup & Ismail, 2008). Also see Karassery (1995).
3 Imru' Al-Qais was a pre-Islamic time Arab poet from the Arabian Peninsula in the sixth century AD.
4 Examples of the historically revered *'ulama* who enjoyed privilege status are the jurist Sheikh Zaiudeen Makhdum of Ponnani of the sixteenth century, Sayyid Fazl Pokoya Thangal of Mamburam from the nineteenth century and Sayyid Alavi Thangal, who was a leading freedom fighter against the British in the Moplah rebellion.
5 In Islamic culture, Muslims usually wear new clothes in *Eid* as a form of celebration. *Khadi* refers to the handloom cloth that was adopted as a counter-colonial strategy by Gandhi.
6 For the English translation, see Makhdoom (2009).
7 The speech was given at MES women's college in Kozhikode. The joke refers to the fact that there is no longer any need to give more attention to women and reserve colleges for them since they outnumber boys anyway in the other mixed colleges.
8 Women would only learn Arabi-Malayalam and the Arabic script to read the Quran. There are many old women who cannot read Malayalam but only the Arabic script. In an interview with a worker at a university canteen, she asserted that she did not go to school and hence could not read Malayalam but she could read and write Arabic because she learnt it at the *madrasa*.
9 For example, when I asked if I was supposed to register my new address, all that my landlord had to do was to meet the police officer by chance somewhere and inform him about me.
10 In addition to the Kashmir House established by the Sunni Markaz, there is a large institution called JDT Islam (Jam'iyyat Da'wa wa Tablighul Islam), which was established as an orphanage in 1922 by Abdul Kader Kasoori from Punjab. Its history dates back to the tragic consequences of the Malabar rebellion. The orphanage was a place for rehabilitation of the orphans of the men who lost their lives. Now it is being funded by the Gulf, especially Kuwait. It also has a hospital called Iqraa International hospital, which is fully funded by Saudi money.
11 It is also argued that the Mappilas preferred the peaceful politics of Muslim League to the communists' because of the 1921 revolt and the devastating effect it had on the Mappilas. As a result, the Madras government legislated land reforms in 1930 to grant tenants protection against eviction and to allow some landless labourers to buy land. This climaxed in the 1969 Kerala Land Reforms, which granted more rights to the

agricultural classes. The importance given to education was another factor, especially with the rise of Mappila-run schools. Educated Mappilas realised that electoral politics was the road to the achievement of gains for the community. The Muslim League started winning seats in the Legislative Assembly by 1945. The Muslim League also considered the formation of a separate state for Kerala to enhance the situation of Mappilas who would constitute, in that case, 20% of the state population. The Muslim League's power was obtained through a dual process: identification with a common problem first and then acquisition of institutional power. In an attempt by the communist government to attract Muslims, it recognised Mappilas as backward and thus secured them a 10% reservation for employment in 1957, and in 1967–69 created the Muslim-majority Malappuram district (Jeffrey, 1992).

12 In Kerala, the word *palli* refers to a Hindu temple or a mosque or church. This is another indicator of the level of social integration.

13 It remains to be said that, despite this change in acquiring a presiding architectural style, their dominance is still not equally compared to the North Indian case where gigantic structures of Vishnu or Hanuman protrude and remind one of their position and difference.

14 A difference in the wrapping style is observed to ensure adherence to Islamic rules, such as covering the midriff and the head.

15 For more details, see Abdelhalim (2013).

16 *Kolkali* is a performing art from Malabar which is taken from the traditional *Kalarippayatt* (a form of Dravidian martial art using small sticks or swords). The change to the Hindu form is that it is accompanied by Islamic songs, the boys are not barechested and their heads are covered with a piece of cloth.

17 The song called *Native Bapa* was made by a group of Muslim students called *Mappila Lahala* in 2013, www.youtube.com/watch?v=opnMreZoRyQ (accessed on 8 May 2014).

18 http://kafila.org/2014/08/24/arrested-for-sitting-during-the-national-anthem-solidarity-statement-with-salman/ (accessed on 24 August 2014).

19 Also known as Haleema Beevi (the transliteration differs in different sources).

20 Haleema Beevi (1920–2000) "Welcome speech at Muslim Women's Conference of the Travancore Muslim Women's Association", Tiruvalla, 15 Edavam (May–June 1938). Muslim Vanita, 1, 4, ME 1113 Mithunam (June–July 1938): 103–7, quoted from Devika (2005, pp. 168–173).

21 This municipality is central in this study for several reasons, including: first, Nilambur is considered the first village in India to achieve a total literacy rate; and second, there is a unique on-going project to make Nilambur the first dowry-free village in India.

22 There is more to this explanation. In private colleges in Kerala, there is a hidden code or stipulation to pay a sum of money in return for a teaching position. Muslim women, being already financially drained because of the dowry obligations and because of being socially more backward than their Hindu and Christian counterparts, cannot always afford to pay this sum of money.

23 Physical Quality of Life Index, which refers to low infant mortality rate, high life expectancy and high level of basic literacy.

24 One of the UDF/Congress Propaganda Brochures for the Kerala Legislative Assembly Elections of 2011 referred to Kerala as "not so shining". It further criticised the LDF's rule as having witnessed *Hawalas*, alcohol, vehicle, sand and sex mafias (UDF Kerala Website, http://udf.org.in/kerala-"not-so"-shining.html, accessed on 14 March 2011).

25 Interview with Jamaati Islami Girls Islamic Organisation activist. For more information on media coverage of 'love *jihād*' see, for example: *Times of India*, Kerala CM reignites 'love jihad' theory, 26 July 2010, http://articles.timesofindia.indiatimes.com/2010-07-26/india/28290879_1_pfi-muslim-women-love-and-money; *Sahil Online*, Karnataka High Court supports true love, not love jihad, 21 January 2010, www.sahilonline.org/english/newsDetails.php?cid=2&nid=7278.

26 There is also a political group that has a thin layer of supporters and is labelled as extremist, or the Muslim counterpart of the Hindu right-wing. This is widely known as NDF (National Development Front), which was transformed into the political party Social Democratic Party of India (SDPI), associated with the Popular Front of India (PFI) and the People's Democratic Party (PDP) of Madani (a famous detained Muslim political leader).

27 For detailed information on KNM, see Osella and Osella (2008). It should be noted that recently KNM has been divided into three groups.

28 These data are obtained from an interview with Hafiz Mohamed. The percentages are obtained through calculating the number of *madrasas* affiliated to each group. Faith-wise, Muslims would actually be divided into four groups, including the Ahmadiyyas, who have their own mosques and act like a clan, and are considered by non-Ahmadiyyas to be untrue Muslims. Politics-wise, Muslims would be divided into three groups. The majority are the Muslim Leaguers, followed by the Jamaati Islami, and finally the NDF supporters (SDPI and PDP).

29 The splitting of Muslim organisations in Kerala eased social control over Muslims. Hussain exemplifies this; in the old days if someone did not attend Jumaa prayer, the *mahals* would enquire about the reason of absence, but now with the tremendous amounts of mosques and factions, people can freely choose which mosque to go to (S. Hussein, author interview, December 2010).

30 The correct reference would either be a verse from the Quran from the story of Joseph (Yusuf) or a *hadith*. The verse reads, "They said if a wolf should eat him while we are a [strong] clan, indeed, we would then be losers" (12:14, Sahih International Translation). As for the *hadith*, it reads:

> The devil continually pursues humans as a wolf pursues sheep. The wolf only dares to attack those sheep which have separated from the rest of the flock and are standing alone. And so, my followers and my devotees! Save yourselves from being caught in the traps of misguidance and firmly remain with the largest and most well-known group of Muslims!
>
> (Imam Ahmed)

31 The biggest mosque in India is going to be built in Kozhikode by the AP Sunni group. This is basically coming from Gulf money.

32 In a visit to a fishermen's village, one of the fishermen showed me his mobile phone with Shehab's photo as the background image. When I commented on this to another fisherman, he said that I would find his photo on everyone's mobile and in everyone's house.

33 For more information on the history of the development of today's Kerala Nadwatul Mujahedeen, see Kutty (1995).

34 Apparently, the figure rose significantly from 600 mosques in 2002, as shown in Zain's (2002) article.

35 The teacher used the word *jahidna* (the verb of *jihād*) to express this struggle.

36 Interestingly until today, the Jamaati are emotionally involved and concerned about the political developments in the Arab world.

37 At the time of my fieldwork in the first half of the year 2011, Jamaati Islami was still proposing the formation of its political party with the aim of giving representation to all marginalised sections. In October 2011, the Welfare Party of India was launched in Kerala.

38 Omar Ibn Al-Khattab was the second Caliph, after Abu Bakr, in the Islamic Caliphate shortly after the death of the Prophet Muhammad; he was also one of his companions.

39 Bint Alshati', or Aisha Abdulrahman, (1913–98) was one of the pioneer Egyptian female writers.

40 According to the Election Commission's polling statistics of the Kerala Legislative Assembly Elections of 2011, 52% of the votes were women's (9,036,356 out of the 17,387,651 votes). The highest women voter turnout was registered in Malappuram

district. Not only in Malappuram, but also in Kasaragod, Kozhikode, Thrissur and Kannur, women outnumbered men in voting (*The Hindu*, Women lead in 1.74 crore votes cast, C. Gouridasan Nair, 21 April 2011).
41 http://indianexpress.com/article/india/politics/muslim-woman-minus-hijab-is-left-choice-in-malappuram/.
42 www.milligazette.com/news/4849-muslim-women-for-social-revolution, accessed on 1 July 2015.
43 The following are links to video clips of these *Mappillapattu* (or Muslim Malayalee songs) which appeared on a reality show on Jaihind channel, which I often watched with the women in the village where I was staying: www.youtube.com/watch?v=1Vx YpATwIA8&feature=related (accessed on 1 November 2011); www.youtube.com/wa tch?v=T8Aka9P2F70&feature=related (accessed 1 November 2011).

References

Abdelhalim, J. (2013). Paradoxes of Pardah and Agency Among Muslim Women in Kerala. *Urban People/Lidé Města*, 15(2), 237–256.
Abdul Samad, M. (1998). *Islam in Kerala: Groups and Movements in the 20th Century.* Kollam: Laurel Publications.
Al-Qasmi, A. G. (2000). *Muslims in Kerala (Almuslimun fi Kerala).* Malappuram: AK MAL Book Centre.
Alexander, J. (2006). Cultural Pragmatics: Social Performance Between Ritual and Strategy. In J. Alexander, B. Giesen & J. L. Mast (eds), *Social Performance: Symbolic Action, Cultural Pragmatics and Ritual* (pp. 29–90). Cambridge: Cambridge University Press.
Bavakutty, M. (1982). Library Movement in Kerala. *Libri*, 32(1), 251–256.
Bayat, A. (2009). *Life as Politics: How Ordinary People Change the Middle East.* Cairo: The American University in Cairo Press.
Bourdieu, P., & Wacquant, L. J. (1992). *An Invitation to Reflexive Sociology.* Cambridge: Polity Press.
Census of India. (2001). Retrieved on 3 July 2012, from www.censusindia.gov.in/2011-common/CensusDataSummary.html.
Dale, S. F. (1980). *Islamic Society on the South Asian Frontier: The Mappilas of Malabar 1498–1922.* Oxford: Clarendon Press.
Devika, J. (2005). *Her-Self: Early Writings on Gender by Malayalee Women 1989–1938.* Kolkata: Mandira Sen.
Devika, J. (2007). *En-Gendering Individuals: The Language of Re-Forming in Twentieth Century Keralam.* New Delhi: Orient Longman.
Eickelman, D. F., & Anderson, J. W. (1999). Redefining Muslim Publics. In D. F. Eickelman & J. W. Anderson (eds), *New Media in the Muslim World* (pp. 1–18). Indiana: Indiana University Press.
Engineer, A. A. (ed.) (1995). *Kerala Muslims: A Historical Perspective.* New Delhi: Ajanta Publications.
Hassan, Z., & Menon, E. (eds) (2005). *In a Minority: Essays on Muslim Women in India.* New Delhi: Oxford University Press.
Heller, P. (2000). Degrees of Democracy: Some Comparative Lessons from India. *World Politics*, 52(4), 484–519.
Hussain, S., & Devika, J. (2010, 10 September). Dressing and Death-Threats in Kerala: Re-former Man's Second Coming? Retrieved on 15 February 2011, from Kafila, http://kafila.org/2010/09/10/dressing-and-death-threats-in-kerala-re-former-man%E2%80%99s-second-coming.

Indian Social Institute. (2009). Minorities: Muslims 2009 – Human Rights Documentation. Retrieved on 10 January 2012, from www.isidelhi.org.in/hrnews/isidownload/Muslim/Muslims-2009.pdf.

Jalal, A. (2008). *Partisans of Allah: Jihad in South Asia.* Cambridge, MA: Harvard University Press.

Jeffrey, R. (1992). *Politics, Women and Well-Being: How Kerala Became a Model.* Houndmills: Macmillan.

Karassery, M. N. (1995). Arabic Malayalam. In A. A. Engineer (ed.) *Kerala Muslims: A Historical Perspective* (pp. 168–173). New Delhi: Ajanta Publications.

Khalil, K. A. (1993). *Al-'aql fil Islam bahth falsafi fi hudood al-sharakah bayn al-'aql al-'ilmi wal 'aql al-deeni (Reason in Islam: A Philosophical Research in the Limits of Partnership Between Scientific Reason and Religious Reason).* Beirut: Dar Al-Tali'at.

Khan, A. M. (2010). *Text and Context: Quran and Contemporary Challenges.* New Delhi: Rupa and Co.

Kunju, A. P. I. (1989). *Mappila Muslims of Kerala.* Trivandurum: Sandhya Publications.

Kurup, K. K., & Ismail, E. (2008). *Emergence of Islam in Kerala in the 20th Century.* New Delhi: Standard Publishers.

Kurup, K. N. (2006). *The Legacy of Islam (Kerala). A Study of the Mappilas of Kerala.* Kannur: Samayam Publications.

Kutty, E. K. A. (1995). The Mujahid Movement and Its Role in the Islamic Revival in Kerala. In A. A. Engineer (ed.), *Kerala Muslims: A Historical Perspective* (pp. 67–82). Delhi: Ajanta.

Makhdoom, S. Z. (2009). *Tuhfat Al Mujahidin: A Historical Epic of the Sixteenth Century* (M. Nainar, Trans.). Calicut: Other Books, & Kuala Lumpur: Islamic Book Trust.

Miller, R. E. (1976). *Mappila Muslims of Kerala: A Study in Islamic Trends.* New Delhi: Orient Longman.

Muslim Youth League. (2014). Bhasha Samaram. Retrieved on 13 March 2014, from www.muslimyouthleaguemlp.org/web/bhashasamaram.asp.

Narayanan, M. G. S. (2006). *Calicut: The City of Truth.* Calicut: University of Calicut.

Oommen, M. A. (2008, 12 January). Reforms and the Kerala Model. *Economic and Political Weekly,* 43(2), 22–25.

Osella, F., & Osella, C. (2008). Islamism and Social Reform in Kerala. *Modern Asian Studies,* 42(2/3), 317–346.

Ottappilakkool, M. (2007). *Role of Ulama in the Anti-Colonial Struggle of India: A Case Study of Malabar.* PhD thesis. Calicut: Calicut University.

Pasha, K. (1995). Muslim Religious Education. In A. A. Engineer (ed.), *Kerala Muslims: A Historical Perspective* (pp. 133–146). Delhi: Ajanta.

Qasmi, M. K. (2005). *Madrasa Education: Its Strength and Weakness.* Mumbai: MMERC and Manak.

Randathani, H. (2007). *Mappila Muslims: A Study on Society and Anti Colonial Struggles.* Calicut: Other Books.

Robinson, F. (2000). *Islam and Muslim History in South Asia.* Oxford: Oxford University Press.

Robinson, F. (2006). Religious Change and the Self in Muslim South Asia Since 1800. In A. Roy (ed.), *Islam in History and Politics: Perspectives from South Asia* (pp. 21–35). Delhi: Oxford University Press.

Siddique, P. A. (2005). Panchayati Raj and Women in Kerala: The Case of Muslims. In Z. Hassan & E. Menon (eds), *In a Minority: Essays on Muslim Women in India* (pp. 284–309). New Delhi: Oxford University Press.

Transparency International. (2005). Indian Corruption Study. Retrieved on 5 January 2011, from www.transparencyindia.org/resource/survey_study/India%20Corruption%20Study%202005.pdf.

Vatuk, S. (2008). Islamic Feminism in India: Indian Muslim Women Activists and the Reform of Muslim Personal Law. *Modern Asian Studies*, 42(2/3), 489–518.

Wilson, C. (2010). *The Commodification of Health Care in Kerala, South India: Science, Consumerism and Markets*. PhD thesis. Brighton: University of Sussex.

Wood, C. (1987). *The Moplah Rebellion and its Genesis*. New Delhi: People's Publishing House.

Zachariah, K., & Rajan, I. S. (2007, December). Migration, Remittances and Employment: Short-Term Trends and Long-Term Implications, Working Paper 395. Retrieved on 1 July 2015, from Centre for Development Studies, http://opendocs.ids.ac.uk/opendocs/bitstream/handle/123456789/3100/wp395.pdf?sequence=1.

Zain, A. (2002). Zakat Cells: A Kerala Model. Retrieved on 20 June 2012, from The Milli Gazette, www.milligazette.com/Archives/01012002/0101200219.htm.

6 Operationalising the sense of citizenship

From Delhi to Kerala

One day while wearing a *burqa*, I went to get phone credit in a shop in an upscale market in southern Delhi. The shop assistant thought I was a foreigner and started talking to me in English even before I opened my mouth. Apparently he had thought I was from the Gulf, although I was dressed exactly like the *burqa*-clad Indian Muslim women. But it was striking to me that it was easier to assume that a woman in a *burqa* in this dominantly Hindu and upper-class area would definitely be a non-Indian; that it was easier to imagine her as a tourist, but not as a local or a fellow Indian.

This obviously meant that the psychological distance was too huge to accommodate a healthy practice of citizenship, especially that the phenomenon of ghettoisation is more evident in Northern India, which, according to an Islamic scholar at Lucknow, appeared after partition as a means to ensure security of the self, belief and livelihood. After Gujarat 2002, citizenship in India was subject to a test. It would be wrong to assume that this incident is a passing irregularity in the stream of events, since only the truth of many things is realised by these fast or spontaneous fragments of happenings. The idea of citizenship after all revolves around the sense of security. Hence, the resulting ghettoisation found in the rest of the country poses substantial threats to a healthy solid formation of citizenship. I ended my fieldwork in India with a short stay in one of these Muslim ghettos in South Mumbai. The words of the Muslim taxi driver that took me to the airport somehow summarises the stories hundreds of interviewees wished to deliver:

> The Muslim area you were staying in is very safe, the Muslims are very united there, no one, except for the police, dares to come and kill, but the other places especially on the outskirts of Mumbai are dangerous and full of problems because of Shiv Sena.
>
> (Mumbai, April 2011)

In operationalising the sense of citizenship among Muslim youth, several aspects have been considered. Citizenship as a set of obligations and rights was measured using indicators such as political rights and duties; voting and political awareness, for example, in addition to cultural rights and perceptions of discrimination.

Voting myths

As the Delhi-based Centre for the Study of Democratic Societies' (CSDS) National Election Surveys (NES) showed, there was no difference in voter turnout between the all-India figures and the Muslim figures. The reliance on the democratic system of governance as a secure haven for the attainment of rights clearly negates any remark on the alienation of Muslims. The data also counters any claim on specificity of Muslims, their passivity and aversion to the democratic process or even that they resort to violence and terrorism. As the Delhi-based journalist, Zafer Aga contends, "Muslim resistance is reflected during elections where they cast their votes; ballots instead of bullets are their weapons" (Zafer Aga, author interview, September 2010).

In my survey of Muslim students, 44.8% of the respondents said they vote in elections on a regular basis, and the figure did not radically change when I included the gender aspect. In my interviews with students, it often seemed ridiculous to them to ask why they vote. For them, voting had become a non-negotiable ritual that does not actually hold rational criteria of judgment. Many laughed when I had asked why they voted, and I had to explain that I was asking this question out of my political background of living in an authoritarian regime where I never had a chance to vote. One female respondent contended, "It is to make the candidate who is worthy of winning (with *iqtidaar*) and who is capable of helping us win." She added that her vote definitely had a high value.

The reasons for not voting as provided by the respondents in Delhi were divided between being away from one's constituency due to studying in Delhi (52% of the cases), not having a voter identity card at the time of the last elections because of their age (35%) and for other reasons related to not finding any of the candidates representative and simply using propaganda tools to gain Muslim votes but not eventually doing anything for their welfare (13%).

As for those who voted, the following gives the reasons for voting and the corresponding percentage:[1]

- 40% see voting as their constitutional and democratic right as citizens of India.
- 38% vote to choose a representative leader.
- 18% vote because of their belief in democracy.
- 7% desire to make a change through voting.
- 5.5% consider voting to be a duty.
- 5.5% vote to help a certain political party win.
- 3.7% vote to follow their family's instructions.

Again in Kerala, the dominance of the rights discourse was hegemonic but with an unequivocal emphasis on the belief in democracy. Of those interviewed, 38.4% said that voting is a right of Indian citizens; this was coupled with 14% who demonstrated a belief in democracy; only 10% viewed voting as a duty of Indian citizens; 11.5% said they voted to make democracy work better. Only 2%

translated their vote into support for Muslims, while 5% translated it into supporting the secular Constitution. The only reason given for not voting was the non-availability of a voter card in the previous elections due to their age.

It is surprising to see that, among those who did not vote, especially in Delhi, none justified their political choice as a translation of an identity-related issue. It was a strictly political choice. "Voting is a political act … being political is a way of being in modern time … and not going for voting is also political … voting is an act of representation" – as one of the respondents noted. Despite the commonly held view that Muslims are alienated and do not vote because they do not feel they belong to this nation but to Pakistan, no respondent ever brought up the issue of belonging.

On the contrary, interestingly, religious identity appeared as an incentive to vote, as a student noted: "I vote because in Islam itself there is a principle to follow the country's rules unless it violates basic tenets of Islam and I have faith in the democracy of my country." There was also an interesting correlation between the level of religiosity and voting, since 54.3% of those who read the Quran always voted.

The discourse of rights and their aptly conscious decision to make use of it also negates the common perceptions on alienation among youth. Although I do not establish an argument of representativeness, these indicators of the politically conscious culture among Muslim youth should not be dismissed. The high percentage of respondents aiming at choosing a representative leader is one significant feature. To many others, however, the only right they could think of possessing as a citizen of India was voting, which was indicative of a shaky sense of citizenship.

Many Muslim scholars have negated the phenomenon of the vote bank. Some asserted that it exists in India on a general basis and is not a Muslim-specific case, but the majority I interviewed held the view that it is a myth and false propaganda. A Muslim scholar at Nadwatul Ulama explained:

> The vote bank is a myth; Muslims are never united on one candidate. Votes are distributed, for example, in a constituency with a majority of Muslims, if a Muslim candidate is nominated, he will win, but if there are several good candidates, votes will be divided, and thus the opposing party will win. Political parties want to make use of Muslim votes, but Muslims are divided because of low levels of correct religious awareness and feeling.... Actually the Muslim candidate never works for the sake of Muslims, usually the Hindu does. A Muslim MP cannot pose questions in parliament concerning Muslims, he does not want to stir trouble for himself … India is the land of wonders, and so in politics, politics is some kind of conspiracy, politics is more of deceit than service.

Collectivity and association

The freedom of association in India is a very important issue that guides the path of democracy in India. In the National Election Surveys, the percentage of membership in religious organisations interestingly rose from 3.4% in 2004 to 12% in

2009 at the all-India level. Reducing the results to Muslims only, the percentage differs slightly: 2.1% in 2004 to 13.5% in 2009 (NES from the CSDS). This might be associated with the rise of 'Muslim' activism after the Babri Masjid demolishment and the Gujarat riots. The survey I conducted among students in Delhi showed a similar result since 15.2% of the students were members of Islamic organisations: 46% of these were affiliated to Jamaati Islami, 23% to Tablighi Jamaati, 23% to Barelvi organisations and 15% to other ones.

In Kerala, the figure is impressively higher since 45.2% are involved in an Islamic student organisation (17.5% females and 87% males). The divisions in the social fabric of the community, as shown in the previous chapter, are reflected in the affiliations of students, where 64.1% are members in Sunni or the traditional Sufi organisations, 22.6% are Mujahids, 9.4% are Jamaati Islami followers and 1% belongs to the Ahmadiyyah group.

As for political parties, 9.5% of the respondents in the Delhi survey said they were members of a party. I noted a slight correlation between membership in Islamic associations and political parties. One factor that should not be omitted is the young age of the respondents and the possibility of them becoming members of political parties in the future, due to the fact that the university workload, the absence of a student union at Jamia, the lifestyle of many youth who need to work during studies to save for the dowry or to take care of their family financially in UP or Bihar do not allow for engagement in political activities. This was reflected even among girls. When I asked one if she was a member of a political party, she said, "Not yet".

The figure in Kerala jumps up to 41.4%. This high level of political-party affiliation reflects the nature of the political culture in Kerala, especially the fact that the majority of Muslims are members of the Muslim League party, followed by the Congress Party.

Political awareness

> Muslims are indeed backward and it is because they are not self-aware. Lā yughayyir allah mā biqawm ḥatta yughayiru mā bianfusihum (God does not change a people unless they change themselves).[2] The soul has to be changed first. Just a feeling of discrimination does not help. With education, it is possible to change the self. Only then we can turn to the government and ask it to be fair and to change its policies and to rely on it to help us, because anyway governments are known to give lots of promises and less action.
>
> (A female PhD student at Jamia, 2010)

Chatting with teenagers, who were ecstatic about finally casting their first vote, about local and national politics, corruption and political choices showed how Indian youth are surprisingly engaged. Nevertheless this is not homogenous across India. In Delhi, only 61% of the respondents could name their MP or MLA. The question was asked in this way: "Can you name the Member of

Parliament or (*aapka netā*) who is representing your constituency?" The reference to the *netā* was made to bridge the political culture gap in the understanding of the representative since not all respondents could understand what an MP or MLA was.[3] This was certainly different in the case of Kerala, where the word MP and MLA did not require any interpretation or explanation, even for rural elderly women who had not finished their basic education; 88% could name one or both of their political representatives, and the female-only figure was still around 84%. Here we can observe a noted gap in political awareness between Delhi and Kerala and between males and females in Delhi, as only 45.2% of the Delhi female respondents could name either the MP or the MLA.

As for reading newspapers, Kerala gave an astonishing figure of 100% readership rate, while Delhi gave 99%. However, the Delhi figure is misleading, because often when I asked some girls about a recent incident, it turned out they had not heard about it. One time I talked to two girls who could only speak Hindi and Urdu, and when I asked whether they read any newspapers, they answered that they read the *Times of India*. When I inquired how they read it since they could not speak English, they said, "Oh, we look at the actors and actresses news."

The division of readership of newspapers according to language radically differed from Kerala to Delhi. Whereas in Kerala, Malayalam newspapers enjoyed the widest readership, in Delhi it was the English ones and not the Urdu one, with the most widely read newspaper being the *Times of India* (38.5%).

Sense of political efficacy and trust

As an operationalised category of citizenship, the sense of political efficacy was tested by the following question: "Do you think your vote is important and makes a difference?" The result was surprisingly high among the respondents in Delhi, with 82.9% giving a positive response. Even the females shared this belief, with 75.6% of them confirming this. Interestingly, the figure did not change in Kerala and was registered at 82.7% overall and 78.8% among females.

When we try to apply these figures to everyday life, we are faced with a paradox. Efficacy for many does not carry much significance. Security, on the other hand, is what eventually counts and forms the essential infrastructure for political action and healthy state–society dynamics. The relationship between the sense of security, an essential requirement of citizenship, and the providers or the police was evident in many narratives of students' lives:

> People come to Delhi and settle here because of job opportunities, then the police come and take the youth, especially those from Azamgarh in fake encounters. There are students who were doing their masters, and they were just picked and thrown in jail for nothing. Now their whole careers are gone, what are they going to do after coming out of prison? Who will employ them? This is why we, as Muslims, do not positively regard the police.
>
> (A male PhD student at JNU, 2010)

Despite the Gulf syndrome in Kerala and the ensuing widespread belief that education is the magical panacea for India, security as a threat to citizenship remains a strongly alarming issue. This is reflected in the words of a Muslim lecturer in Kerala:

> The state should provide security and only then we could say we are proud of being an Indian. But if being an Indian Muslim does not give one security, then there is a real problem with Indian democracy and secularism. Everyone should be able to speak about being a Muslim; otherwise there is no meaning of any democratic right being present in India.

According to the survey I conducted among students in Delhi, the majority (35.4%) showed moderate support of the Indian political system. Figure 6.1 shows the percentages of trust that North Indian Muslim youth have in certain institutions on a scale of 1–5, where 1 is the least and 5 is the maximum.

In Kerala, the percentages increase, as 58.7% show moderate support of the political system (Figure 6.2). The corresponding trust levels are as follows: the central government got 50.4%; 40% of the respondents showed trust in the state government, at an average level of 2.5; the local government got a slightly higher trust level at an average of 3.2 (32.5%); the legal system also had 32.5% of the respondents giving it an average of 3.2; the Election Commission had the highest trust level as 35.7% of the respondents gave it a 4, with an average of 3.5. The police got a higher trust level than in Delhi, with an average of 2.8 as 39.1% of the respondents gave it a 3. The Muslim clergy got a similar trust level as in Delhi, with an average of 3.5 and 30.1% ranking it with a 4. Finally, 37.6% of the respondents gave the media an average of 3.

If 1 is the least and 5 is the maximum, how would you rate the level of your support to the Indian political system?

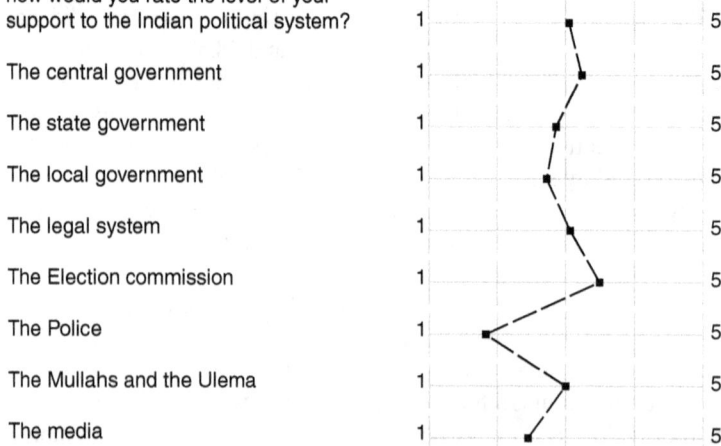

Figure 6.1 Trust levels among the youth in Delhi (source: own survey).

If 1 is the least and 5 is the maximum, how would you rate the level of your support to the Indian political system?

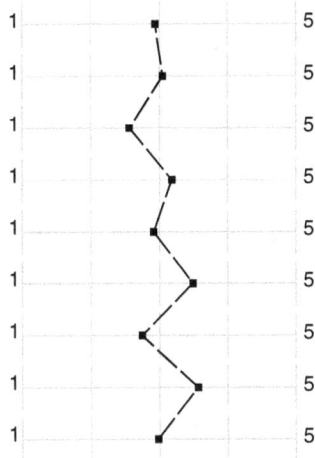

Figure 6.2 Trust levels among the youth in Kerala (source: own survey).

Despite the high level of trust for the police and media in Kerala, in-depth interviews with people belonging to the *'ām ādmi* category or the working class have reflected a disparate image. The results of the survey were skewed to the 'better' or rosy position due to the outnumbering of females. Being confined to the safe realms of their home, their hostel or their campus, they did not encounter many problems with institutions and the police. However, interviews with working students or destitute fishermen showed cases of police bias based on their economic class, not to mention their caste. Many of these interviews refer to the notorious Marad massacre in the coastal village near Kozhikode and the ways both the police and the media biasedly dealt with the issue.[4] In the words of a Muslim fisherman:

> It was seen that the police in Marad was angry with the Muslims. It depends upon the area. My aunt lives there in Marad. Her son has been in jail for seven years. When we go there we feel that the police is angry with our people. And so is the media. When they give some news about the first Marad riot it would be given in the first page, but when it is about the second Marad riot they put it in the inner pages. They left the Hindus who were captured. Now our people are in prison.
>
> (A Muslim fisherman, in a coastal village in
> Malappuram district, December 2010)

Instead of the discourse on religion-based reservations, which does not always find resonance among Muslims, due to the fear of the hegemony of the Muslim upper class, emphasis is cast on the enforcement of law and the eradication of corruption and discrimination. In Gupta's words, "Citizenship becomes a viable project when the enforcement of law respects the individual as a citizen and does not make concessions to sentiments of 'the people'" (Gupta, 2007, p. 43). The sense of security is hence directly related to the efficacious practice of citizenship rights. The sense of citizenship and belonging of the part (the citizen) to the whole (the *patria* and the homeland) necessitates cooperation and integration of issues that are of relevance to the part but influence the whole. The uniqueness about the Indian experience is the hybrid creation of this formula.

This is also realised through a process of accepting the system's legitimacy. Interestingly, throughout my conversations with students in Delhi, it was apparent that most of them did not know what legitimacy meant. Some girls did not know the word democracy in the first place (in both its English and Urdu variants), and most were not cognizant of what authoritarianism referred to. Political terminologies seemed to carry different connotations. For one female student, legitimacy was linked to the Commonwealth Games and how the country was not prepared for it. For another male student, he saw the central government as corrupt, especially after the Commonwealth Games deal. He had read in the Hindi newspaper *Jansakta* how the money that was spent on the Commonwealth Games could have fed rice to all of India, and could have given free medical services to Indians for the next eight years.

This means that the level of trust is contingent upon events unveiling corruption deals, for instance. The same is the case for the police and *'ulama*. The police, for many, are a body that works solely via bribes and hence only the rich can get away with anything. The similarity in the support level to the central government is directly linked to the fact that it was a Congress government at the time of my survey. Respondents in both the regions affirmed that, as long as it was a Congress government, then it was the best among the worse.

Although there is a realistic difference between what an *'alim* refers to and what a *mullah* is since *'alim* (singular of *'ulama*) is a learned scholar of Islam, with a higher educational status than a *mullah*, the two words are used interchangeably among Indian Muslims. Very few students actually managed to differentiate between them in their conversations. This is the reason I grouped them in one category despite my acknowledgment that they are not synonymous. As for the *mullahs*, the low level of trust cast by some of the students was due to their frequent political inclinations. Another reason was explained by a female PhD student who, despite her *madrasa* educational background, had a low level of trust in the *'ulama*. She argued that it was because they saw every matter with the lens of Islam and belief. However, according to her, not everything was linked to faith: "It should be a little neutral, liberal and not narrow."

What should also be noted is not only that the role of *'ulama* is surprisingly stronger in Kerala, but that there is also a big difference between female and male support. In Kerala, only 17.2% of the females showed maximum trust in the *'ulama*, in contrast to 45.5% of the males. In Delhi, it was the opposite: 25% of females gave the highest rank, while only 17.9% of the males did. This could be attributed to the system of education and the process of political socialisation and social engineering produced in different colleges.

The stance from Islamic ideals and socio-political concerns

> I always thank Allah that I have been born in India. Muslim nations are des-
> potic, running governments against basic principles of Islam. Sometimes I
> laugh at them. Saudi Arabia has a declared monarchy. There were socialist
> monarchies in Egypt, Syria and Iraq under Saddam. At least I can say
> loudly: Give me my right. At least I can confront the government when it
> turns majoritarian.
>
> (Navaid Hamid, member of the National Integration Council, Delhi, 2010)

> Democracy is a good system because a human being gets heard in it, he has
> the right to ask, but in the other systems he can only answer.
>
> (A Muslim taxi driver, Mumbai, April 2011)

Burgat (2008) differentiates between two processes and levels of analysis of
Islamism. The first is identity-centredness, which occurs when a generation
chooses to 'speak Muslim' and to resort to a central and privileged lexicon
derived from Muslim culture in order to counter the categories of the colonial
discourse that were imported and imposed. The second level is the diversified
uses of this lexicon which are contingent on multiple variables, varying with the
kind of political claim and mobilisation for which they are utilised (ibid.,
pp. 8–9). Applying these analytical tools to the case of India, one notices the
intricate usage of the democratic spaces to channel 'religious' demands, but at
the same time the aversion to utilise narrowly religious language or to 'speak
Muslim'.

One of the major aims of this research was to check how the attitude to the
democratic ideal differs between a place where Muslims are in a majority and
where they constitute a minority. Is the commonly held conviction that Muslims
would automatically opt for a *shari'ah*-based Islamic system of governance
valid? Or has the long political socialisation process affected the political psyche
of the community in a manner leading it to prefer the secular democratic option?
The most interesting result from the interviews and the survey conducted among
the youth was that there was no difference either in the perception of India as a
democratic state or in the preference of democracy as a system of governance. In
Kerala and Delhi, the majority affirmed that they supported democracy in India,
although they acknowledged its deficiencies and how it is not functioning on all
terms; the figures were 68.2% and 68.7%, respectively. On a more critical note,
not all students could display an argumentative stance of their perception of
democracy. As a Muslim female teacher informed me after a focus group I had
with Muslim students:

> It was only when I had gone to Qatar that I understood the meaning of
> democracy. If you ask these students of their opinion, they would not be
> able to answer, they cannot understand what democracy is because they
> have not seen the other side. Here in India we see the debates on laws

months before it is passed, but in Qatar, people heard about the laws one day before it is passed or even after it is passed.

(Mampad College, Malappuram district, March 2011)

Many respondents in the survey confirmed the disparity between the constitutional aspect of India's democracy and the empirical reality of malpractice of the democratic ideal:

> The system is democratic but not on all terms. Nothing in India is fully operating in a specific way on all terms. There is always corruption and lack of transparency. Although India is the biggest democracy in the world, this system is not always functioning. People usually sell their votes to criminals (*goondas*). Elections in Bihar are an example of this – no one can be sure about the result or how it went. The criminals play a very big role in the election process. The voters are silent. Money and *goondas* determine the result.
>
> (A female student at Jamia, November 2010)

Discrimination and the minority discourse feature as critical aspects of the democratic malfunction. No mention of discrimination could be complete without a reference to the Gujarat riots of 2002 and its aftermath on the psyche of Muslim youth and their collective memory. In Delhi, there was a noted difference in the attitude to the memory of communal riots. Whereas some students claimed that they had no idea about what happened in Gujarat in 2002, others chose not to speak, and some spoke of how it was a wakeup call for Muslims to realise their place in the Hindu *rāshtra*.

What is interesting to note is how some students adopted a similar attitude to that of the former Gujarati Vice Chancellor of Darul Uloom Deoband, Maulana Vastanvi, who was forced to step down from his post after his remarks on Gujarati Muslims.[5] This was evident in the emphasis of many students to move beyond discrimination and fear of violence, and to see the real reasons behind Muslims' backwardness. In a meeting on the Vastanvi issue in Delhi, the following statement was uttered: "Most of us have tired of the *jalsa-jaloos* [procession-protest] politics of the Muslim leadership" (Subrahmaniam, 2011).

The Gujarat carnage does not prominently feature in the discourses presented by the Muslim Keralites, whether in media or everyday life. Nevertheless, as I deduced from many conversations, it was the RSS that was cultivating the worries of many young Muslims since apparently the number of RSS branches is the highest in Gujarat, followed by Kerala (this negates the perception that RSS is weak in Kerala; it is powerful yet invisible). Kerala, having had a background of militant Islamism as evident in the ISS (Islamic Sevak Sangh)[6] or the current Popular Front of India, has presented a clear response to Hindu nationalistic activities. However, this type of political activity has been met with conflicting reactions; some either condemned it as an initiator of communalism or it was met with limited support, or as a college lecturer informed me, it was not even seen as a counterpart to RSS:

We cannot group RSS and PFI in one group because RSS has gotten the power with them; democracy and human rights in India are defined by RSS. The RSS controls visual and print media, and even government holidays, even without resort to evident violence. The RSS is responsible for setting the standards for who should be a good Muslim.

(Kozhikode, April 2011)

Whereas 76.9% of the respondents in Delhi claimed that they felt they belonged to a minority, this feeling was registered at 43.8% in Kerala (despite the fact that they constituted a majority in the district where the survey was held). The numerical idea did not dominate their mode of thinking while answering this question. Being empowered was the main driving force behind locating oneself as a minority or not. Here the gender variable does not present us with interesting results but, in the case of discrimination, it seems significant.[7] More females in Kerala (16.7% as compared to 9.4% of males) confirmed they had encountered discrimination mainly at their educational institutions and, to a lesser extent, at their home. This is in contrast to the case of Delhi, where the males encountering discrimination outnumber the females. When asked about their future, 53% feared discrimination in finding a job (unlike in Delhi, where the highest percentage went to finding a house), followed by governmental offices and their homes. Since discrimination in Kerala was based more on gender rather than on religion, this explains the high percentage of scepticism about finding a job since the majority of respondents were female.

The first point to be made is the majoritarian feature of Muslims in Northern Kerala. The establishment of a long democratic culture and competitive politics away from communalism and the memory of partition was also a reason for the disappearance of the feeling of being a minority and for a strong faith in constitutional guarantees:

We do not feel we are a minority here because we have considerations and rights. There is justice. India is not a Muslim country, all people are here, but the Indian Constitution gave Muslims the right to live like they wish, especially concerning education and *da'wah*. There are good chances for *da'wah* here in India; we cannot do *da'wah* in Saudi Arabia as freely as we can do it here.

(Mujahid-affiliated college in Malappuram district, January 2011)

Unlike the case in North India, where 21.3% of the male respondents in my survey complained that they have been accused of being a Pakistani or non-Indian, none in the Kerala sample encountered this problem. In an interview with the principal of a Jamaati-affiliated Islamic college, he asserted the difference in the accommodation of religion between the North and the South: "In the North, Hindus accommodate Islam, whereas in South India, it is the Muslims who accommodate the Hindu culture." The strong difference between Kerala and

Delhi reflects the historical context of a shared belonging. Thus, the communal harmony existing in Kerala makes it hard to imagine a system of difference for civil codes, for example, although it is actually practised and many might not be aware of its actual manifestations. This difference was translated in the 32.3% in Kerala who supported having different civil codes for different communities in comparison with 52.4% in Delhi.

Another contested issue of identity that has assumed huge political space is the Babri Masjid conflict. In September 2010, the Allahabad High Court pronounced the famous Ayodhya verdict, dividing the disputed land into three parts. Whereas the Muslim press showed significant turmoil over the verdict (as Figure 6.4 shows), Muslim youth shared a different opinion (see Figure 6.3, in response to the question "Do you think that the Ayodhya verdict on 30 September concerning Babri Masjid was fair to the Muslims of India?"). It remains to be said that the 'No opinion' answer is a politically burdened one. It was not chosen by the respondents to convey political ignorance or unawareness, but to assert a statement. Students were often critical of the question in the first place, since, to them, it was not a matter of justice or not. It was rather a matter of common sense. In other cases, students did not want to sound too critical of the High Court since it is unacceptable for an Indian citizen to challenge a court's decision.

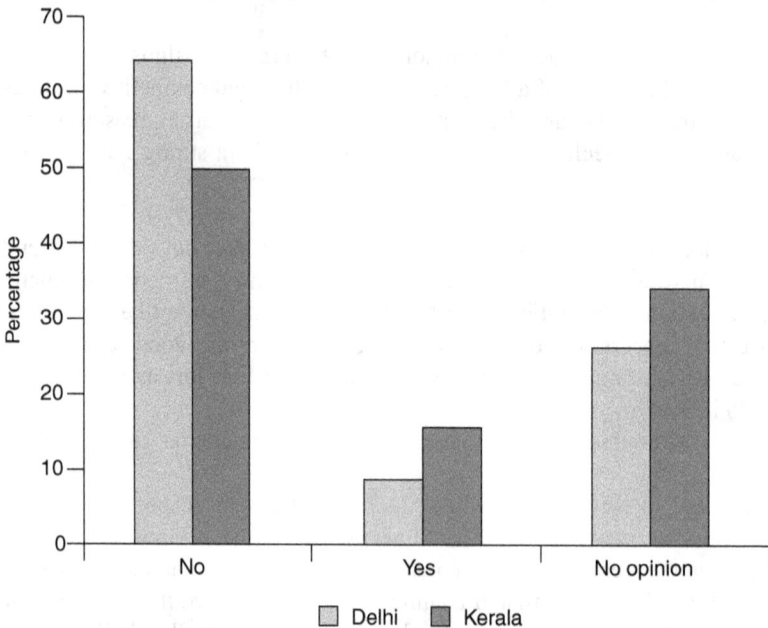

Figure 6.3 Response to the question: "Do you think that the Ayodhya verdict on 30 September concerning Babri Masjid was fair to the Muslims of India?".

Indian Muslims' Leading English Newspaper, published since January 2000

www.milligazette.com ISSN 0972-3366

MG THE MILLI GAZETTE

Fortnightly   258 Vol. 11 No. 20   16-31 October 2010   32 pages   Rs 10

On the basis of faith

On the basis of facts

2/3 for 1st Class Citizens

1/3 for 2nd class citizens

This is victory of aastha

Saffron faith

YusufIMG

Babri Masjid Verdict

The Second Demolition

Pages: 2, 3, 5, 6-7, 8-9, 12, 13, 14, 18-19, 20, 21

We will never accept second class citizenship

The Lucknow bench of Allahabad High Court has grossly overstepped its limits proving what we knew all-along that some people were more equal than others even in the eyes of law in this secular and democratic country. What was *de facto* until yesterday is *de jure* today. The court was supposed to basically decide the title suit of the disputed land. It did so but relying not on evidence and history but on *aastha*, faith, and said so unabashedly.

This verdict has smashed our trust in the Indian judiciary. It reveals it as a Hindu and politicised system, not one strictly bound by law and constitution. The verdict has left the Babri issue an open wound for all time to come and any temple built on the site by this sleight of hand will always be seen by us, Indian Muslims, as a monument of injustice and unfairness.

I have been proud of our judiciary and have been saying so openly to the whole world. We considered it a safety valve for the country's myriad problems and one reason why the Indian Muslim was so law-abiding and peaceful. Now that trust stands smashed and shattered.

Babri was never a land ownership issue. It is a ploy of the majority community fanatics whose plan is to marginalise the minorities, especially Muslims, to force them to accept the status of second class citizens in their own country. Until that aim is fulfilled, they will keep finding one issue after another. These fanatics have a very long list of monuments including Taj Mahal and Delhi's Jama Masjid, which they claim either stand on the sites of "razed" Hindu temples or are "Hindu" monuments whose names were changed by Muslim rulers (Taj Mahal, they claim was Tejo Mahlaya). Pre-British historical records, including the books written by Hindus themselves have no such indication. The Hindutva list is very elastic and includes anything from three to three

thousand monuments, mainly mosques. The idea is to perpetually keep Muslims occupied in mandir-masjid issues, polarise the Hindu voters in favour of the BJP and show the Muslims their place as second class citizens in their own country. The example of one of the first three mosques demanded by Hindutva zealots shows that they will not be content with any compromise short of complete surrender to their dictates. Under a mutual settlement overseen by the local court and district authorities, Muslims of Mathura had handed over about half of the land of the Mathura Eidgah (a *masjid*) in October 1968 to a trust headed by Hari Dalmia, head of the VHP. The matter was closed and a magnificent temple was built on the land given by the Muslims while their dilapidated mosque does not even have a proper approach. Yet, despite that solemn agreement, they are now demanding the other half of the site on which the actual Eidgah stands today. Let the fanatics know we are equals, we will never accept to live as second class citizens.

ZAFARUL-ISLAM KHAN

Figure 6.4 The cover of *The Milli Gazette* following the Ayodhya verdict, October 2010 (source: author's own collection).

Agency dynamics

> We walked through dirty alleys. She apologised that her house is very small. She also told me, "Muslim areas are very dirty". I told her, "I noticed this, but why?" She said, "Because they have dirty minds". I told her, "But Islam encourages cleanliness". She said, "Yes, they clean their houses very well and throw the garbage outside on the roads". I asked, "Do they expect the government to clean it?" She said, "No one expects the government to do anything. The government promises a lot. But people are supposed to clean themselves."
>
> (Excerpt from my field notes on a day I spent with a female Muslim student in Batla House, 2010)

When asked what steps should be done for Muslims to achieve educational advancement and to overcome their economic backwardness, a strong sense of a need for agency and a belief in the responsibility of the self in the deterioration of Muslim conditions and as a solution were noted in the replies of the readers of a Jamaati Islami magazine opinion poll. Minimal mention was noted of any assumed or aspired role for the government to take. Instead, the mosque appears as a recurrent tool and space for reform. Through the mosque, several readers mentioned how primary education could be enforced, and networks of these primary educational centres could be coordinated on panchayat, village and block levels. After the *fajr* prayer, the poor and the rich should then convene and decide on the possibility of donations and funds according to the educational and economic needs of their neighbours. In the commentator's opinion, this should be done on a daily basis, following a tradition that was performed in the Prophet's Mosque in Medina.

This emphasis on the self as an initiator of change is central to Islamic conceptualisation (Robinson, 2006). In the Quran, it is asserted that God does not change a people's conditions unless they change what is in themselves first (13:11), a verse that was regularly cited by respondents. Almost all Islamic organisations adopt this methodology in their work. An example of this is the Tablighi Jamaat, which is famous for its worldwide proselytising work, or the Jamaati Islami, with its intermingling between the role of religion and politics. If we overlook the intensity of orthodoxy and rigid rules adopted by these organisations, we will find unprecedented spaces created for individuals to exercise their sense of agency in self-change. Jamaati Islami builds a network in which the youth are creatively engaging in leadership roles and career building. Tablighi Jamaat offers a vast space for women to become preachers and to exercise limited mobility. In an interview at Jamia, a PhD student researching early Urdu women novelists emphasised how she was an active member at Tablighi, which she joined because of her grandmother, who was also a member. This student was responsible for a weekly programme of *da'wah*, in which she gathered some girls who discussed religion together. However, this young woman was not seeking employment, but she was studying out of interest – the same answer I got from a girl at the *madrasa* in Lucknow. She referred to the importance of education, especially when her children would go to school and how it differs when the child realises how educated his mother is, and also how the school sees that the mother is highly educated. Education thus opens up spaces not only for agency but also for challenging orthodox and widely accepted ideas like the ban on intermingling between males and females. According to this woman and to many others, although this intermingling is *harām*, there is no problem when it comes to seeking education at the university. In the words of a Muslim scholar at Nadwa: "India is a democratic country; because of this, Muslim girls find spaces for education, they progress while conserving their *shari'ah* simultaneously."

This is a clear and outspoken defiance of the commonly established *fatwa* on the separation between women and men in public spaces. The secular democratic nature of India makes the realm of *fatwas* a deeply contested one. This was mostly obvious after the Shah Bano case. In a society where citizens are free to opt between civil or religious laws governing their personal lives, the scope of agency increases. However, the power the *'ulama* class is invested with makes this choice almost absent in many cases.

Increasingly, the realm of *fatwas* trespassed its 'personal law' boundaries and assumed significant presence in the political arena. As I mentioned in the previous chapter, many *'ulamas, mullahs* and *imams* produce what could be termed a political *fatwa*, such as banning the singing of the *Vande Mataram*, or preferring a specific political candidate in elections. Through amplifying the negative impact of the politics of *fatwas*, many notable Muslim figures first condemn these *fatwas*, like Zafrul Islam Khan, who contends that *fatwas* are only followed by the media. Second, they dissolve the conceptual chaos of terming political opinions or appeals endorsed by Muslim *'ulama* as *fatwas*. Upon asking him whether the *muftis* give any political kind of *fatwas*, the *imam* of the Fatehpuri Masjid in Delhi vehemently argued:

> No, there aren't two kinds of *fatwas*. Those related to *shari'ah* are considered *fatwas*, but those *Vande Mataram*-like ones are not *fatwas*, these are opposition *fatwas*. They are not based on *shari'ah*. *Fatwas* should be based on *shari'ah*. If there is a political candidate in front of us, a non-Muslim who is better than the Muslim, we will just help the non-Muslim. This *imam* who does this is not an *imam* of a mosque, but an *imam* of politics.

On the mass level, there was no consensus as to whether the public follows the *fatwas* or not. The *'ulama* assume their power in many cases from the inefficiency of the Indian court system, which takes many years to make a ruling. Thus in personal matters, most Muslims go directly to the *'ulama* to solve their problems, especially if it is a woman seeking a divorce:

> Very few people go to Indian courts. The case there goes on for ten, fifteen, twenty, thirty, to forty years. *(She starts giggling)*. It goes on forever. Because our Personal Law Board people know *hadith* and Islamic law, that is why any need of going to Indian courts does not arise. Of course we do follow the *fatwas*. Darul Uloom Deoband is the number one in Asia, but people following *barelwi* ideas and those coming from Western UP do not follow Deoband's *fatwas*.
>
> (A middle-class woman I met at the Jama Masjid Delhi, December 2010)

Because I can read and figure out for myself then I follow only those *fatwas* I see right. Most *fatwas* issued related to women aim at keeping them backward, for example, women cannot be judges or Sania Mirza cannot wear shorts. So do they expect her to play tennis with a *burqa*? There are so many people around me whom I can ask questions relating to religion, I do not need to go and ask a *sheikh*, I would never actually.

(A female student at Jamia)

Although we are *madrasa* graduates, we do not always follow *fatwas* issued by the *'ulama*, and there are specific institutions like Darul Uloom Deoband, which we think are too extremist, narrow-minded and irrational and therefore we do not follow their *fatwas*. We follow only those appealing to our hearts.

(A male student at JNU)

When asked in Delhi if they follow *fatwas* issued by the *'ulama*, 29.1% of the surveyed students said they always do, 37.9% said sometimes and 33% negated this action. Interestingly, for females, the figures differed since only 14.6% said they always follow the *fatwas*, 36.6% said sometimes according to what they are convinced of, and 48.8% said they never do.

Unlike in North India, it is argued that there is no *fatwa* culture in Kerala, but only a 'whispering effect' (Hafiz Mohamed, author interview, January 2011). The 'whispering effect' refers to the action by upper-caste Muslim religious leaders (the *Thangals*) who hold a weekly ceremony of inviting people to their houses and then offering them some healing rituals by whispering a set of Islamic codes and writing then some Quranic verses on a piece of paper. The practice is not isolated from the North Indian Sufi rituals of healing, as I will show; however, the authority imbibed by the *Thangals* led to an interesting case. Despite the emergence of other series of political authority and affiliations with the Indian Union Muslim League, these *Thangals* did not engage in the traditional politics of *fatwa* that were common in North India. In Kerala, *fatwas* are not the business of ordinary *imams*; nevertheless, as a Jamaati Islami leader informed me, while the *imams* and *khateebs* do not issue *fatwas*, their organisations do. It is here that politics of hidden *fatwas* emerge. For example, despite the dearth of any direct opposition to women's reservations in the local government bodies, Islamic organisations have issued *fatwas* stating that no woman should be out after 6 p.m. In other words, these organisations have clearly placed hurdles against women's public work.

Another issue that has to be emphasised is the transnational aspect of *fatwas* followed by Indian Muslims, especially in the South. Due to the Gulf connections, the literary and intellectual ties with the Arab world precipitated in a situation where Indian Muslims inherited a literary heritage from the Arab world and translated it to Malayalam.[8] This practice is still prevalent and has migrated to the realm of religious writings. I was fascinated to see, on several occasions, students sitting on campus reading a Malayalam translation of Al-Qaradawy's books. In one of my interviews, a student told me:

We do not care about local *fatwas* issued by *musliyārs* (local *imams*). We are only concerned about international ones like Al-Qaradawy's. We cannot depend on the local *fatwas*; one has to check whether it suits contemporary requirements of commitments or not.

In my attempt to excavate the role of *fatwas* in Muslims' lives, the following narrative from a visit to Chandni Chowk in December 2010 is insightful. I went to Jama Masjid looking for the office of the *shāhi imam*. I sat there with the secretary and I asked him if there is any collection of *fatwas*, he explained to me that the *imam* does not give any *fatwas* and that I should go to Fatehpuri mosque, so I took a rickshaw and went there.

I entered the mosque and saw several small groups of young men sitting and learning with an *'alim*. There were doors and windows on two of the sides of the mosque's inner courtyard. I walked around trying to find a sign of the *imam's* office. A young man looked at me suspiciously and I knew at once that I was out of place. Then I found an old guard who guided me to the *imam's* assistant. As I got to know from him, they all belonged to the Sufi *naqshabandi tariqah* (tradition), and they were specialised in spiritual healing. After introducing myself, he instantly told me I could talk to any of the two *muftis* at the mosque and that he could tell me his opinion as well.

Throughout our conversation, he emphasised four times that whatever he said was his personal opinion and did not represent the general opinion of Muslims. He started by asserting, "If there is no ban on our fundamental rights and if we are freely allowed to practise these rights, then we fully recognise and accept the government."

The major point is that they have the freedom to adopt *shari'ah* as their law and that the non-Muslim government would not interfere with it or ban it. As long as the basic rights of practising Islamic rituals of fasting, praying, *haj* and *zakat* are not in conflict with any law, then they would be loyal to the state. Loyalty also stems from *shari'ah*, in which it is stated that in *darul harb* if the state allows Muslims to practise their religion, then they should accept their status and be loyal to the state.

He further emphasised how democracy is given in Islam; the Caliphate system is the best example of this through the *shura* system. Before this, the world never witnessed such an example of democracy where people would elect their ruler. Another ideal is non-violence, which was also first mentioned in the Quran through the concept of *ṣabr* (patience). According to him, the three concepts of *akhlāq* (morals), *maḥabah* (love), and *ṣabr* (patience) constitute the essence of non-violence in Islamic thought.

The *shari'ah* system was referred to upon discussing justice. To him, the Indian state could never be just because it does not apply *shari'ah*, and voting, as a political right, is not enough to maintain a just system:

The judicial system takes years to solve any dispute, unlike *shari'ah*. *Shari'ah* says if someone steals and there are witnesses to his act, then his hand should be chopped off. The penalty in Islam is instant. But look at the Indian court system. I will give you an example. Here is a coin. If someone stole it, and there are witnesses, and I go to the court and sue him. The court will first put hand on my coin, it will become legal property, the thief will pay his bail and be released and live his life normally, then they will take fifteen, twenty, twenty five years to reach a verdict. I may not be alive to witness the verdict, but even if I am alive, I will not remember if this coin was the one stolen from me twenty five years ago, and anyway what would its value then be.

The following day, I went to meet the *imam*. There was no place for me to pray *dhuhr* (noon prayer) and, when I remarked on this, I was told in a matter-of-fact way, "Yes, there is no place for women's prayer." I ended up sitting in a room filled with women (some had their husbands with them) and many children. Both Hindus and Muslims came to find solutions; one had a baby whom she said cried nonstop at night and people recommended that she come to consult the *imam* so that he would give him his blessings. After many conversations with Muslims, I began to realise that the realm of political *fatwas* is a media-created myth. Paradoxically, the *'ulama* played a great role in the common people's lives (the *'ām ādmi*), but they seldom appeared as political experts. Among many Muslims, the corruption of some of the *'ulama* tainted their reputation, especially when they saw their divisions concerning worldly purposes:

> In India, Muslims are looked upon as being weak. But where is their weakness? It is in their partiality and lack of political power. Discrimination is not just practised by the non-Muslims. It is also practiced among Muslims themselves. The major reason behind the difference in the development of Muslims in the North and the South is funds and resources on the one hand, and infrastructure on the other. *'Ulama* are to blame for the problems of Muslims. I admit there is strong corruption among them. We have to learn who a Muslim is, we have to know first who we are, only then we could be powerful and see where we stand.
>
> (An informant at Fatehpuri Masjid, Delhi, December 2010)

Concluding remarks on the sense of citizenship

Citizenship as a 'sense of comfort' in the public sphere (Bhargava, 2010, quoted in Mitra, 2012, p. 91) is composed of a moral commitment to defend one's place and a legal right to where one is (Mitra, 2012). This chapter has aimed at projecting how widely this is shared among the youth in Delhi and Kerala. This task was not conducted in a direct or prescribed manner. The means of operationalising citizenship remains a hugely contested domain and certainly differs from one context to the other. This is clearly manifested by the participants in this study. The initial hypothesis was that regional contexts with different problematic aspects incur different degrees of a sense of full and equal citizenship. The result, as I showed, proved otherwise. In fact, the other variable, which led to a noted degree of difference in the sense of citizenship, was gender.

This was, nevertheless, significant only in Kerala. When asked if they feel in reality that they have equal rights as a citizen, 50% of the respondents in Delhi confirmed this. The figures did not change when we considered the gender aspect: always (50%), sometimes (28.6%) and no (11.9%). However, when I moved to Kerala, and carried out the same survey, I arrived with interestingly different results, especially with the gender variable taken into consideration (Figures 6.5 and 6.6).

Unlike in Kerala, where the word citizenship (*paurutum* in Malayalam) had a clear conceptual clarity, when I had mentioned the word citizenship to North Indian students, not everyone could understand the political content of the concept. They all knew the word citizenship but in its Hindi form, *nāgriktā*, and less in its Urdu form, *shehreyet*. For many female students, it meant being born in India and thus being an Indian by birth. However, when I mentioned the concept of rights and obligations, this was one answer:

> We do have the right to choose our leaders and our political system, but unfortunately there is no transparency. Theoretically and constitutionally, there is the right to vote granted to everyone on equal terms. But at the end, all these rights are on paper only. In reality, there is no equality in rights. There is discrimination everywhere. No one is given equal rights.

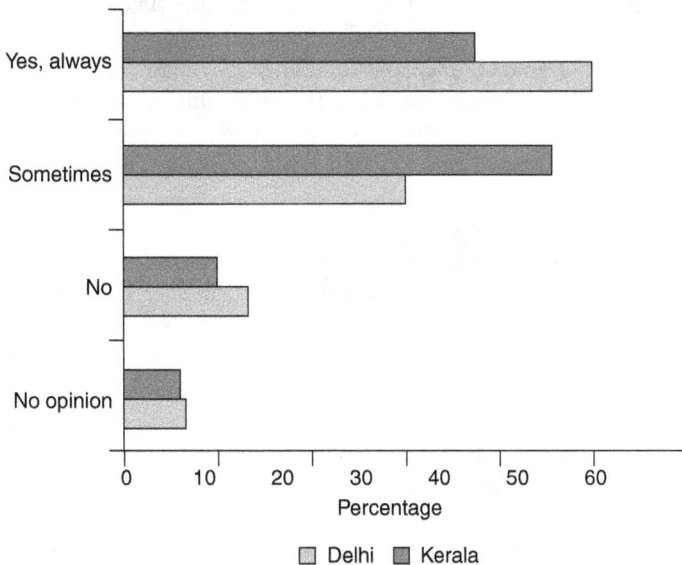

Figure 6.5 Sense of equal citizenship in Kerala and Delhi.

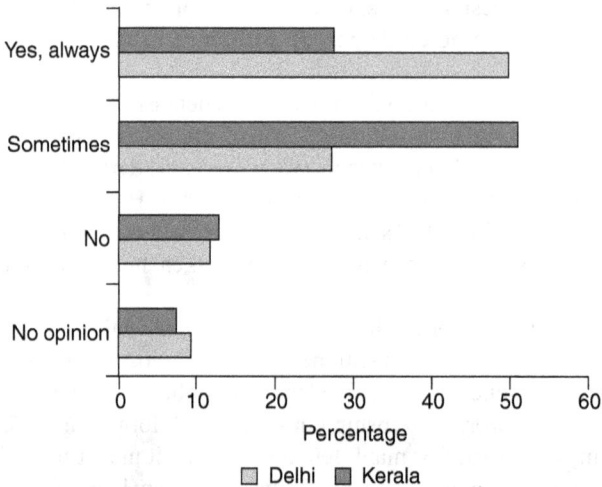

Figure 6.6 Sense of equal citizenship among females in Delhi and Kerala.

In order to put the comparative map in perspective by looking at what other non-Muslims think of this debate on rights, it is noteworthy to point out that, in the National Election Surveys, conducted by the CSDS, respondents were asked whether they agreed or disagreed with the statement "Everyone enjoys equal rights." There was absolutely no difference between the Muslim response and the national average; the percentages that agreed with the statement both amounted to 47%.

The spaces of freedom granted in the Constitution led eventually to a change in the sentiments of Muslims towards the state. However, this is considerably limited to the educated. Education clearly leads to a change in the conception of rights and obligations in the framework of citizenship. In the words of a Muslim scholar at Nadwa:

> Muslims feel responsible towards the state. They implement governmental laws in their everyday life because these laws keep our lives safe. As for religion and what concerns our daily life (what to eat and how to preserve our religious concerns), if it conflicts with governmental law, we will follow Islamic principles. If a court or parliament issues a law contradicting Islamic *shari'ah* in inheritance or marriage or divorce, then we apply Islamic *shari'ah* and ignore this rule. Because of the nature of life, there are increasingly new issues coming up needing new *fatwas*.

The result is the activation of the practice of *ijtihād* or independent reasoning among both scholars and common people who are educated enough to be able to read the Quran and its translated interpretation, as we have seen from conversations with students. Several Muslim scholarly leaders have contributed to the establishment of this trend. Historically, we saw the role played by Maulana Madani in producing the concept of composite nationalism. Contemporary scholars like the late Asghar Ali Engineer in Mumbai, Maulana Wahiduddin Khan in Delhi and many reformist Mujahid scholars in Kerala are examples of those who try to raise positivity among Muslims and ensure Hindu–Muslim relations prosper. The youth I interviewed supported this argument and emphasised how India is now witnessing a different development since the government has been active in disclosing right-wing Hindus and even *sadhus* who are behind terrorist activities like the Mecca Masjid and the Malegaon blasts. Ensuring justice is interlinked to the increasing sense of responsibility on the part of Muslims. The coming out of the victimisation mentality is another by-product:

> All government schemes are badly managed; therefore those for Muslims are also badly managed. It is the responsibility of Muslims to monitor the implementation.
>
> (S. Mehdi, former vice chancellor of Jamia,
> author interview, December 2010)

> Even poor people here think of their citizenship. They love their *watan*, their religion, and also their country. This is a good citizen. When you look around, you see signs saying this is your city, so keep it clean. A good citizen takes care of the beauty and the development of the place he lives in.
>
> (Imam Makrami, author interview, December 2010)

Before I started the survey from which I obtained my statistics for this research, I had conducted a pilot survey study, which had an initial question that I eventually removed from the final questionnaire. The question was: "Do you call yourself an Indian Muslim or a Muslim Indian?" Not only did many condemn this question, but some could not fathom what I wanted to ask. Some considered the two terms to be equal, and some even told me that I am a Muslim Indian, because we are all Indians, but few Indians are Muslims – an answer that reflected no political consciousness of one's identity. However, those who were politically conscious would echo Maulana Abul Kalam Azad's statement: "I am an Indian first, then I am a Muslim."

The inclusion of religion in the citizenship formula necessitated another question reflecting the common derogatory reference to Indian Muslims as being supporters of Pakistan. I have previously alluded in this chapter to an alarming percentage among youth in Delhi who have been accused of being Pakistani. Interestingly, some of the respondents asserted that this was not very common in everyday life in India, but it happened only during cricket matches. Cricket erupted as an intriguing space where identity was contested. One of the young engineering male students at Jamia told me that I should also include the following question: "Do you support India or Pakistan in cricket matches?" He emphasised:

Fifty per cent of them would tell you that we support Pakistan. But actually in my opinion, Pakistanis are not good people because they call Indian Muslims *kafirs*. Actually if you see the reality in the Gulf states, it is the Indian Muslims who have a better reputation. *Pakis* call us *kafirs* because we are friends with Hindus but actually the Quran says that no Muslim should befriend the Jews. The Quran does not mention Hindus, so there is no problem being friends with Hindus.

Despite this widely shared sentiment, it was noted how, unlike in Kerala, the common spaces required to establish a coherent sense of citizenship was missing in the case of Delhi. Despite being the capital, it did not reflect many of the 'citizenship' attributes of common existence and transcending religious barriers that were found in peripheral towns and villages. The urban-ness did not necessarily lead to a case of urbane-ness.

Notes

1 The figures do not add up to 100% because some respondents gave more than one reason for why they vote.
2 This is a verse from the Quran (Ar-ra'd (13): 11).
3 The question changed from Delhi to Kerala. In Delhi, I just asked about the MP or the *netā*, and I added this question of naming him/her to check the percentage and the honesty. In Kerala, my research assistant modified the question to include MLA and MP since the political culture is different and it is unquestionable that everyone knows the MP.
4 The Thomas P. Joseph Commission of Inquiry report can be accessed at www.mathrub-humi.com/2006_customimages/news/PF123172_marad01.pdf; for a sample of media coverage see, for example: V. R. Krishna Iyer, The Marad massacre, *The Hindu* 31 May 2003, www.hindu.com/2003/05/31/stories/2003053100621000.htm; *rediff.com*, Marad riots: Five years on, sixty-three found guilty, 27 December 2008, www.rediff.com/news/2008/dec/27marad-riots-five-years-on-63-found-guilty.htm; George Iype, Marad: How politicians fanned a communal riot, *rediff.com*, 28 September 2006, www.rediff.com/news/2006/sep/28gi.htm.
5 Maulana Vastanvi, a former rector of Darul Uloom Deoband *madrasa*, made positive comments about Muslims' development in Gujarat and had urged Muslims to overcome what happened in 2002. Some people interpreted this as a reminder to the Muslims of the role of Gujaratis as businessmen and therefore of the importance of an atmosphere of communal harmony to the thriving or mere existence of their business and thus livelihoods. Others, mainly embodied in the majority of the *Majlis-e Shoora* or the Advisory board of the Deoband seminary, had voted in favour of his ouster since they interpreted his remarks as praise for Narendra Modi (the Chief Minister of the state of Gujarat), in addition to not being from Uttar Pradesh, unlike his predecessors.
6 The ISS was created by Madani in Kerala as a response to the Bhagalpur riots of 1991.
7 In Delhi, 65% of females showed their sense of being a minority. This was in contrast to 38.2% in Kerala. The figures for males were 84.4% and 52.8%, respectively.
8 For example, Arabic colleges in Kerala typically teach the literary works of Egyptian writers such as Taha Hussain, Al-'Aqqad and Naguib Mahfouz.

References

Burgat, F. (2008). *Islamism in the Shadow of al-Qaeda.* (P. Hutchinson, Trans.). Austin: University of Texas Press.

Gupta, D. (2007). Citizens Versus People: The Politics of Majoritarianism and Marginalization in Democratic India. *Sociology of Religion*, 68(1), 27–44.

Mitra, S. K. (2012). Turning Aliens into Citizens: A 'Tool-Kit' for a Trans-Disciplinary Policy Analysis. In S. Mitra (ed.), *Citizenship and the Flow of Ideas in the Era of Globalization: Structure, Agency, and Power* (pp. 82–154). Delhi: Samskriti.

National Election Studies. (1999, 2004, 2009). Center for the Study of Developing Societies, Delhi.

Robinson, F. (2006). Religious Change and the Self in Muslim South Asia Since 1800. In A. Roy (ed.), *Islam in History and Politics: Perspectives from South Asia* (pp. 21–35). Delhi: Oxford University Press.

Subrahmaniam, V. (2011, 3 April). *Breaking the Muslim Stereotype.* Retrieved on 3 April 2011, from The Hindu-Opinion Page, www.thehindu.com/opinion/lead/article1506918.ece?homepage=true.

7   Conclusion

This book started by presenting the historical context in the post-partition era and how the notion of the community was theorised and presented within both the broader and global Islamic discourse and the local context of India as a case study. This impelled me to look at the myth of the *Ummah* as a component of what can be termed transnational citizenship as a new level of analysis in global politics. The Indian case presented us with, first, a postcolonial order of an application of a liberal conception of citizenship, coupled with an invention of minority status and adjustments guided by a uniquely secular Constitution. Second, these adjustments led to devising new concepts such as composite nationalism. By this, the Indian case sets a historically fascinating precedent in global history; the majority of Indian religious leaders (*'ulama*) acted as motivators for choosing the secular democratic option versus the promised Islamic regime.

The role of *'ulama* is highly significant since classical Islamic jurisprudence dealt only with a situation in which Muslims assumed political power, while the question of Muslim minorities had been neglected from traditional analysis. This had necessitated a drive towards *ijtihād* among Islamic scholars worldwide. Reconciling faith with citizenship was a major innovation of the Indian Muslim *'ulama*. The classical fascination with *darul Islam* versus *darul ḥarb* was replaced by multiple variants, such as *darul waṭan*. The love of the *waṭan*, hence, was asserted as an integral part of faith. Muslims were assigned a dual responsibility demanding that they should take an active interest in the affairs of their country (Nadwi, quoted by Sikand, 2004, pp. 81–85). As I have shown, Azad and Madani's ideas of composite nationalism embodied the result of these new interpretations of Islamic laws and called for a unique adjustment and accommodation of the Islamic identity to a new one – that of being a 'citizen minority' in a secular democratic setting.

In the analysis of the treatment of Islamic political thought to the idea of the political home (*dār*), Indian Muslim *'ulama*, by the introduction of the term *darul waṭan* as a source of legitimacy, managed to establish a discovery of an entity both modern and Islamic. This had further implications on the way the notion of the community or the *Ummah* was conceived. We saw from the examples set in this study how *Ummah* consciousness was not a myth but was realised through solidarity networks established chiefly by Muslim organisations such as the Jamaati Islami, the Popular Front of India and the Jamiat Ulama-e-Hind. The relevance of the *Ummah* took additional transnational turns, as Muslim youth expressed their opinion on international issues, such as Kashmir, Palestine, Pakistan and a critique of India–US and Israel relations.

Through a comparative study between Delhi and Kerala, the book argues that, through means of argumentative and spiritual *jihād*, Indian Muslims strive towards a realisation of citizenship ideals as inscribed in the Constitution, regardless of being in a majority or minority setting. To operationalise *jihād*, I started by emphasising its exact definition and its moral component. Self-rule, education, striving for social mobility and patience are all operationalised mechanisms of what *jihād* means for Indian Muslims. The practice of *jihād* was forged along different regional and historical experience, interestingly intertwined with a nationalist cause, where a religious tool and objective became mingled with a pragmatically political one.

Analysing the dynamics of politicising a religious identity is a complex endeavour. First, there is a strong role played by collective memory and hence a community identity. Second, socio-religious structural changes in the fields of education, personal laws and caste associations also interfere with the political power sphere. Finally, we find internal struggles among the *'ulama* or the religious institutions over power and authority.

Unravelling the means by which Indian Muslims accommodate Islam with the reality of being citizens in a secular democratic state was one of my main concerns as I embarked on this research. The answer I got could be summarised in the Fatehpuri Mosque's *shāhi imam's* statement: "Accommodating Islam was not difficult: the public sphere is left open to propagate freely on the one hand, and on the other hand, the Constitution is not biased to any religion." Fieldwork-based research revealed that the decision to support secularism and to actively engage in the democratic process is not seen as a desperate person's last refuge in constitutional rights, but is surprisingly often emerging out of Islamic incentives. Hence this drove to a deeper analysis of the reasons behind creating enclaves, which are fundamentally prompted by the demand for security and filling gaps in the sense of citizenship. The reasons for these gaps have proven to be gender-related and not only emerging from the traditional religious minority discourse.

The high level of political efficacy projected by students touches on the hypothesis generated in this study concerning the paradoxical situation of Indian Muslims in which the sense of deprivation and discrimination does not diminish their faith in democracy and in the value of their votes. The falsification of this hypothesis is also valid, as many citizens have expressed the Hinduisation of the Indian state and how the benefits of Muslims could never be forwarded or their rights guaranteed.

Reference is hence made to policy implications concerning the betterment of the life-space in which citizenship is practised and felt. In my opinion, I think one of the most important measures to be undertaken is to organise illiteracy programmes managed by *madrasa* and university students. This would be considered part of obligatory social work. In addition to this, the translation of historical *'ulama* writings from Urdu to English and Hindi might also enhance the spread of social reform among the public and counter the Hindu right-wing propaganda against Muslims.

The most important measure is to make sure the gap in the Muslim middle class is overcome. Policy analysis, instead of being influenced by an alleged relationship between Islam and educational backwardness, should take into consideration spatial contexts and socio-economic indicators. Empirical studies have proven how there is no unilinear process in conceptualising religious differences when it comes to literacy and levels of education; on the contrary, demographic and socio-economic indicators determine the rate of educational development (Alam & Raju, 2007). The religion-based explanation of the low rate of Muslims' enrolment in natural sciences and engineering should be surmounted:

> Muslim students cannot simply qualify to medical and engineering sciences, because their economic situation makes it very hard to compete with others. High tuition fees and exam preparation procedures always disqualify them from entering such fields, in addition to the fact that *madrasa* education is not recognised in many universities or for many disciplines. That is why they are mostly in Urdu, Arabic or Islamic studies.
>
> (An interview with a Muslim University scholar, Delhi, December 2010)

Examples of Muslims, especially girls, being able to acquire an educational habitus, to borrow Bourdieu's term, and thus induce different levels of social change, have been presented throughout this study. In more desolate cases, such as the survival after riots, especially in the Gujarat experience, the attempt to arrive at normalcy and to move from victim to survivor status should not be omitted from analytical observations.

The predicaments Indian Muslims face in several parts of India, where their sense of security is critically low, convey a significant part of the story. However, the other less narrated stories are of youth redefining the meaning of safe spaces. This is realised primarily through women's efforts. The case of the fight for mosque entry and inclusion in the job market in Kerala is such an example. Another prominent case presented through this study was the programmes organised by Jamaati Islami's female wing, which campaigned in the drug and prostitution zones in Kozhikode. Eventually, youth overcame the dualistic imagination of political realities of Muslims in India. In both North and South India, illiberal spaces were gradually transformed to accommodate liberal ideas and spaces. The intersection of the perception of a common reality led, on the social and political level, to circles where Hindus are working with Muslims and essentially for Muslim causes, especially on the civil society level. This negates the classic remark that Muslims are obsessed with a desire for Muslim representatives.

The idea of 'composite nationalism' that Madani forged in the first half of the twentieth century as an answer to the partition call was central to this study.

Examples in everyday life were presented: Muslim women taking their children to Hindu ceremonies at school, Muslims celebrating national holidays in an entirely Muslim manner, youth getting socialised to the idea of being 'Indian Muslims' and 'Muslim Indians' simultaneously, without a preference to an identity over the other, holding mass demonstrations and public rallies that carry purely Islamic causes but utterly respect Indian legal regulations. All these are manifestations of how 'composite nationalism' is indeed a basis of citizenship in a diverse society.

Many interlinked networks are formed through the role of the state (materialised in the surveillance by the police), the locality (represented in the mosque committee), the individual and collective level of non-resident Indians, religious leaders and organisations who manage to establish transnational connections with the Gulf. These networks provide the intricate spaces in which citizenship ideals are created and transmitted in a complex manner, arriving at an embodied sense of composite nationalism.

The dynamics of political action and awareness, expressed through the Indian Muslims' acquisition of a 'citizen minority' identity, contribute to a subversion of the stereotyped identities ascribed to them. I devised the term citizen minority to describe the status of Indian Muslims who are full citizens, yet possess in differing contexts different minority cultures. The inability to be critical of the Babri verdict, for example, and hence of the Indian legal system, as shown through many interviews and review of the press, represents an inclination towards a process of self-marginalisation and a construction of an idea of 'model citizenship' to which an Indian Muslim strives. However, this struggle is combined with another crucial one: the search for life's security.

It remains to be said that only in a diverse country like India would one find travel agencies advertising for a *haj* package coupled with a visit to Israel and Egypt. There, conceptions such as the religious intermingle with the 'anti-Muslim' and the pagan to create an essentially transcultural awareness, allowing a rare sense of acceptance of the other.

References

Alam, M. S., & Raju, S. (2007). Contextualising Inter-,Intra-Religious and Gendered Literacy and Educational Disparities in Rural Bihar. *Economic and Political Weekly*, 42(18), 1613–1622.

Sikand, Y. (2004). *Muslims in India Since 1947: Islamic Perspectives on Interfaith Relations*. London: RoutledgeCurzon.

Index

For Product Safety Concerns and Information please contact our EU
representative GPSR@taylorandfrancis.com
Taylor & Francis Verlag GmbH, Kaufingerstraße 24, 80331 München, Germany